Why are you a part of today's Messianic movement? Since the beginning of the Messianic Jewish movement in the late 1960s to the present, we have witnessed a generation of Jewish people come to faith in Israel's Messiah, retaining their Jewish heritage. Since the mid-to-late 1990s to the present, we have also witnessed a great number of evangelical Protestant Believers be sovereignly called by God into the Messianic movement, to join in and participate with their fellow Jewish Believers in the restoration of Israel. Many are of the sincere conviction that the end-time prophecies involving a massive salvation of Jewish people (Romans chs. 9-11) and the nations coming to Zion to be instructed in God's Torah (Micah 4:1-3; Isaiah 2:2-4), are simultaneously occurring in this hour.

Today's Messianic congregations are often places where these two dynamics emerge, and people from diverse backgrounds fellowship with one another on a regular basis in a local assembly or fellowship of brothers and sisters. What are some of the things of what it means to be a Jewish Believer in Yeshua of Nazareth? What are some of the things of what it means to be a non-Jewish Believer in the Messianic movement? How do we pool the strengths and virtues of our Judeo-Protestant heritage, as we anticipate and work toward the salvation-historical trajectory of "all Israel will be saved" (Romans 11:26) and the return of Yeshua to Planet Earth?

Messianic Apologetics editor J.K. McKee has developed the workbook *The Messianic Walk* to specifically aid in acclimating people to today's Messianic movement. This resource is a primer, divided into six units, covering: (1) The Messianic Experience, (2) Shabbat, the Appointed Times, Jewish Holidays, (3) Kosher and Torah-Based "Means of Grace," (4) The Contours of Jewish Evangelism, (5) Our Place in the Congregation, and (6) A Survey of Messianic Theology. *The Messianic Walk* has been written in an as user-friendly and easy-to-read style as possible, as it introduces students to the Messianic congregational experience as it has developed by the third decade of the Twenty-First Century. It is a resource intended to be used in the new members classes of today's Messianic congregations, either on its own or in concert with other materials.

THE MESSIANIC WALK

THE MESSIANIC WALK

THE END-TIME MOVE OF GOD

J.K. McKee

MESSIANIC APOLOGETICS
messianicapologetics.net

THE MESSIANIC WALK
THE END-TIME MOVE OF GOD
© 2018, 2020 John Kimball McKee
All rights reserved. With the exception of quotations for academic purposes, no part of this publication may be reproduced without prior permission of the publisher.

Cover Image: GidonPico via Pixabay

ISBN 978-1983946752 (paperback)
ASIN B07G5MN3XV (eBook)

Published by Messianic Apologetics, a division of Outreach Israel Ministries
P.O. Box 516
McKinney, Texas 75070
(407) 933-2002

outreachisrael.net / outreachisrael.blog
messianicapologetics.net / messianicapologetics.blog

Fair Use Notice: This publication contains copyrighted material the use of which has not always been specifically authorized by the copyright owner. We make use of this material as a matter of teaching, scholarship, research, and commentary. We believe in good faith that this constitutes a "fair use" of any such copyrighted material as provided for in section 107 of the US Copyright Law, and is in accordance with Title 17 U.S.C. Section 107. For more information go to: https://www.law.cornell.edu/uscode/text/17/107

Outreach Israel Ministries is a non-profit 501(c)3. All prices listed on the publications of Outreach Israel Ministries and Messianic Apologetics are suggested donations.

TABLE OF CONTENTS

Introduction xi

A Spiritual Scavenger Hunt xv

UNIT ONE
THE MESSIANIC EXPERIENCE

The Messianic Mission 1

An End-Time Move of the Holy Spirit 15
Mark Huey

A Torah Foundation 27

UNIT TWO
SHABBAT, THE APPOINTED TIMES, JEWISH HOLIDAYS

Introducing the Biblical Appointments 53

Remembering Biblical and Jewish Holidays as a Messianic Believer 61

Controversies Involving Biblical and Jewish Holidays
as a Messianic Believer 71

UNIT THREE
KOSHER
TORAH-BASED "MEANS OF GRACE"

Kosher and Torah-Based "Means of Grace" 85

Our Family Experiences Going Kosher 95
Margaret McKee Huey

Controversies Involving Torah-Based "Means of Grace" 101

UNIT FOUR
JEWISH OUTREACH AND EVANGELISM

The Contours of Jewish Evangelism 115

How Do We Know that Yeshua of Nazareth is the Messiah? 125

The Wild and Wonderful World of the Broad Messianic Movement 147

UNIT FIVE
OUR PLACE IN THE CONGREGATION

What Does It Mean to Participate in a Messianic Congregation? 161

Navigating Through a Very Small Messianic Movement 171

The Calling of Ruth and Non-Jewish Believers
in Today's Messianic Movement 181

UNIT SIX
A SURVEY OF MESSIANIC THEOLOGY

A Survey of Messianic Theology 195

How Do You Study the Bible? 205

Moving Forward in Your Messianic Experience 215

About the Author 229

Bibliography 233

Statement of Faith 243

Abbreviations and Special Terms

The following is a list of abbreviations for reference works and special terms which are used in publications by Outreach Israel Ministries and Messianic Apologetics. Please familiarize yourself with them as the text may reference a Bible version, i.e., RSV for the Revised Standard Version, or a source such as *TWOT* for the *Theological Wordbook of the Old Testament*, solely by its abbreviation. Detailed listings of these sources are provided in the Bibliography.

ABD: *Anchor Bible Dictionary*
AMG: *Complete Word Study Dictionary: Old Testament, New Testament*
ANE: Ancient Near East(ern)
Apostolic Scriptures/Writings: the New Testament
Ara: Aramaic
ASV: American Standard Version (1901)
ATS: ArtScroll Tanach (1996)
b. Babylonian Talmud (*Talmud Bavli*)
B.C.E.: Before Common Era or B.C.
BDAG: *A Greek-English Lexicon of the New Testament and Other Early Christian Literature* (Bauer, Danker, Arndt, Gingrich)
BDB: *Brown-Driver-Briggs Hebrew and English Lexicon*
C.E.: Common Era or A.D.
CGEDNT: *Concise Greek-English Dictionary of New Testament Words* (Barclay M. Newman)
CGL: *Cambridge Greek Lexicon* (2021)
CHALOT: *Concise Hebrew and Aramaic Lexicon of the Old Testament* (Holladay)
CJB: Complete Jewish Bible (1998)
CJSB: Complete Jewish Study Bible (2016)
DRA: Douay-Rheims American Edition
DSS: Dead Sea Scrolls
EDB: *Eerdmans Dictionary of the Bible*
EJ: *Encylopaedia Judaica*
ESV: English Standard Version (2001)
Ger: German
GNT: Greek New Testament
Grk: Greek
HALOT: *Hebrew & Aramaic Lexicon of the Old Testament* (Koehler and Baumgartner)
HCSB: Holman Christian Standard Bible (2004)
Heb: Hebrew
HNV: Hebrew Names Version of the World English Bible
IDB: *Interpreter's Dictionary of the Bible*
IDBSup: *Interpreter's Dictionary of the Bible Supplement*
ISBE: *International Standard Bible Encyclopedia*
IVPBBC: *IVP Bible Background Commentary (Old & New Testament)*
Jastrow: *Dictionary of the Targumim, Talmud Bavli, Talmud Yerushalmi, and Midrashic Literature* (Marcus Jastrow)
JBK: New Jerusalem Bible-Koren (2000)
JETS: *Journal of the Evangelical Theological Society*
KJV: King James Version
Lattimore: The New Testament by Richmond Lattimore (1996)
LITV: *Literal Translation of the Holy Bible* by Jay P. Green (1986)
LES: *Lexham English Septuagint* (2019)
LS: *An Intermediate Greek-English Lexicon* (Liddell-Scott)
LSJM: *Greek-English Lexicon* (Liddell-Scott-Jones-McKenzie)

LXE: *Septuagint with Apocrypha* by Sir L.C.L. Brenton (1851)
LXX: Septuagint
m. Mishnah
MT: Masoretic Text
NASB: New American Standard Bible (1977)
NASU: New American Standard Update (1995)
NBCR: *New Bible Commentary: Revised*
NEB: New English Bible (1970)
Nelson: *Nelson's Expository Dictionary of Old Testament Words*
NETS: New English Translation of the Septuagint (2007)
NIB: *New Interpreter's Bible*
NIDB: *New International Dictionary of the Bible*
NIV: New International Version (1984)
NJB: New Jerusalem Bible-Catholic (1985)
NJPS: Tanakh, A New Translation of the Holy Scriptures (1999)
NKJV: New King James Version (1982)
NRSV: New Revised Standard Version (1989)
NLT: New Living Translation (1996)
NT: New Testament
OT: Old Testament
REB: Revised English Bible (1989)
RSV: Revised Standard Version (1952)
t. Tosefta
Tanach (Tanakh): the Old Testament
Thayer: *Thayer's Greek-English Lexicon of the New Testament*
TDNT: *Theological Dictionary of the New Testament*
TLV: Messianic Jewish Family Bible—Tree of Life Version (2014)
TNIV: Today's New International Version (2005)
TWOT: *Theological Wordbook of the Old Testament*
UBSHNT: United Bible Societies' 1991 Hebrew New Testament revised edition
v(s). verse(s)
Vine: *Vine's Complete Expository Dictionary of Old and New Testament Words*
Vul: Latin Vulgate
YLT: Young's Literal Translation (1862/1898)
WMB: World Messianic Bible (2020)

Introduction

The Messianic movement is a vitally important community of people, Jewish and non-Jewish alike, who have been called at this point in time, **to be involved with some very important salvation historical work**. At no other time in human history, since the First Century C.E., have we seen Jewish people coming to faith in their Messiah in significant numbers, and non-Jewish Believers tangibly embracing their spiritual heritage in Israel's Scriptures, **and both** joining together as "one new humanity" (Ephesians 2:15). In today's Messianic congregations and synagogues, there is a broad conviction that we are seeing a return to something that was lost almost two thousand years ago. In fact, we are all a part of something which will culminate in "all Israel will be saved" (Romans 11:26) and the return of Yeshua to Planet Earth.

Centuries ago, if you were a Jewish person who expressed faith in Israel's Messiah, it was widely believed by Christian authorities that you could no longer regard yourself as being Jewish anymore. Today's Messianic Jewish movement has rightly corrected this—as Jewish Believers in Yeshua hardly stop being Jewish! Today's Messianic movement is a safe place for Jewish Believers to maintain their Jewish heritage and culture, without fear of reprisal and/or assimilation. More recently, if you are a non-Jewish Believer investigating and appreciating his or her spiritual heritage in the Old Testament and Judaism, you likely have received many accusations and insults levied against you, rooted in misunderstandings of Jewish history and tradition, by Christian people who have never really bothered to do their homework. Today's Messianic movement has become a safe place for non-Jewish Believers who have been called, at this time in history, to join with their Jewish brothers and sisters to participate in the restoration of Israel's Kingdom (cf. Acts 1:6). When we can all come together as one in the Lord, and employ the various strengths and virtues from our shared Judeo-Protestant heritage, I certainly believe that a great deal of significant progress can be made for the Kingdom of God!

Being a part of **the Messianic walk** is something that does not just have individual components to it, but it affects the corporate Messianic community, albeit a still-developing and still-emerging movement. Being a part of the Messianic walk involves each of us comprehending (1) the Messianic vision, (2) understanding and appreciating Biblical and Jewish holidays, (3) having a fair-minded approach to external expressions of God's commandments, (4) **actively participating in**

The Messianic Walk

Jewish outreach and evangelism, (5) actively participating in the life and fellowship of a local Messianic congregation, and (6) staying up to date with developments in Messianic theology and Bible teaching. Whether you choose to employ *The Messianic Walk* workbook for individual or group edification, the Messianic movement at the beginning of the 2020s offers each of us a venue to grow substantially in our faith and make a difference.

This workbook is a direct product of me teaching the New Foundations-New Members class at my own Messianic congregation, Eitz Chaim (EC) of Richardson, Texas (www.ecdallas.org). In the Spring of 2016, I was given the responsibility of taking over the New Foundations-New Members class, but would only do it on the condition of me being given a free hand to teach the class on my own terms. The materials which had been employed for the class, were certainly important staples for any Messianic library, and were books with which I was familiar. Originally, the class for EC was taught with *Jewish Roots: A Foundation of Biblical Theology* (Shippensburg, PA: Destiny Image, 1995) by Dan Juster, and *Our Hands Are Stained With Blood* (Shippensburg, PA: Destiny Image 1992) by Michael Brown. When I took the New Foundations-New Members class in the Spring of 2014, a different workbook was being employed, *Messianic Judaism Class* (Copenhagen, NY: Olive Press, 2011), by James Appel, Jonathan Bernis, and David Levine. This workbook was much easier for most students to follow, but many of the questions were formulated in the sense of "Tell us what Bible verse XYZ means..." Bible verse XYZ could have a dozen different meanings...

Originally when I took the EC New Foundations-New Members class, the facilitator would take around eighteen weeks to take people through the *Messianic Judaism Class* workbook, and each class would essentially be spent by going through the different study questions. When the eighteen weeks were over, the class might have gotten through about two-thirds of the material. *This was hardly useful, given the fact that* **the most important information** *for people becoming members of a Messianic congregation, is going to be found in the final chapters of the book(s) they are employing.* When I took over the New Foundations-New Members class, I streamlined everything to nine weeks. Students would have to do work on their own in the *Messianic Judaism Class* workbook, and when they came to the congregation, I would give them a brief presentation on the subject matter—but most especially would then discuss what the subject matter meant for our local congregation in North Dallas, and our interactions with both the Jewish and evangelical Protestant communities. Given some of the limitations of the *Messianic Judaism Class* workbook, I would also recommend that students purchase its associated Teacher Book, which would offer various answers to its questions.

Today, with the 2020s literally on our doorstep, the *Messianic Judaism Class* workbook and Teacher Book, are resources dated to the late 1990s. This new workbook, **The Messianic Walk**, has been produced as a direct result of me

Introduction

teaching the Eitz Chaim New Foundations-New Members class from *Messianic Judaism Class*, and various discussions with my congregational leadership and students. I am also directly affected by my ongoing ministry work with Outreach Israel (www.outreachisrael.net) and Messianic Apologetics (www.messianicapologetics.net), as today's Messianic movement does not exist in a bubble, and there are subjects mentioned which reflect our current times. *The Messianic Walk* is indebted to the previous work of many leaders and teachers in today's Messianic Jewish movement, **and should be employed in concert with the *Messianic Judaism Class* Teacher Book,** as there will be various references and quotations made.

At the same time, *The Messianic Walk* workbook also represents a capstone to much of the labor that I have conducted since being called into full-time Messianic ministry in 2003. *The Messianic Walk* workbook is not designed to answer every single question that you have about the Messianic movement and its purposes—but it is designed to acclimate you enough to this journey, and it will point you in the right direction where you can be further informed and educated.

J.K. McKee
Editor, Messianic Apologetics

The Messianic Walk

A Spiritual Scavenger Hunt

Every single one of us, as a redeemed man or woman of faith, has been on some kind of life journey that has led us to the salvation of Yeshua the Messiah, and hopefully into a place of contributing to the purposes of the Kingdom of God. One of the questions that I frequently ask myself, as a person who has been involved in the Messianic movement since 1995, very much is: *How did I get here?* A follow up question to this is: *What does God actually want me to do here?*

I truly came to dynamic saving faith on August 8, 1995. While this concerned dealing with some demonic issues from my family's past, as well as some issues involving the death of my father in 1992[i]—within several months of repenting of my sins and being born again I was in the Messianic movement. My mother Margaret, and her new husband Mark Huey, had gone on a Zola Levitt tour to Israel in December of 1994, where they had the impression that when returning to the United States, they needed to be focusing on the Biblical feasts of the Lord (Leviticus 23). And, by the Fall high holidays of 1995, we were attending a Messianic Jewish congregation, and getting acclimated to things like the weekly *Shabbat*, a kosher-style of diet, and various mainline Jewish traditions and customs.

One of the things that was very appealing for Mark and Margaret Huey, entering into the Messianic movement, was the fact that my mother was an Arminian, and my new stepfather was a Calvinist. While we all came from a broadly evangelical Protestant background, this new blended family knew that it was going to have to chart a new spiritual course. Throughout the second half of 1995 and into 1996, we tried attending *Shabbat* services on Saturday, while also going to Sunday Church. By the Spring of 1996, we had fully crossed over to the Messianic Jewish congregation. Not only was our faith in the Messiah being enriched and enlivened at new levels—with there being significant "hands on" spiritual activities

---

[i] Some of my experience in coming to salvation is covered in my article "The Assurance of Our Salvation" (appearing in *Introduction to Things Messianic*) and *Why Hell Must Be Eternal*.

The Messianic Walk

to be considering—the Jewish community is one which indeed likes to talk about significant issues. Fellowship times either before or after the service, or getting to know new friends at their homes, was a substantial blessing. *We were a family that liked to talk about the Bible, things of the Lord,* and *current events.*

Our full transition into the Messianic movement was also enjoined in the Spring of 1996 by our family encountering a number of—at the time—compelling voices, "quasi-Messianic" we would say now, who were making significant predictions about the end-times, the return of Yeshua, and the Middle East peace process. In the Summer of 1996, my parents made a point to attend both the MJAA Messiah conference in Grantham, PA and the UMJC conference in Sturbridge, MA, mainly with the purpose of getting acclimated to this movement we were getting involved with. But when they returned home to Dallas, they got plugged in more and more to the prophecy teachings and predictions. Certainly for a new family, with three children who had lost their father several years earlier, the thought that Yeshua was soon going to return, was something that grabbed our attention. In fact, it grabbed our attention for a number of years!

At the beginning of 1997, our family moved out of Dallas to a small farm north of the city. Over the course of 1997, while we continued to maintain our connections to the local Messianic Jewish congregation, my stepfather helped host a series of prophecy conferences. In March of 1997, I launched my first website, where I posted a number of opinion articles on both end-time prophecy and Messianic themes. On August 15, 1997, I started the website Tribulation News Network or TNN Online. And, in forecasting the future with the close of the Millennium and Y2k impending, my stepfather actually got involved with a shortwave radio operation based out of Central Honduras. In the Spring of 1998, and with some end-time concerns being present, my family sold its major assets and sent two containers with all of our possessions to the island of Roatán in the Bay Islands of Honduras.

It was my stepfather's plan in 1998 to go back and forth between Roatán and the mainland, doing work for the shortwave radio venture and some real estate consulting in the Bay Islands. We would then see what the global-prophetic situation in the world would be. None of this came to pass. For eight months (April-December) we rented a number of picturesque homes on Roatán, with our two containers still on the dock waiting to be opened. Due to the intervention of Hurricane Mitch in October-November 1998, one of the deadliest storms on record, we knew it was time to return to the United States. An opportunity opened for my stepfather to do some consulting work for a ministry in Oklahoma. We are thankful that we did not lose anything due to Hurricane Mitch!

I am most especially thankful that even though my high school career was not what others would have wanted it to be, that I did finish my senior year through a homeschooling correspondence program, and that in the Fall of 1999 I was able to

A Spiritual Scavenger Hunt

enroll at the University of Oklahoma. As we returned to the United States in 1999, any end-time preoccupation, fear, or paranoia did get removed from us, and we instead returned to witnessing what God was doing through an increasingly expanding and diversifying Messianic movement. As I was finishing up the first year of my college studies in 2000, my parents accepted an offer to consult with another ministry out of Central Florida. This venture ended in 2002, but by this time we had become a part of an independent Messianic assembly in the Greater Orlando area.

Throughout my college studies at the University of Oklahoma, my TNN Online website, Theology News Network, was something which definitely kept my attention, and it also kept me away from associating with the wrong crowd. I was working on my bachelor's degree in political science, and as a result took classes not only in political philosophy and theory, but also in histories ancient and modern relevant to Biblical Studies, and was able to take some modern Hebrew and classical Greek. Being on my own for these years, with my website as a hobby, did get me to focus on what being part of the Messianic movement *meant to me.* I was not really a part of a Messianic congregation or fellowship, and so I instead would spend *Shabbat* often in Bible study or in writing for my website. I did try to be a part of various on campus ministry groups, which had some success for a season, but eventually did not work out too well by the time I graduated. While there were sincere evangelical Christian people at OU, it was obvious that the Messianic movement, its focus on Israel, and reconnecting with the Tanach or Old Testament, were just too foreign. And, I do have to admit that I was not always too kind or graceful in response to criticism I would receive. *It was good that this happened while I was in college, and not when I entered into full time ministry.*

In the Fall of 2002, my parents launched Outreach Israel Ministries, which at the time had a very broad vision of incorporating many different possible ventures. When I graduated from college in 2003, I returned to Central Florida, TNN Online became a division of OIM, and our ministry began releasing its first series of educational resources. For the most part, these books, bearing titles like *Hebraic Roots: An Introductory Study* and *Introduction to Things Messianic*, were written with the intention of helping aid many non-Jewish Believers, like our family, in getting acclimated to the Messianic movement.

To be sure, as we got started in the first full two years of ministry, in 2003-2005, we had a lot to learn. Mark Huey and I did some speaking trips throughout the U.S., Canada, Israel, and the United Kingdom. In 2005, I started attending the Orlando campus of Asbury Theological Seminary, where I would work on my M.A. in Biblical Studies. As a result of our major travels in 2004, where we encountered all sorts of people identifying with the label "Messianic"—Jewish Believers, non-Jewish Believers, people part of Messianic Judaism, people part of break-off sects

The Messianic Walk

and new sects bearing provocative labels[ii]—**we realized that we had a huge amount of work ahead of us, and that even some of our own attitudes and viewpoints needed to change.** As a result of the first few semesters of attending Asbury Seminary, where I was able to reconnect with much of my Wesleyan upbringing, I was having, for the first time, to deal with the Holy Scriptures and the world of the Bible in a much more complex and detailed way. In learning new skills involving Biblical exegesis, Hebrew and Greek, and accessing technical commentaries and resources—I found myself being much better equipped to defend many of my convictions as a part of the Messianic movement. I also realized in 2005-2006, that a number of the things that our family picked up in our early days entering into the Messianic movement, were in serious need of reevaluation, even dismissal, being rather simple and downright unsupportable.

My seminary experience from 2005-2008 is something which I have not commented about too frequently among Messianic people, precisely because I know that on the whole many Messianic people are skeptical, if not hostile, to religious studies education. *I did not attend seminary to "convert" people to my Messianic beliefs.* I attended seminary to acquire skills, and be able to join into a larger conversation of Biblical Studies. And this is something that I was able to do. When I graduated in Spring of 2009, I was blessed to receive the Zondervan Biblical Languages Award for Greek. But immediately following seminary, our ministry would have to start absorbing all of the new knowledge and resources that I had access to, and things certainly started to change.

One of the biggest things that shifted for us in 2009 was seeing that our ministry books be transferred out of spiral combs and into printed paperback books. It was at this time that I was able to totally dedicate all of my time to ministry work, and as titles were prepared for paperback release, updates reflecting my seminary training and degree would be steadily reflected. Yet as we all know, God has a unique way of being able to "jump start" things...

As the 2000s came to a close, and in particular as my youngest sister Maggie started finishing high school, our family knew that our time in Central Florida would be concluding. In the Summer of 2009, my mother, Maggie and I went on a college scouting trip out to the University of Oklahoma. I had not been back since my graduation. When the three of us walked into the Armory at OU, where the Naval ROTC unit was based, we all received the distinct impression that Maggie was going to OU. Of course, this did not affect me directly; I would be returning to Central Florida and be continuing my work of editing our books for paperback release, and working on new Bible studies. In the late Spring of 2010 we again went on a roadtrip out to OU, as Maggie had been accepted and was getting ready to start college in

---

[ii] These provocative labels included, but were not limited to, the Two-House and One Law/One Torah sub-movements.

A Spiritual Scavenger Hunt

the Fall. My work was continuing.

Our family had originally believed that were we to move out of the Orlando area, that we would move northward to Jacksonville, where we have extended family. In late August 2010, my mother and I went to Jacksonville to help move my grandmother from her assisted living unit into a new memory care unit. While we were there, my stepfather Mark was on a trip visiting friends and other family members. I remember distinctly walking out of the Allegro in Orange Park, and telling my mother that I would seriously consider moving back to Dallas rather than move to Jacksonville. *This was quite a change, because neither one of us ever wanted to live in Dallas again.* Yet, with my sister Maggie now at the University of Oklahoma, and knowing that there was a vibrant and significant Messianic community in the DFW Metroplex, we definitely started feeling the pull West.

We announced our intention to relocate to North Texas in the Fall of 2010, but we had no idea that it was going to take us over two years to do it. For my part, I knew that I had to gear up, seeing that all of our books were prepared for paperback release—and that if the Lord wanted us to go through any major theological changes, namely in the form of refining and expanding our teachings on various issues, **now would be the time to do it.** While 2011-2012 were hardly easy years for me, 2011 was a significant year for some theological transitions. 2012 was spent formatting all of our ministry books for both paperback and eBook release. At the end of 2012, my parent's house in Kissimmee, FL finally sold, and by December we were all living in North Dallas once again—in the same exact zip code where we had originally moved in 1994, no less!

The Spring of 2013 was widely spent getting reacclimated to the DFW area, after being gone for fourteen years. What was most important to us was getting reconnected with the Messianic friends we knew from our early days in Messianic Judaism, back in 1995-1998. By the late Summer of 2013, we quickly got plugged into Eitz Chaim Messianic Jewish Congregation, as we had been good friends with the main leaders, Rabbi David and Elizabeth Schiller, in the late 1990s. Because EC is an assembly which encourages participation from members, by the Winter of 2014 we had all taken the New Members class, our family began helping out with the different festivals (in particular the congregational Passover *seder*), and by the Fall of 2014 Mark Huey had been asked to become a *shammash* (deacon), by the Fall of 2015 being further elevated as an elder. I had given several teachings on *Shabbat*, and had renewed my own friendship with David that I had back in 1996-1997 when I was in my teens.

2014-2015 were important years not just in terms of transitioning to a new life back in North Texas, to take on new theological and spiritual challenges, and to consolidate ourselves—they were also very important as we began to discern what our own long term purpose would become as a family ministry. While we all agree that moving back to Dallas was the best decision we ever made, because we are

The Messianic Walk

human, no place on Earth is entirely perfect. Things in the United States shifted immeasurably with the legalization of homosexual marriage in the Summer of 2015. When this happened, I actually felt in a similar manner to how I did in 1996-1997, when we were encapsulated with end-time prophecy. If anything, American society crossed a Romans ch. 1 "red line," **and we were all shown a "road sign" that End Game is approaching.** I myself have had the distinct supernatural impression that with as many things that I have researched and written on, that I would have to be targeted with my life, and would not be able to have all of the same opportunities that those who preceded me had. In June of 2015, the tnnonline.net domain was actually stolen from me during the few hours that the domain was needing to be re-registered, and so I made the necessary upgrade from TNN Online to **Messianic Apologetics**. This was a vital change for the future!

Mark and Margaret Huey like to frequently describe the journey our family has been on as a "spiritual scavenger hunt." *We went from one place and experience...to another place and experience...and so on...* The journey of human life is always something that is ongoing. We learn new things every day through our experiences and interactions, with both the Lord and other human beings, as to how to be more effective in His service. But as far as the bulk of experiences that our family has had—in moving from place to place, in being called into Messianic education, and in interacting with broad and diverse sectors of this emerging faith community—on the whole our "spiritual scavenger hunt" is over. Much of what we are involved with today concerns our effectiveness as Messianic people, fine-tuning our strengths and abilities, and with new stages of development which are likely to equally excite and frighten us all.

Our family was first called into Messianic ministry to help others from evangelical backgrounds, adequately transition into a Messianic lifestyle—extending grace and mercy to others who were not similarly called (at present), and making sure that this was a genuine work of the Holy Spirit in their lives (cf. Jeremiah 31:31-34; Ezekiel 36:25-27). Our ministry experiences to the present day included things that we could both anticipate and not anticipate. Like everyone, we have had our good days and our bad days, we have had to firmly stand up for the truth of God's Word, and we have had to admit where we have made mistakes and correct them.

Salvation history is on a decisive trajectory: "all Israel will be saved" (Romans 11:26ff). This is something that involves not only a massive salvation of Jewish people, but will culminate in the return of Israel's Messiah—and with it the completion of not only many prophecies regarding the restoration of Israel's Kingdom, but will involve Yeshua Himself reigning over this planet. Today in the Messianic community, we see Jewish people coming in substantial numbers to Messiah faith. We also see non-Jewish Believers embracing their Hebraic and Jewish Roots in substantial numbers. Together, we should not only be united as

A Spiritual Scavenger Hunt

"one new humanity" (Ephesians 2:15, NRSV), purged of old hostilities and mistrust of the other—but we should be employing the virtues and strengths of our shared Judeo-Protestant heritage for what is to be anticipated in the future.

If there is anything that I have learned on the spiritual scavenger hunt, it is that suspicion, division, and rivalry begin when we fail to communicate with one another, and when we do not even bother to consider the vantage point or perspective of someone else. A figure like Paul knew better than this, when going out to reach the diverse groups of people in the First Century Mediterranean (1 Corinthians 9:19-23). My many writings and studies to date bear significant attention to detail. For some, this is just information overkill. For others, it is a documented record of wanting to not only hear multiple witnesses in a case (Deuteronomy 19:15), it demonstrates a deep seated commitment on my part to be fair, and even what it means to "love one another with mutual affection; outdo one another in showing honor" (Romans 12:10, NRSV).

Your journey into the Messianic movement is not the same as my family's journey. Your journey may have been less, or even more, difficult. Like all people in this unique and special move of the Holy Spirit, there are things we have had to give up. I personally take a great deal of comfort from Yeshua's word, "And everyone who has left houses or brothers or sisters or father or mother or children or property, for My name's sake, will receive a hundred times as much, and will inherit eternal life" (Matthew 19:29, TLV). Yet, each one of us needs to maintain a sense of purpose, a steadfast will, and a consistent resolution to accomplish the Messianic mission—and to arrive at the culmination of history. *May we stay true to the call!*

The Messianic Walk

THE MESSIANIC EXPERIENCE

UNIT ONE

The Messianic Mission

Why are any of us involved in today's Messianic movement? The answers that we might provide to this question are likely varied, and they each involve a number of distinct life circumstances and encounters. Hopefully the main answer that each of us would have to this question is: *God wants us here.* If you are a Jewish person raised with a knowledge that your ancestors definitely stood at the base of Mount Sinai, hearing the Ten Words from the Almighty, then you have found your promised Messiah and may be considered a completed Jew. If you are a non-Jewish person, likely raised in an evangelical Protestant home, then you have connected with your Hebraic Roots in the ancient Scriptures of Israel, your Jewish Roots in the Synagogue, and have joined with your Messianic Jewish brothers and sisters in an important move which will culminate in the return of Israel's Messiah.

My family has been involved in the Messianic movement since 1995, has been called into full time Messianic educational ministry since 2003—and in the process we have encountered many valuable, but also varied, approaches to what the Lord is doing in this hour. For many of today's Messianic Jews, the modern Messianic movement has been a significant lifeline, not only as a faith community where they do not have to give up on their Jewish heritage as Believers in Israel's Messiah, assimilating into the larger pot or tossed salad of non-Jewish Christianity—but where they can anticipate being part of a significant salvation historical trajectory, involving not only the salvation of many more of their fellow Jews, but the restoration of the Kingdom to Israel as anticipated by the Disciples (Acts 1:6). For many of today's non-Jewish Believers, specially called by the Lord into the Messianic movement at this phase of its development, the Messianic movement has provided them a venue to not only tangibly partake of things like the Passover *seder* or a weekly *Shabbat* rest, but for them to connect with the Tanach (Old Testament) and the ways of Yeshua and His first followers in a very significant manner.

The Scriptures direct us regarding the truth of how, "Without a prophetic vision, the people throw off all restraint" (Proverbs 29:18, CJB/CJSB). At the close of the 2010s, it is fairly witnessed that many people across the Messianic spectrum have their own view(s) about what the Messianic movement is all about, or will become. Far too frequently, the perspectives that people have regarding the future vision, mission, or purpose of the Messianic movement are a bit too *individualistic*, meaning that they do not tend to take into account what God is doing with the *corporate* Body of Messiah. Many of us are conditioned by a modern Western mindset which is so hyper-individualistic, that we think that our faith in God only concerns our individual selves and God—and not our individual selves, our fellow brothers and sisters in the Messiah of Israel, and God's Kingdom purposes for this hour. In Romans 12:1, the Believers were actually admonished to look at themselves **not** as *individual* living sacrifices, but as individuals making up a *corporate* living sacrifice: "I urge you therefore, brothers and sisters, by the mercies of God, to present your bodies as a living sacrifice" (TLV). If there is any big difference between Judaism and Protestantism, it is that the former will emphasize the interconnectivity of the people of God involved in the purposes of God, as they anticipate the world to come.

The Prophet Habakkuk was communicated Divine messages from the God of Israel, who directed him to record His word, with it stressed that what was to take place would take place: "Write down the vision, make it plain on the tablets, so that the reader may run with it. For the vision is yet for an appointed time. It hastens to the end and will not fail. If it should be slow in coming, wait for it, for it will surely come—it will not delay" (Habakkuk 2:2-3, TLV). This *chazon* or vision would only take place at the Lord's pre-determined "season" (YLT), yet it would be up to the people of God to have the perseverance for God's plan to take shape on God's timetable. Many of us, Jewish and non-Jewish alike—with our many gifts, talents, and skills endowed by our Creator—are indeed part of *the end-time move* of God. But it is also required of us to know how we got to this point in history, so that we can be effective and not grow weary, with the work and labor that are necessary as we see this unique and special Messianic movement enter into its own.

The First Century Believers

One of the most significant "revelations," as it were—not only to evangelical Protestant people investigating their Jewish Roots, but even Jewish people reading the Apostolic Scriptures or New Testament—is that Yeshua of Nazareth and His first followers were all Jewish. Many evangelical Protestants, when they read the Gospels, at least subconsciously transfer a Western (particularly conservative, Southern American) experience into what the Messiah and His Disciples are saying and doing. This is reflected in a great deal of contemporary Christian preaching and teaching, which contemporary Jews—even those who are open-minded to hearing new ideas—consider to be largely irrelevant and unimportant to them and their religious and cultural heritage. However, the accounts are vast and diverse from many of today's Messianic Jewish Believers, that when they finally read the sayings

The Messianic Mission

of Yeshua and His interactions with the Jewish religious leaders and ancient contemporaries, that Yeshua was obviously acting and speaking very similar to many of the Rabbis of His time. For certain, Yeshua spoke and acted with the same authority and presence as one of the Prophets of Ancient Israel. Yeshua also frequently employed colloquial expressions such as "Whatever you prohibit on earth will be prohibited in heaven, and whatever you permit on earth will be permitted in heaven" (Matthew 16:19, CJB/CJSB), which may require some investigation with Second Temple Jewish literature.

So what has been the disconnect between many of today's Jewish people, not frequently seeing the Jewishness of the Gospels and Messianic Scriptures—and most especially today's non-Jewish evangelical Protestant Believers not seeing the importance of a spiritual heritage going back to Second Temple Judaism, Mount Sinai, and the Patriarchs Abraham, Isaac, and Jacob? The factors that play into this are broad and diverse, some of them involving an ignorance of Biblical history, some of them involving poor and errant decisions made by religious leaders in the past, and some of them involving a close-mindedness and prejudice that need to be jettisoned.

One of the biggest mistakes that does not get challenged enough **is that the First Century C.E. followers of Yeshua of Nazareth were not the Sunday, church going "Christians" that many people automatically assume them to be.** The first group of First Century C.E. followers of Yeshua of Nazareth were Judean and Diaspora Jews, raised in a society that recognized the One God of Israel, and were trained in the Scriptures of Israel, the Tanach (an acronym for *T*orah/Law, *N*evi'im/Prophets, *K*etuvim/Writings) from birth. They remembered the weekly *Shabbat* or seventh-day Sabbath, the annual appointed times or *moedim* of Leviticus 23, they followed the kosher dietary laws, and they circumcised their sons. Many of them were also fiercely protective of their integrity as a community, wanting to keep pagan influences out.

The second group of First Century C.E. followers of Yeshua of Nazareth were mainly Greeks and Romans, who were raised in a polytheistic society that worshipped the gods and goddesses of classical antiquity. Because of their paganism, they were frequently derided by the Jewish community for their sexual immorality (cf. Romans 1:26-28). Many of them were notably attracted to the Jewish Synagogue, its morality, and its monotheism, and as God-fearers were among some of the first non-Jews who would receive Israel's Messiah. Many of them were attracted directly to Israel's Messiah from paganism (1 Thessalonians 1:9). And many of them, when encountering Israel's Messiah, found it difficult to adhere to the four, non-negotiable requirements for entry into the assembly as issued by the Jerusalem Council: abstinence from idolatry, fornication, things strangled, and blood (Acts 15:20, 29). Clearly *if followed*, the Apostolic decree would serve the purpose of seeing the new Greek and Roman Believers severed

The Messianic Walk

from their old spheres of social and religious influence, hence making their new sphere of social and religious influence one where the Scriptures of Israel were honored (Acts 15:21).

The First Century *ekklēsia* or assembly, in the Land of Israel, was exclusively Jewish, and centered around Jerusalem. James (Jacob) the Just, Peter, and John were recognized as being pillars of the Judean community of Jewish Believers (Galatians 2:9). As James would report of many of the Jewish Believers in and around Jerusalem, "{Look at} how many myriads there are among the Jewish people who have believed—and they are all zealous for the Torah" (Acts 21:20, TLV). While some of this may have involved some of the fierce Jewish nationalism and Zealotry of the mid-First Century, what is seen is that belief in Yeshua as Israel's Messiah hardly meant casting aside one's Jewish heritage. In later centuries, Church leaders considered that if a Jewish person professed faith in Jesus, that he or she would become a "Christian," and have to give up on his or her Jewish heritage completely.

In view of the Great Commission given by Yeshua to go out and make disciples of the nations (Matthew 28:19-21; Acts 1:8), Bible readers' understanding of the First Century Believers widely comes from the letters of Paul, with significant background often witnessed in the Book of Acts. Paul had a distinct assignment from the Messiah to go out into the Mediterranean, and witness to Jews, Greeks, and Romans (Acts 9:15). The assemblies planted by the Apostle Paul, often first involved his traveling to a city where there was a Diaspora Jewish synagogue, he would declare the good news of Israel's Messiah, where a group of Messiah followers from among Jews, God-fearing Greeks and Romans, and perhaps also pagans from the local community, would steadily form. Sometimes after a period, Paul and his company would be forced to leave the local Jewish synagogue, but not always. Each of the assemblies and groups of Messiah followers established or influenced by Paul, had their own advantages, disadvantages, and challenges. While Paul is seen to have a significant Jewish heritage and pedigree (Philippians 3:5-6), he is also one seen to emphasize the centrality of placing one's faith or trust in the sacrificial work of Yeshua (Galatians 2:16; Philippians 3:9).

First Century Warnings Gone Unheeded

While the good news or gospel message of salvation in Israel's Messiah going out to the whole world, was a critical imperative issued by the Lord Himself to His first followers—the good news going out to the whole world was actually a critical component of the restoration of Israel's Kingdom. The steadfast word of Isaiah 49:6 proclaims, "It is too trifling a thing that You should be My servant to raise up the tribes of Jacob and restore the preserved ones of Israel. So I will give You as a light for the nations, that You should be My salvation to the end of the earth" (TLV). Yeshua the Messiah did not simply come to restore Israel proper, but also

The Messianic Mission

to be the *or goyim* or "light to the nations." **The restoration of Israel's Kingdom is something which is to affect the entire world.**

Ancient Israel's obedience to God's Instruction, and hence their being blessed, was to serve as a testimony to others and consequently to draw others to the Lord (Deuteronomy 4:5-8). At the construction of the First Temple, Solomon prayed that foreigners would hear of it and come to a knowledge of the God of Israel (1 Kings 8:41-43). Themes of Israel being a light to the nations, the Messiah being a light to the nations, and the restoration of Israel affecting the entire world, are all detectable throughout the Apostolic Writings and the evangelistic works undertaken in the First Century Mediterranean. In Ephesians 2, those of the nations who came to faith in Messiah are described as being a part of the Commonwealth of Israel (Ephesians 2:11-12), "brought near" (Ephesians 2:13; cf. Isaiah 57:19), and being "fellow citizens with the holy ones, and of the household of God" (Ephesians 2:19, author's rendering). Jewish and non-Jewish Believers in Israel's Messiah, purged of the effects of sin, were to come together as one in Him, forming a one new man or one new humanity (Ephesians 2:12), able to accomplish the purposes of God in the Earth.

A figure like Paul believed that those of the nations, having received the Jewish Messiah, were indebted to help their fellow Jewish Believers in the First Century in their material needs (Romans 15:27). As he puts it, "For it is not relief for others and hardship for you, but as a matter of equality. Your abundance at this present time meets their need, so that their abundance may also meet your need—so that there may be equality" (2 Corinthians 8:13-14, TLV). Jewish and non-Jewish Believers were to come together as one in the Lord, equals in the Messiah (Galatians 3:28; Colossians 2:11), and pooling all of their gifts, talents, and resources—becoming steadily inter-dependent, reliant, and mutually respectful of each other.

While it can be recognized that in the Second-Fourth Centuries, some terrible, and indeed damning, anti-Semitic and anti-Jewish statements were made by leaders of the emerging Christian Church, as Roman Catholicism began to form—it has to also be acknowledged that the warnings issued by a figure like the Apostle Paul, in Romans chs. 9-11, were largely not heeded. When Paul wrote the Romans, he recognized that more people from the nations were receiving Israel's Messiah than his fellow Jews. This, he concluded, was a part of God's plan, and that "by their transgression salvation *has come* to the nations, to make them jealous" (Romans 11:11, author's rendering). With non-Jewish people receiving the Jewish Messiah, and hence benefitting from promises originally given to Ancient Israel, Jewish people should be provoked to jealousy *to want* what these various Greeks, Romans, and others have—which they had an ancestral claim to. Yet, Paul had to warn against possible arrogance issued by non-Jewish Believers to the Jewish people who had widely dismissed their promised Messiah. As he says in Romans 11:18-21,

The Messianic Walk

"[D]o not boast against the branches. But if you do boast, it is not you who support the root but the root supports you. You will say then, 'Branches were broken off so that I might be grafted in.' True enough. They were broken off because of unbelief, and you stand by faith. Do not be arrogant, but fear—for if God did not spare the natural branches, neither will He spare you" (TLV).

Non-Jewish Believers, by their faith in Israel's Messiah, might be grafted-in to Israel's olive tree (Jeremiah 11:16-17; Hosea 14:1-7), but that does not give them any right **to be arrogant or boastful over the Jewish people who have widely dismissed their Messiah.** Instead, as Paul directs in Romans 11:30-31, "For just as you once were disobedient to God but now have been shown mercy because of their disobedience, in like manner these also have now been disobedient with the result that, because of the mercy shown to you, they also may receive mercy" (TLV). The non-Jewish Believers were told to be vessels of mercy and kindness to Jewish people who had not yet encountered their Messiah, in an effort to see them saved from their sins!

Unfortunately, in the many centuries of Christianity that have taken place since Paul wrote some of these words, his instruction has never been fully implemented, *at least until today. . .* Today, via the emergence of the modern Messianic movement in the past half-century or more, we have seen Jewish people come to faith in their Messiah in significant numbers, and we have seen non-Jewish Believers embrace their faith heritage in Israel's Scriptures. Most importantly, we have seen the words of Ephesians 2, Romans 9-11, and even Yeshua's prayer of John 17:22—"The glory that You have given to Me I have given to them, that they may be one just as We are one" (TLV)—take on dimensions which have not been seen since the First Century. Much of original setting and issues, witnessed in the Apostolic Writings or New Testament, does not seem so abstract any more—because Messianic congregations and fellowships indeed have Jewish Believers and non-Jewish Believers present within them, with each sorting out what it means to place their trust in Israel's Messiah, desiring to see Him return and reign from Jerusalem.

Breaking With Judaism

While in the First Century C.E., there was a noticeable and sizable number of Jewish Believers in Israel's Messiah, following the death of the Apostles and many of their second generation successors, the numbers of Jewish Believers dramatically decreased. Some of this was caused by the outcome of the Jewish Revolt and the destruction of Jerusalem in 70 C.E. by the Romans. Anti-Semitism flared up significantly in the Roman Empire, and did not help the burgeoning assemblies of followers in Israel's Messiah, especially among Greek and Roman Believers who may not have been too keen on Jewish sensitivities. By the Second and Third Centuries, though, leadership of the now emerging Christian Church was

The Messianic Mission

almost entirely non-Jewish, and far from the Apostle Paul's direction of Romans chs. 9-11 being heeded, supersessionism or replacement theology began to take significant hold. It was widely believed that God had rejected Israel and the Jewish people, replaced Israel with a new "Church" entity, and had transferred His promises to Israel to this new entity. Here is a small summary of some Second Century Christian views of the Jewish people:

> "This is He who was put to death. And where was He put to death? In the midst of Jerusalem. By whom? By Israel...O Israel, transgressor of the Law, why have you committed this new iniquity" (Melito c. 170).

> "Inasmuch as the former [the Jews] have rejected the Son of God, and cast Him out of the vineyard when they slew Him, God has justly rejected them. He has given to the Gentiles (outside the vineyard) the fruits of its cultivation" (Irenaeus c. 180).

> "Thus has the 'lesser' people—that is, the elder people—overcome the 'greater' people. For [the lesser] have acquired the grace of divine favor, from which Israel has been divorced" (Tertullian c. 197).

> "Let the Jews recognize their own fate—a fate which was constantly foretold as destined to occur after the advent of the Christ. This fate was on account of the impiety with which they despised and slew Him...Thereafter, God's grace desisted among them. And, 'the clouds were commanded not to rain a shower upon the vineyard of Sorek,'—the clouds being celestial benefits" (Tertullian c. 197).[1]

Witnessing the fall of Jerusalem to Rome, a widescale Jewish dismissal of Yeshua of Nazareth, and scores of Greeks and Romans recognizing Israel's Messiah in some way—far from being moved with mercy and empathy for the Jewish people, Christian leaders of the Second-Fourth Centuries instead believed that God was finished with them. If you were a Jewish Believer in Yeshua in the early Second Century, you would find yourself not only a minority in the *ekklēsia*, but you would not find your commitment to your Biblical and ethnic heritage in the Torah something to be too honored. Concurrent with the idea that God was finished with Israel, was also that He was finished with the Law of Moses and its rituals. Christian leaders like Justin Martyr did think that Jewish Believers could continue to practice things like circumcision or the Sabbath, and that non-Jewish Believers could join with them in fellowship, although the former were weak-minded:

---

[1] "Jew, Jews," in David W. Bercot, ed., *A Dictionary of Early Christian Beliefs* (Peabody, MA: Hendrickson, 1998), pp 375, 376.

The Messianic Walk

"'There are such people, Trypho,' I answered; 'and these do not venture to have any intercourse with or to extend hospitality to such persons; but I do not agree with them. But if some, through weak-mindeness, wish to observe such institutions as were given by Moses, from which they expect some virtue, but which we believe were appointed by reason of the hardness of the people's hearts, along with their hope in this Christ, and [wish to perform] the eternal and natural acts of righteousness and piety, yet choose to live with the Christians and the faithful, as I said before, not inducing them either to be circumcised like themselves, or to keep the Sabbath, or to observe any other such ceremonies, then I hold that we ought to join ourselves to such, and associate with them in all things as kinsmen and brethren" (*Dialogue with Trypho* 47).[2]

In such an environment—where one's ethnic and cultural heritage *in Israel's Scriptures* would be barely tolerated—it was far easier for Jewish people to not have anything to do with the emerging Christianity of the Second-Fourth Centuries. Of course, even though various religious leaders and ecclesiastical authorities would have their negative words to issue against Judaism and the Jewish people, there were many individual non-Jewish Believers who would, in various ways, be drawn to the Jewish community and Synagogue. Church councils, however, would make it illegal for any Christian person wanting to commemorate the Resurrection of Yeshua in association with the Passover, or remember the seventh-day Sabbath.

The Council of Antioch (341 C.E.) decreed that anyone caught celebrating the Lord's resurrection ("Easter") at the same time as the Jewish Passover would be excommunicated from the Church, and be considered to be causing destruction to his soul:

> But if any one of those who preside in the Church, whether he be bishop, presbyter, or deacon, shall presume, after this decree, to exercise his own private judgment to the subversion of the people and to the disturbance of the churches, by observing Easter [at the same time] with the Jews, the holy Synod decrees that he shall thenceforth be an alien from the Church, as one who not only heaps sins upon himself, but who is also the cause of destruction and subversion to many; and it deposes not only such persons themselves from their ministry, but those also who after their deposition shall presume to communicate with them (Canon 1).[3]

The Council of Laodicea (363 C.E.) decreed that Christians should not rest on the Sabbath, but instead observe "the Lord's Day":

---

[2] *The Post-Nicene Fathers*, P. Schaff, ed.; Libronix Digital Library System 1.0d: Church History Collection. MS Windows XP. Garland, TX: Galaxie Software. 2002.

[3] Ibid.

The Messianic Mission

> Here the Fathers order that no one of the faithful shall stop work on the Sabbath as do the Jews, but that they should honor the Lord's Day; on account of the Lord's resurrection, and that on that day they should abstain from manual labor and go to church. But thus abstaining from work on Sunday they do not lay down as a necessity, but they add, 'if they can.' For if through need or any other necessity any one worked on the Lord's day this was not reckoned against him (Canon 29).[4]

These kinds of sentiments, most lamentably, have not gone away, and are still alive and well in the hearts and minds of many of today's evangelical Protestant theologians, ministers, and laypeople. Yeshua, the Messiah and King of Israel, decreed the ongoing continuance of the Torah or Law of Moses and its commandments—albeit centered around His interpretation and application (Matthew 5:17-19)—yet throughout too much of Christian history, many purported followers of Israel's Messiah have wanted little to do with Israel's Scriptures and its instruction.

Today's Protestants would be fair to recognize that the forced conversions and baptisms of Jewish people, often on the threat of death by Roman Catholic leaders, is a Middle Aged tragedy that does not reflect on the love of Jesus and the character of those truly born again. Likewise, the social oppression and discrimination of the Jewish people throughout European history, for certain, is something that today's evangelical Protestants would likewise eschew and treat with disdain. At the same time, even though Protestants have been keen to recognize the anti-Semitic stain of Medieval Catholicism on the Jewish people and Jewish-Christian relations—social and religious anti-Semitism are still alive and well throughout many denominations and theological traditions of Protestantism. Many of today's evangelical non-Jewish Believers are of the mindset that they have replaced Israel and the Jewish people in the intentions of God. They actually consider the Scriptures of Israel, the Tanach, to be something foreign and alien—and no different than some of the Church Fathers of the Second-Fourth Centuries, would at best tolerate today's Jewish Believers remembering the Sabbath or circumcising their sons as some part of their (backward) cultural heritage.

A Movement Reborn

With the death of the original Messianic Jewish Disciples and their second generation successors, and the emergence of Roman Catholicism by the Fourth Century C.E., the numbers of Jewish Believers in Israel's Messiah for many centuries were scant at best. Catholicism, in no uncertain terms, demanded that Jewish people who profess belief in Yeshua of Nazareth, quantitatively abandon their Jewish heritage. Perhaps during the Middle Ages, various religious and

---

[4] Ibid.

The Messianic Walk

political authorities were ignorant of the Scriptures, and were grossly misguided. But, their negative legacy has left its impact.

While hardly perfect, the Protestant Reformation was a necessary and required step forward. Seeing the corruption and opulence of Roman Catholicism reach intolerable levels, figures such as Martin Luther and John Calvin were used by the Lord, in the Sixteenth Century, to help the Body of Messiah return to a foundational grounding in the Holy Scriptures, and that faith in the Messiah alone is what provides salvation to a person. The Reformation exposed many of the non-Biblical and pagan traditions of Catholicism, and helped to formulate an ideology where individual people did not have to rely upon Catholic priests and rituals in order to have redemption. To be sure, when individual people can read the Bible for themselves, many unique and diverse interpretations arise—hence the wide number of Protestant theological schools and denominations.

Because of the diverse number of Protestant denominations—with huge dividing lines emerging by the Seventeenth Century between Calvinists and Arminians—there have been different approaches witnessed in the relationship that Protestant Christians have had with Judaism and the Jewish people. Many have continued to promote supersessionism or replacement theology, the belief that God is finished with Israel and the Jewish people, and that "the Church" has inherited all of Israel's promises. At the same time, there have been Protestant Christians who have interpreted the Tanach or Old Testament more literally than not, and who several centuries ago made efforts to oppose anti-Semitism, establish dialogue with their Jewish neighbors, and reach out to the Jewish people with the good news of the Messiah. From the period of the American Revolution, the Great Reform Bill of 1832 in Great Britain, and even the Napoleonic Wars—the Jewish community in the West was afforded social emancipation and equal rights along with their Protestant Christian neighbors. Exchanges of theological ideas *and* religious literature, which had been limited or even prohibited before, was now permitted.

The Nineteenth Century saw the rise of the different Protestant evangelistic societies, aimed at seeing Jewish people come to faith in Israel's Messiah. At the turn of the Twentieth Century, the Hebrew Christian movement saw many Jewish people express faith in Jesus as the Messiah. The Hebrew Christian movement was mainly an association of enclaves of Jewish Believers, who attended mainline Protestant denominations and who were integrated into Christianity, but who did maintain some cultural association with their Jewish heritage and traditions. The Hebrew Christian movement certainly was an important step forward—especially with the Zionist movement, promoting a Jewish homeland in the Middle East also arising in the late Nineteenth Century—but there were many limitations. The Hebrew Christian movement encouraged a large amount of intermarriage between Jewish and non-Jewish Believers, and since fidelity to a Torah lifestyle was perceived in only cultural terms, many of the children and grandchildren of the Hebrew Christian movement assimilated into non-Jewish Christianity, eventually forgetting their Jewish heritage.

The modern State of Israel was created in 1948, in the aftermath of the Second World War and Holocaust of Nazi Germany. As Isaiah 66:8 declares, "Who ever heard the like? Who ever witnessed such events? Can a land pass through travail in a single day? Or is a nation born all at once? Yet Zion travailed and at once bore her children!" (NJPS). This is commonly viewed as being a prophecy detailing the establishment of modern Israel. Certainly with the State of Israel on the scene, many things shifted spiritually, as many Christian people who looked forward to a Jewish homeland being recreated—as a definite sign of the Messiah's approaching return—were vindicated. Other Christians, holding on to replacement theology, viewed the State of Israel as only important for Jewish self-determination, but nothing involving prophecy or the Second Coming. Many of them now consider the State of Israel as a great danger to world peace.

Much of what we are witnessing today, in the Messianic movement, can trace its path back to the late 1960s, and Israel's recapturing of the Old City of Jerusalem in 1967. Many are of the opinion that with Jerusalem and the Temple Mount fully in Jewish hands, that the "times of the Gentiles" (Luke 21:24) were concluded, and that some end-time countdown has started, eventually to culminate in the Messiah's return. Once again, many things shifted spiritually, the most significant being the transition of the Hebrew Christian movement into the Messianic Jewish movement. The Messianic Jewish movement, unlike many of its Hebrew Christian forbearers, would be a movement which would hold its congregational services on *Shabbat*, it would observe the Biblical festivals and Jewish holidays, it would keep (some form of) kosher, it would circumcise its sons, and it would encourage participation of Jewish Believers in the Jewish community. Most importantly, the Messianic Jewish community would maintain fidelity to the commandments of the Torah as a part of the prophesied New Covenant (Jeremiah 31:31-34; Ezekiel 36:25-27), not just as something as a part of their ethnic or cultural heritage.

The 1970s-1990s saw a significant expansion of Messianic Jewish congregations throughout the world, with congregations in Israel, Europe, the former Soviet Union, North and South America, Australia, South Africa, and elsewhere. The main bulk of the Messianic Jewish movement is in the Diaspora, and in North America at that. Common estimates to our present time is that there are over one-hundred thousand Messianic Jewish Believers. The salvation, and the unique testimonies, of today's Messianic Jewish Believers who have come to faith in Israel's Messiah, is a sure sign of fulfillment of Romans 11:15: "For if their rejection leads to the reconciliation of the world, what will their acceptance be but life from the dead?" (TLV).

The Messianic Walk

The Messianic Jewish mission has always been rightly focused around Jewish outreach, Jewish evangelism, and Israel solidarity. But the Messianic Jewish mission would not be possible without a strong basis of support, both spiritual and material, from non-Jewish Believers, who have been called to join in common cause and unity, with today's Messianic Jewish Believers. From the 1990s to our present, large numbers of non-Jewish Believers have entered into the Messianic movement. The main, overarching reason for this, is that these people have come to a conscious recognition of the Jewishness of Jesus the Messiah. Messianic Jewish rabbis and teachers frequently go to evangelical churches during the season of Passover, to teach on how the Last Supper meal of Yeshua was actually a Passover *seder*. Wanting to experience "Jesus in the feasts" of Israel, is *the significant magnet* for non-Jewish Believers entering into the Messianic movement. And, just as a massive salvation of Jewish people is to be anticipated in the end-times, so too it is prophesied that the nations will come to Zion to be instructed in God's Law, resulting in worldwide peace (Isaiah 2:2-4; Micah 4:1-3). This is a conscious reality present in today's Messianic movement as well.

What is the Messianic Jewish movement? You will certainly receive a wide number of answers from the people involved in it today! The workbook *Messianic Judaism Class* offers the following fair summation:

"Messianic Judaism is a movement that gets its motivation from the Spirit of God. . .[It involves] Jewish people following Yeshua while retaining their Jewish lifestyle, traditions, and culture. It is not a new sect of Christianity. There are a few churches from Christian denominations that have adopted a Messianic Jewish flavor, but in these cases it is them who are joining us. Messianic Judaism has never been Jewish people joining Christianity. There are many people who class themselves 'Jewish Christians' who are Jews who have joined Christianity, but that is not Messianic Judaism."[5]

Those who are involved with today's Messianic movement might indeed benefit from a shared Judeo-Protestant spiritual heritage—but they are part of something that surely *transcends Christianity*. It is something that focuses one's spiritual attention on Israel, the Jewish people, and on the return of the Messiah to Jerusalem. It is something that has definite origins in the experiences of Yeshua and His first disciples.

The Messianic Mission and Our Future

All of us, who have been called into today's Messianic movement, have a distinct witness of the Spirit that we are involved in something very, very big. We know that the Holy Scriptures, Genesis-Revelation, are relevant instruction for

---

[5] James Appel, Jonathan Bernis, and David Levine, *Messianic Judaism Class*, Teacher Book (Copenhagan, NY: Olive Press, 2011), 10.

The Messianic Mission

each follower of Israel's Messiah. **We know that God's promises to, and purposes for, Israel, remain true.** We know that we are part of an end-time move of God, which is going to culminate in the Messiah ruling and reigning over this planet. So significant are God's promises to Israel, that He declares that the rules of space-time which govern the universe would have to be altered, in order for there to be no seed of Israel:

"'Thus says ADONAI, who gives the sun as a light by day and the fixed order of the moon and the stars as a light by night, who stirs up the sea so its waves roar, ADONAI-Tzva'ot is His Name: Only if this fixed order departs from before Me'—it is a declaration of ADONAI—'then also might Israel's offspring cease from being a nation before Me—for all time'" (Jeremiah 31:35-36, TLV).

Yeshua Himself declared in His Olivet Discourse on the end-times, "Yes! I tell you that this people [this race, *hē genea*] will certainly not pass away before all these things happen" (Matthew 24:34, CJB/CJSB), a sure word on the continuity of the Jewish people to the time of the end. In spite of the anticipated disobedience of Ancient Israel (Deuteronomy 31:16-17) and a reduction of their numbers (Deuteronomy 28:62-64), the Lord promised a regathering of His people to the Promised Land (Leviticus 26:38-45). There will be a great victory and a vindication by the Lord, for His people (Zechariah 12:1-9), resulting in a great salvation (Zechariah 12:10-13).

Although more is coming in the future, we have seen the rebirth of the State of Israel in 1948, the recapturing of the Old City of Jerusalem in 1967, and the emergence of the Messianic Jewish movement in the late Twentieth Century.

Many of those, who are involved in Messianic Jewish congregations and fellowships, have the distinct impression that not only are we part of something special and important—which will culminate in the return of Israel's Messiah—but that the Body of Messiah is actually getting a "second chance" to do things the way that the original Disciples and Apostles wanted them to take place. As my own local congregation, Eitz Chaim of Richardson, Texas, considers itself: "Our community seeks to be like the first Jerusalem congregation where both Jew and non-Jew are as one new man, equal before G-d (Acts 2)." While we are all equal in the Messiah, whether we be Jewish or non-Jewish, we are hardly all the same—**but we have far more in common than not.** Our differences of background or perspective on the issues of life, from our shared Judeo-Protestant heritage, will need to be considered as we anticipate the challenges coming for the final stretch of human history.

The Messianic movement is a restoration movement, as we recapture a First Century theology and faith experience, in the Twenty-First Century. As the Messianic movement gets larger and expands, it is a sure sign that we will be getting closer and closer to the Messiah's return. The original Messianic Jewish pioneers emphasized a mission of **Jewish outreach, Jewish evangelism, and**

The Messianic Walk

Israel solidarity. Today, this is a mission which must remain at the forefront of what the Messianic movement is, because it decisively places each of us on the salvation-historical trajectory of Romans 11:26-27: "in this way all Israel will be saved; just as it is written, 'THE DELIVERER WILL COME FROM ZION, HE WILL REMOVE UNGODLINESS FROM JACOB. AND THIS IS MY COVENANT WITH THEM [Isaiah 59:20-21], WHEN I TAKE AWAY THEIR SINS' [Isaiah 27:9; Jeremiah 31:33-34]" (author's rendering).

Getting closer to the Messiah's return, it is hardly an enigma why many non-Jewish Believers have been called into the Messianic movement as well, with a dual mission now having emerged, as these people need to be trained and educated in the importance of their Hebraic and Jewish Roots. But seeing non-Jewish Believers come to an appreciation of their faith heritage in the Tanach Scriptures and practices of Yeshua, should not only be for the purposes of their personal enrichment and enlightenment; it must be done with the expressed intent of joining into the purposes of Jewish outreach and evangelism, and standing with Israel and against anti-Semitism. Frequently, the presence of non-Jewish Believers—who understand their faith heritage in the Tanach and in Judaism—can at times be most vital for the purposes of seeing Jewish people come to Israel's Messiah. I can testify to how the extended family members of my Messianic Jewish friends, who do not know Yeshua, have asked me, a non-Jewish Believer, about my faith and why I am in the Messianic movement—more than they would have the courage to ask their relatives about Yeshua, who are Jewish Believers. But in order to answer their questions and communicate properly, I have had to learn a great deal about not only the Tanach and Second Temple Judaism, but also the Jewish experience and struggle throughout history since.

Being a part of the Messianic mission, joining into the Messianic Jewish outreach to Jews who need to know the Messiah of Israel, and seeing all Believers educated and trained in the practices of the Messiah of Israel—**is something which will give you a dynamic faith, challenging your heart and mind in new and wonderful ways!** You will have your spiritual hunger satiated, and your spiritual thirst quenched. *We sincerely hope that each of you has indeed been called to join!*

An End-Time Move of the Holy Spirit

Mark Huey

Generally speaking, the children of God, who rely upon the inspiration of the Holy Scriptures, have been fascinated with the coming of the Messianic Age and/or the end of time for thousands of years, particularly in relation to their personal eternal destiny.[1] Such is humanity's self-centered finite nature, whether inherited in the fallen nature of Adam or even when enlightened by the indwelling presence of the Holy Spirit. This is to be expected, because according to the Book of Ecclesiastes, the Creator has uniquely placed eternity in people's hearts, with a specific caveat that they will **not** find out all the work that God has done from the beginning to the end, in spite of the insatiable curiosity. Consequently, given such a warning, Qohelet or the Preacher added that people should instead rejoice for God's gift of life, and devote their lives to do good works, until one departs from this world:

"I have seen the task which God has given the sons of men with which to occupy themselves. **He has made everything appropriate in its time. He has also set eternity in their heart, yet so that man will not find out the work which God has done from the beginning even to the end.** I know that there is nothing better for them than to rejoice and to do good in one's lifetime; moreover, that every man who eats and drinks sees good in all his labor—it is the gift of God" (Ecclesiastes 3:10-13, NASU).

However, regardless of the wisdom conveyed by the Preacher in this ancient text, with everything made appropriate in its time, even Yeshua's God-fearing disciples affirmed humanity's fervent desire to know the unknowable, when they questioned Him about what the signs of His coming would entail. Almost two thousand years ago, given all of the spiritual dynamics that the Disciples had been

---

[1] This article originally appeared in the December 2013 issue of Outreach Israel News.

The Messianic Walk

exposed to in the previous few years, while following and listening to the Messiah's teaching and claims, they anticipated the commencement of the Messianic Age and sought specific answers from Him to eternity-related matters:

"Yeshua came out from the temple and was going away when His disciples came up to point out the temple buildings to Him. And He said to them, 'Do you not see all these things? Truly I say to you, not one stone here will be left upon another, which will not be torn down.' **As He was sitting on the Mount of Olives, the disciples came to Him privately, saying, 'Tell us, when will these things happen, and what *will be* the sign of Your coming, and of the end of the age?'** And Yeshua answered and said to them, 'See to it that no one misleads you. For many will come in My name, saying, "I am the Messiah," **and will mislead many'"** (Matthew 24:1-5, NASU).

In the Olivet Discourse, Yeshua stated more about the End of the Age than anywhere else in His teachings. Forebodingly, His initial reaction, to these logical queries from His most intimate followers, was to caution them *not to be misled* when it came to the destruction of the Temple, the sign of His coming, and/or the End of the Age. Without hesitation, Yeshua categorically warned His Disciples that over time, many will come as professing followers ("in My name"), who declare Him to be the Messiah, and yet, they will mislead many. Many false teachers and false prophets, who will claim to be Christians or followers of Yeshua, will whether knowingly or unknowingly, mislead many undiscerning souls. *The ash heap of history is littered with too many examples to mention.* Their false teachings, misguided prognostications, and errant predictions about the End of the Age or the return of the Messiah, generally prey on people's fear of what only the Creator God knows, as stated by the Preacher above, and affirmed by Yeshua's declaration to His Disciples:

"But of that day and hour no one knows, not even the angels of heaven, nor the Son, but the Father alone" (Matthew 24:36, NASU).

Nevertheless, despite these revealing Scriptural statements—because eternity has been placed in the hearts of people—there is still a voracious appetite for many seekers of God to want to know the signs of the end of time. Over the ages and increasingly at this late hour, eschatology or the study of the end times has blossomed and grown. The distance from Yeshua's First Coming lengthens, and the End of the Age is almost two thousand years closer. At this time in salvation history, a virtual cottage industry of books, movies, video games, DVDs, CDs, and other assorted paraphernalia that are related to the end of time, the return of the Messiah, or apocalyptic themes, are introduced every year by those who claim to be followers of the Messiah. Of course, the proliferation of ear-tickling teaching, and now eye-catching video presentations, should be anticipated, as was forewarned about by the Apostle Paul, in some of his final instruction, delivered to his faithful disciple Timothy:

Testimonial An End-Time Move of the Holy Spirit

"For the time will come when they will not endure sound doctrine; but *wanting* to have their ears tickled, they will accumulate for themselves teachers in accordance to their own desires, and will turn away their ears from the truth and will turn aside to myths" (2 Timothy 4:3-4, NASU).

Today, a resurgence in obscure teachings about the Nephilim described in Genesis 6:4 and Numbers 13:33, in light of the technological advances in genetic engineering, has another generation of seekers speculating about things that the Lord has kept unknown for His purposes, as noted in Ecclesiastes 3:11 above. Yet the curious nature of human beings, with eternity embedded in their hearts, makes people susceptible to teachings that rely heavily upon non-canonical writings which are suspect in origin. Consequently, inquisitive people have an inherent tendency to spend an inordinate amount of time talking about and contemplating theories that do not necessarily enhance a person's walk with the Messiah. But instead, due to these thought-provoking distractions and vain speculations (1 Timothy 1:4), people are kept from doing the good works that please the Almighty during their limited time on Earth.

It has been nearly two thousand years since the death, burial, resurrection, and ascension of Yeshua the Messiah. Certainly the world is closer to the End of the Age and His return today, than it was in the First Century. Additionally, with the technological advances of the past century in transporting people and electronically transmitting information, knowledge and the availability to information are increasing rapidly. With these present-day realities, many prophecy teachers have surmised that a statement regarding a "time of distress," coupled with the resurrection of the dead found in the Book of Daniel, is on the verge of being fulfilled:

"Now at that time Michael, the great prince who stands *guard* over the sons of your people, will arise. **And there will be a time of distress such as never occurred since there was a nation until that time; and at that time your people, everyone who is found written in the book, will be rescued. Many of those who sleep in the dust of the ground will awake, these to everlasting life,** but the others to disgrace *and* everlasting contempt. Those who have insight will shine brightly like the brightness of the expanse of heaven, and those who lead the many to righteousness, like the stars forever and ever. **But as for you, Daniel, conceal these words and seal up the book until the end of time; many will go back and forth, and knowledge will increase**" (Daniel 12:1-4, NASU).

Some interpreters of the Book of Daniel have concluded that proper interpretation and understanding of Daniel's concealed prophecies are finally happening, because his book is being unsealed, as the end of time approaches. Hence, given human beings' innate curiosity regarding eternal questions about the End of the Age that has prevailed for millennia, a reasonable question in an attempt

The Messianic Walk

to discern the times, given the increased access to information and knowledge about salvation history, naturally arises:

> *Is the explosive growth in the past several decades of the Messianic movement among Jewish and non-Jewish Believers a sign that the End of the Age is approaching?*

Clearly, the worldwide emergence of the Messianic community of faith, over the past century, is a palpable result of the Holy One doing something radically different among His chosen ones from Jewish and non-Jewish backgrounds. Most assuredly, our family believes that the preponderance of non-Jewish followers of the Messiah of Israel—who have been drawn into the Messianic movement, coming from strong evangelical backgrounds with generations of godly people preceding us—can be considered a significant move of the Holy Spirit. Personally, we have no other way to explain our conscientious and, we believe, Spirit-led actions to leave the relative familiarity of evangelical Christianity, and instead seek to conduct our lives in a manner more consistent with the way Yeshua and His Disciples walked. Now through the eyes of enlightened hearts (Ephesians 1:18), spiritual passages like the following from the Apostle Paul to Believers in Asia Minor, regarding how the sacrificial blood of the Messiah established the framework for the "one new humanity" to develop in Israel's Messiah, with the enmity between people groups abolished, is better understood with a similar emergence of modern-day Messianic congregations and fellowships:

"Therefore remember, that once you, the nations in the flesh—who are called 'Foreskin' by the ones called 'Circumcision,' *which is* in the flesh, made by hands—*remember* that you were at that time separate from Messiah, alienated from the Commonwealth of Israel, and strangers from the covenants of the promise, having no hope and without God in the world. But now in Messiah Yeshua you who were once far off, have been brought near in the blood of Messiah. For He is our peace, who made both *groups* one, and broke down the middle wall of partition, **having abolished in His flesh the enmity, the *religious* Law of commandments in dogmas, that He might create in Himself the two into one new humanity, *so making peace,*** and might reconcile them both in one body to God through the wooden scaffold, having killed the enmity by it" (Ephesians 2:10-16, author's rendering).

In many ways, this First Century revelation about the "one new humanity"—with the relatively recent formation of Messianic communities of faith—affirms the choices, made by unknown thousands from the nations, to pursue a Torah observant Messianic lifestyle in the modern era.

However, to consider the above question, I must first confess my own inclination to want to understand the times and discern them like one of the sons

Testimonial An End-Time Move of the Holy Spirit

of Issachar, who were **"men who understood the times, with knowledge of what Israel should do"** (1 Chronicles 12:32a, NASU). But rather than theorize or speculate about the aforementioned topics relating to the End of the Age, because we view spiritual things through a "mirror dimly" (1 Corinthians 13:12), I want to instead use personal testimonies (one of the weapons of spiritual warfare described in Revelation 12:11) to conclude that the Messianic movement is an end-time move of the Holy Spirit. After all, for a non-Jewish family like ours to willfully choose to be totally dedicated to ministering to those called into the Messianic community of faith, we have had to firmly believe that the emergence of the Messianic movement was, and most assuredly is, an end-time move of the Spirit of God. Let me share a few of our collective testimonial highlights...

Back in 1992, after having been born again for fourteen years, and while in a season of spiritual searching enduring a life trial, I came across a book written in 1956 by Arthur Wallis entitled, *In the Day of Thy Power*, which chronicled many of the "awakening" spiritual movements that had taken place since the Middle Ages. While the historical aspect of what the Spirit of God had done down through the centuries was intriguing, there was an anonymous quote defining what "success" was from a spiritual perspective, located on a page between the Table of Contents and the Introduction, declaring,

> *Success: If you would make the greatest success of your life, try to discover what God is doing in your time, and fling yourself into the accomplishment of His purpose and will.*

I was so impressed by the profundity of this statement that I typecast and framed it, placing it on my desk to ponder for years. Thinking back on that action and how the Lord used these words to encourage me to discern what He was doing before flinging myself into work for Him, brings back great memories. Perhaps others can relate to certain things the Lord providentially placed in their lives, to guide them into the decisions and choices which have ultimately led them into the Messianic community of faith. Clearly, this quote was used back then and even to this very day, to inspire me to personally pursue the Lord with zealous abandon, upon discerning what He was or is doing at different points in salvation history.

Within the next year of seeking to discover what God was doing (1993), the Lord brought a precious believing woman into my life, who shared a godly heritage, a profound admiration for history, and most especially, a deep love for Him. At that time, Margaret was a widow with three children, whom I had dated one time twenty-one years prior, during our undergraduate years at college. After our romance blossomed and we were married in 1994, her strong Wesleyan Methodist upbringing and my Calvinistic Bible Church perspectives did not necessarily line up theologically, as we were unable to solve the centuries-old debate regarding the

The Messianic Walk

responsibility of man and the sovereignty of God. So the Lord led us to compromise, by attending some Charismatic churches, desperately seeking to discover what the Lord was doing at that hour with us and in the Body of Christ. While courting we concluded that, for His purposes, He had allowed two marriages to dissolve, through a premature death and a divorce—but had allowed us to get reacquainted in order to fall in love and remarry, **only** after He responded to our heartfelt pleas for guidance with tangible answers. We both were convinced that the trials of life we had endured, had simply honed us for the work where the Father would eventually lead us. Of course, we never suspected that He would, in about a year of searching, lead us to a Jewish Messianic congregation and show us by His Spirit that the much prophesied restoration of all things (Acts 3:19-21) was what He was in the process of accomplishing!

However, before we sought out a Messianic group to celebrate the Fall feasts, we went on a tour to Israel led by Zola Levitt Ministries. This trip to Israel was conducted in lieu of going to Toronto, where we were being told by those who had returned from the Toronto Blessing phenomenon that "the Spirit of the Lord was being poured out, and everyone needed to go to get a touch from the Lord." The peer group pressure to go to Toronto fomented in the Charismatic circles we were frequenting was extreme. The following verse, Acts 3:19, "Therefore repent and return, so that your sins may be wiped away, in order that times of refreshing may come from the presence of the Lord" (NASU), was being liberally referenced in messages about God's "time of refreshing" His people. So one day while I was out jogging in preparation for an upcoming marathon, I debated in my mind whether we should go to Canada—because at this stage in our spiritual walks, we both wanted to do what the Lord was doing, and perhaps, despite some of the craziness we witnessed, we thought that maybe this unusual activity in Toronto could be God's Spirit at work. Instead, toward the end of my workout, I got a visual image in my mind's eye of the Lord pouring out His Spirit on the Land of Israel, with a direct splash going up in the air, circling around the globe, and descending upon Toronto. In a flash, the word "Jerusalem" came to my heart and mind, and I ran home and declared to Margaret that rather than go to Toronto, maybe we should go to Israel and receive a "direct" outpouring. Without much hesitation, she responded with this suggestive remark, "Well, if we are going to Israel, we should go with Zola Levitt, because who other than a Messianic Jew would you want to guide you on your first tour of Israel?" Since I knew Zola from his ministry efforts in Dallas, I immediately retorted affirmatively, and we were soon booked on the next tour in December 1994. It was there in Israel on our tour that the Holy Spirit, among some significant and wonderful encounters with Him, prompted us specifically to celebrate the feasts of the Lord upon our return to the United States.

It took about nine months, but by the time *Rosh HaShanah* of 1995 arrived, after we commemorated the Fall feasts of the Lord, we had a congregation to

Testimonial An End-Time Move of the Holy Spirit

attend. Over the next few months, as we continued to attend the *Erev Shabbat* and *Shabbat* services, it became readily apparent to us that this is where the Spirit of God was truly ministering to our souls, so we discontinued going to church. We soon joined the new members class at the synagogue and began to take Hebrew. Before long, we were fully integrated into the Messianic Jewish assembly.

Since those early days and our years of pursuing the Lord from a Messianic perspective, as He has led us into full time ministry, we have discovered through interactions with a wide assortment of people from around the world, that they also were awakened to their Hebraic and Jewish Roots in roughly the same time period from 1995-1997. These testimonies have helped confirm to our family that we had discovered one of the major global moves of God's Holy Spirit in our lifetime! Providentially, this move of the Spirit was not being orchestrated by some huge ministry with all sorts of resources making their claims from satellite TV stations. But instead, this was something being led and nurtured by people just like our family, who were unknown people from various walks of life scattered around the world. From 1998-2000, as we were led to help small Messianic ministries grow and flourish, we were eventually led to fling ourselves without reservation into the accomplishment of His purposes and will—after much prayer, Biblical research, and confirmation coming from a variety of sources. In our personal analysis from a historical and Scriptural perspective, what we witnessed firsthand made increasingly more sense, as we studied and got more comfortable with the Torah and the prophecies found in the Tanakh. Thankfully, our fervent family pursuit of serving the Holy One of Israel was confirmed over and over again that we were being led by the Spirit of God.

Broadly speaking from a historical point of view—given the relatively recent history of the past century or so—one discovers that the Lord has been working on parallel tracks with many Jews and Christians around the world, to accomplish His will. The Zionist movement was promoted effectively by Theodor Herzl and birthed in Europe in the late Nineteenth Century. Zionism ignited a passion among many oppressed Jews to leave Russia and Eastern Europe and emigrate to the Ottoman Empire's Palestinian province, in order to establish a permanent home on the ancient land from which they were dispersed. For nearly two millennia, in what is known as the Diaspora, Jews sought contentment, but until this time had never had a concerted successful attempt to return to the land of their ancestors and reestablish the State of Israel. The time was just not right. However, in His time during the late 1800s and early 1900s, the Lord raised up people such as Eliezer Ben Yehudah to revive the Hebrew language into a modern version that was eventually restored to the Jews who formed the modern State of Israel. Here was another tangible indication that the Lord was starting to do something unique with the Jewish people, who had been entrusted with the oracles of God (Romans 3:2). Eventually through the traumas of persecutions, pogroms in Russia, and ultimately

The Messianic Walk

the Holocaust in Germany, in the Twentieth Century, the Lord used world powers such as Great Britain with the Balfour Declaration in 1917, to lay the groundwork for the new Jewish State of Israel.

This activity among the Jewish people was being paralleled in the Christian world, with the growing acceptance of the dispensational teaching of John Nelson Darby and the Plymouth Brethren in the late 1800s. This pre-tribulation rapture teaching impacted C. I. Scofield, who first published the influential Scofield Bible in 1909 among evangelicals, which readily embraced the return of the Jewish people to the Promised Land. This enhanced the dispensational message and established a basis for what would later be termed "Christian Zionism." At the same general time, the 1904 revival in Wales and the 1905-1915 Azusa Street Revival, in the first decade of the 1900s, was reintroducing the concept that the gifts of the Spirit were not just for the early Church, but available throughout the ages. New understanding, about the promised restoration of the Jewish people to the Land of Israel, made verses like the following much more understandable *today*—because more than a simple refreshing was expected, but ultimately "the restoration of all things," as prophesied by many of the ancient prophets:

"Therefore repent and return, so that your sins may be wiped away, in order that times of refreshing may come from the presence of the Lord; and that He may send Yeshua, the Messiah appointed for you, whom heaven must receive **until the period of restoration of all things about which God spoke by the mouth of His holy prophets from ancient time**" (Acts 3:19-21, NASU).

Perhaps as many concluded regarding the End of the Age, the books of prophecy were finally being unsealed and understood, as suggested by Daniel 12:4 above. After all, for the first time since the early centuries of the post-resurrection assemblies, Jews were coming to faith in Yeshua, and non-Jews were being drawn to return to the Hebraic Roots of the faith. The Messianic community of faith, unlike any other spiritual entity we know of, is perhaps preparing a people for the coming time of distress mentioned in Daniel 12:1 and/or Jacob's distress found in Jeremiah 30:7, by training up a group of Believers who exemplify this verse found in the Book of Revelation:

"Here is the perseverance of the saints who keep the commandments of God and their faith in Yeshua" (Revelation 14:12, NASU).

There is coming a time of great turmoil in the world when the holy ones of God will be at war with the Beast System that will dominate human affairs. But according to Revelation 12:17 and 14:12, despite the emergence of the antimessiah, who will be at war with them (Daniel 7:21; Revelation 13:7), there will continue to be a remnant of Believers, who have a testimony of faith in the Messiah Yeshua, while seeking to keep His commandments. We believe that the Messianic community of faith, despite its differences of opinion on many non-essential matters, is widely representative of who those "end-time saints" are going to be.

Testimonial An End-Time Move of the Holy Spirit

Yet, having been a marathoner in my youth, patience and perseverance have had to become essential attributes when seeking spiritual understanding. In fact, through prayer, serious Bible study, continual analysis and research about the Messianic movement over the past two decades of reading accounts, talking to firsthand witnesses, and/or personal experiences in a wide array of Messianic settings—we have come to some conclusions about the future of the Messianic movement and its relationship to the End of the Age.

If one takes the more recent history of the Messianic movement from the 1960s to the present, there are some continuing parallels in light of what the Holy One has been doing with the Jewish people and the State of Israel, and the Body of Believers over the past sixty years or so. The initial, most significant event was the formation of the State of Israel in 1948, following the horrific consequences of World War II and the Holocaust. Many Christians at that time were astonished that an ancient prophecy found in the Book of Isaiah was being fulfilled:

"Who has heard such a thing? Who has seen such things? **Can a land be born in one day? Can a nation be brought forth all at once?** As soon as Zion travailed, she also brought forth her sons" (Isaiah 66:8, NASU).

At Israel's modern-day re-formation, the dispensationalists were ecstatic, as the relatively recent eschatological theories about the pre-tribulation rapture took on added significance. (Please note that I am *not* a supporter of the pre-tribulation rapture belief.) Support for the State of Israel and the Jewish people returning to their ancient homeland from the evangelical community began to grow exponentially. Ministry efforts developed from a wide array of Christian sources. But as the reconstituted State of Israel struggled to survive in a hostile environment surrounded by Arab and Muslim enemies, various Christian-oriented countries increasingly lent support either economically, diplomatically, or at times, even militarily. About twenty years later, on June 7, 1967 in the midst of what has been labeled the Six Day War, the Israelis finally liberated Jerusalem from the Jordanians after nearly 2,000 years under Gentile control. In what can be considered a unique victory over extraordinarily superior forces, the fledgling country not only survived, but expanded its borders to the Jordan River forcing back the Jordanians, captured the Golan Heights from Syria, and occupied the Gaza Strip and Sinai Peninsula from Egypt. The testimonies of miracles on the battlefield are incredible to hear or read about! The omnipotent Creator God favored His chosen people against their adversaries, and freed the City of David from its oppressors!

On a spiritual plane, during the half-dozen years or so, until the Yom Kippur War of October 6-25, 1973, there was a period of time in Christian circles known as the "Jesus Movement," when the Spirit of God brought to faith a growing number of young Jewish and non-Jewish people. Many of the Jews were children of Holocaust survivors, or had simply been caught up in the hippie and anti-war

The Messianic Walk

movements that thrived during this era. This "Baby Boomer" generation, born after the end of World War II, has had a tremendous impact on the growth of the Messianic movement. In fact, major Messianic groups were fortified during this era, as the Spirit of God rose up visionary leaders to restore a Jewish expression of worship and service gleaned from childhoods spent attending Orthodox, Conservative, and Reform Jewish synagogues. Believing in Yeshua as the Messiah of Israel became the common denominator, as these Jewish pioneers of Messianic Judaism endured being ostracized by their families and relatives, if not persecuted by other Jews who did not believe that Yeshua was the Savior.

Yet, as the Messianic Jewish movement of the 1970-1980s began to mature in the 1990s, all of a sudden, the Spirit of God was drawing non-Jewish Believers from evangelical Christian backgrounds (like us) into many Messianic places of worship. Eventually, as the non-Jewish congregants began to explode and numerically dominate most Messianic Jewish assemblies and celebrate the feasts of the Lord, some people would conclude that this was in many ways a realization of these verses prophesied by Zechariah millennia ago:

"Thus says the LORD of hosts, 'The fast of the fourth, the fast of the fifth, the fast of the seventh and the fast of the tenth *months* will become joy, gladness, and cheerful feasts for the house of Judah; so love truth and peace.' Thus says the LORD of hosts, '*It will* yet *be* that peoples will come, even the inhabitants of many cities. The inhabitants of one will go to another, saying, "Let us go at once to entreat the favor of the LORD, and to seek the LORD of hosts; I will also go." **So many peoples and mighty nations will come to seek the LORD of hosts in Jerusalem and to entreat the favor of the LORD.' Thus says the LORD of hosts, 'In those days ten men from all the nations will grasp the garment of a Jew, saying, "Let us go with you, for we have heard that God is with you"'"** (Zechariah 8:19-23, NASU).

From another perspective, the increasing amount of tourism that has brought millions from around the world to Israeli-controlled Jerusalem, to seek or entreat favor from the Lord since the liberation of the Six Day War, can also be noted from these verses.

However, despite the scores of prophecies being realized in this era with the birth and emergence of the Messianic community of faith around the world, it continues to have challenges—primarily from *within* rather than from *without*. Pioneers in any field of endeavor, be it business, education, government, technology, or in this case, spiritual matters—often do not have the skillset or the personalities to lead a movement during the building or development stage, after the pioneering stage wanes. The pioneers have to give way to the builders, if any enterprise or endeavor is going to survive and thrive. Perhaps just like Ezra, Zerubbabel, and Nehemiah were used to return the Jewish exiles to Jerusalem, and the Apostles were chosen to spread the good news of the Messiah to the First

Testimonial An End-Time Move of the Holy Spirit

Century world, or the founders of the United States were assembled to launch a unique form of government—the people who followed each set of pioneers had to build on what had been started by those chosen to be the pioneering generation.

This leads me to quote from the Book of Acts, when the highly respected Torah scholar Gamaliel was giving some sound advice to his students and followers, who were very concerned about what was transpiring among the followers of Yeshua. Citing a number of examples about purported moves, perhaps of God's Spirit among different people, Gamaliel made these statements about the Apostles, in attempting to discern if these followers of Yeshua were a genuine move of God:

"So in the present case, I say to you, stay away from these men and let them alone, for if this plan or action is of men, it will be overthrown; but if it is of God, you will not be able to overthrow them; or else you may even be found fighting against God" (Acts 5:38-39, NASU).

I cite this ancient warning by Gamaliel, because it can apply to the "pioneer generation," who are reluctant to relinquish their roles and responsibilities to the maturing "developer generation" of the Messianic movement.

We believe that the Messianic movement is one of the end-time moves of the Spirit of God, which is preparing a future generation for the return of Yeshua the Messiah. We do not speculate on when that time will be, but rather fall back on the Preacher's sage advice to spend our time on Earth joyfully doing the good works that we have been called to do. Above all, we want to point people to Yeshua and His saving grace, freely available to those who truly repent, and believe in the sacrificial offering He made for their individual sin. Because eternity has been placed in our hearts, we pray that when our individual or collective time comes to be with the Lord, He would receive us with the words, "Well done, good and faithful servant!" To hear these words from the Lord would absolutely affirm that our life on Earth has been a resounding **success**!

We give thanks for the pioneers! But it will soon be time for them to release the reins of responsibility to the builders, who we believe will be supernaturally empowered to take the Messianic movement into its next stage of development and maturation. In so doing, may the Holy One receive all honor and praise for what He is going to do through those called unto His service during this end-time move of His Spirit, while advancing His Kingdom, until the restoration of all things. . .

The Messianic Walk

A Torah Foundation

When people attend a Messianic congregation, they are immediately struck with a connection to traditions and practices of not only today's Jewish Synagogue, but of antiquity long standing. For Jewish Believers in Israel's Messiah, entering into a Messianic congregation for a Saturday morning *Shabbat* service—there is an instant connection not only to one's Biblical heritage, but also one's ethnic and cultural heritage going back millennia. When the traditional liturgy and prayers are recited—which incorporates Scripture, hymns once sung in the Temple, and compositions from post-Second Temple Judaism lauding the Creator—Jewish Believers feel a strong comfort level, as they seek to live out their Messiah faith by embracing and not rejecting their Jewish heritage.

Non-Jewish Believers from Protestant backgrounds, visiting or attending a Messianic congregation, have varied reactions to the traditions of the *Shabbat* service. Many are sincerely intrigued, and they appreciate the structure and reverence of a worship time with Hebrew and English liturgy. Many indeed appreciate the ancient tradition of reading from the Torah scroll, seeing that canting the Hebrew aloud to the assembly is an ancient art to be greatly cherished. Others, however, do not see the value of liturgy or canting from a Torah scroll, considering these to be vain human practices. In fact, many—visiting a Messianic congregation almost entirely out of curiosity—are actually quite negative toward anything having to do with the Torah.

There is no question when reading the historical record of the Tanach (Old Testament) that obedience to God's Instruction is required of His people. Israel's obedience to the commandments of God's Torah or Law was to bring it great blessings and fame (Deuteronomy 4:5-10), but disobedience would bring judgment (Deuteronomy 30:1-2). The history of Israel throughout the Tanach is, unfortunately, one of frequent disobedience—and Bible readers often witness the required punishment or chastisement of Israel by God (Deuteronomy 27:26). As soon as the Ancient Israelites entered into the Promised Land, one encounters how the period of the Judges was one where "Everyone did what was right in his own eyes" (Judges 17:6, ESV). The Kingdom of Israel was split in two by the

The Messianic Walk

disobedience of King Solomon to God's Law (involving incessant polygamy, idolatry, and child sacrifice!), although there was a period of critical reform during the reign of King Josiah, which saw a renewed appreciation for God's Torah (2 Kings 22:1-23:28; 2 Chronicles 34:1-35:27). Following the Southern Kingdom's return from Babylonian exile, the custom of publicly reading the Scriptures to the community became established (Nehemiah 8:1-3). If the exile was caused by disobedience to God's Word, then it is logical that the Jewish community assemble to hear God's Word, so that such disobedience would never take place again.

The Torah Cycle

In today's Messianic community, just as in today's Jewish Synagogue, a major feature of the *Shabbat* service is reading from the weekly Torah portion. While Jewish history indicates that there have been different ways that the Synagogue has approached reading the Torah, with both annual and triennial cycles employed[1]—the practice of the Jewish community reading through the Torah *is ancient*. In fact, the oblique statement appearing in Acts 15:21, "For from the earliest times, Moshe has had in every city those who proclaim him, with his words being read in the synagogues every *Shabbat*" (CJB/CJSB), is an historical attestation of the Torah being read and discussed in the ancient Synagogue.

Two significant Jewish figures from the First Century indicate how important it was for members of the Jewish community to come together, hear the Torah declared, and for it to be the centerpiece of education in holy conduct. The Jewish philosopher Philo, who lived in Alexandria and was contemporary to Yeshua and Paul, stated, "And would you still sit down in your synagogues, collecting your ordinary assemblies, and reading your sacred volumes in security, and explaining whatever is not quite clear, and devoting all your time and leisure with long discussions to the philosophy of your ancestors?" (*On Dreams* 2.127).[2] The historian Josephus recorded how members of the Jewish community were permitted "to leave off their other employments, and to assemble together for the hearing of the law, and learning it exactly, and this not once or twice, or oftener, but every week; which thing all the other legislators seem to have neglected" (*Against Apion* 2.175).[3]

It is seen in the evangelistic efforts of Paul, that after the public reading of the Torah and Prophets (Acts 13:15), that he would use the opportunity to speak of the salvation of Yeshua the Messiah. Within today's Messianic movement, the weekly

---

[1] Consult Louis Jacobs. "Torah, Reading of," in Encyclopaedia Judaica. MS Windows 9x. Brooklyn: Judaica Multimedia (Israel) Ltd, 1997.

[2] Flavius Josephus: trans. William Whiston, *The Works of Josephus: Complete and Unabridged* (Peabody, MA: Hendrickson, 1987), 805.

[3] Philo Judeaus: trans. C.D. Yonge, *The Works of Philo: Complete and Unabridged* (Peabody, MA: Hendrickson, 1993), 397.

Torah portion, and its associated Haftarah reading from the Prophets, frequently tends to be a venue for considering the work of Israel's Messiah. This is an excellent way to testify of Yeshua to Jewish non-Believers, and to see evangelical Protestant Believers drawn to Messianic things, significantly connect with their faith heritage in the Scriptures of Israel. Today's Messianic movement, on the whole, follows an annual Torah cycle, divided into 54 Torah portions. In addition to the associated Haftarah from the Prophets, Messianics also have tended to incorporate associated readings from the Apostolic Scriptures (New Testament).

The Bible of Yeshua

One of the significant pulls for many evangelical Protestant people, drawn by the Lord into the Messianic movement, is reconnecting with the Tanach or Old Testament Scriptures. As obvious as it may be, **the Tanach was the Bible of Yeshua and His Disciples.** Yeshua Himself spoke of how "all things which are written about Me in the Law of Moses and the Prophets and the Psalms must be fulfilled" (Luke 24:44, NASU). When a figure like Paul speaks of how "All Scripture is God-breathed and is useful for teaching, rebuking, correcting and training in righteousness" (2 Timothy 3:16, NIV), much of what we today call the "New Testament" had yet to be collected together or even written. The Scriptures to which Paul was referring would have composed the "Old Testament." Theologian John Goldingay emphasizes,

"One of the New Testament's own convictions is that the Old Testament is part of the Scriptures (indeed, *is* the Scriptures). . .and that the Old Testament provides the theological framework within which Jesus needs to be understood. The New Testament is then a series of Christian and ecclesial footnotes to the Old Testament, and one cannot produce a theology out of footnotes."[4]

The Tanach Scriptures, and consequently also the Messianic Writings, are built upon the foundation of the Torah (the Pentateuch or Chumash). If you do not understand the Torah, you are liable to misunderstand what is being said in the remainder of Scripture. You have to understand the foundational stories of the Patriarchs of the faith: Abraham, Isaac, and Jacob, and the formation of Ancient Israel as a nation. **Understanding the Exodus is imperative to properly appreciating one's salvation and the sacrifice of Yeshua as the Lamb of God.** You have to understand that the theological patterns established in the Torah are repeated in the remainder of the Tanach, and indeed also, in the Apostolic Scriptures. The Torah forms the foundation of the Bible and Scripture progressively builds upon it as God's plan of salvation history unfolds. The ethical

---

[4] John Goldingay, *Old Testament Theology: Israel's Gospel* (Downers Grove, IL: InterVarsity, 2003), 24.

The Messianic Walk

and moral values of the Torah, for certain, affected the worldview and perspectives of Yeshua and His Disciples!

As Jon D. Levenson remarks in *The Jewish Study Bible*, "both Jewish and Christian traditions view the books Genesis through Deuteronomy in this order as a single unit, standing first in the Bible. The unanimity of tradition and the initial placement of these five books reflect their significant place within religious life. In Judaism, the Torah is accorded the highest level of sanctity, above that of the other books of the Bible."[5] Even though Christianity does accord the Torah some strong status, this status is not as high as it is in Judaism. W.D. Davies notes in *IDB* that "The coming of Jesus has inaugurated a new order in which, in some sense, the law is superseded."[6] While the Messiah Yeshua is always to be our primary focus of faith as Believers, and Yeshua as God in the flesh and thus our "Lawgiver" (James 4:12) must by necessity exceed the Torah itself in importance, does Yeshua supersede and make the Torah to none effect? Or, is the Torah fully realized in Yeshua, who has final authority?

How should we approach the Torah of Moses?

While the Torah of Moses is the foundation of the rest of Scripture—and all Bible readers should have a good understanding of it—it would be a mistake to say that with the coming of the Messiah, there have not been some changes resultant of His sacrifice for human sins. In Protestant theology, for certain, there are varied approaches witnessed to the role that the Law of Moses plays in the life of a Believer. There are theological traditions such as Lutheranism which see a strong contrast between the law and grace of God, considering the Torah to be a part of a previous time. There are other theological traditions such as Calvinism and Wesleyanism, which have historically sub-divided the Torah's commandments into the civil law, ceremonial law, and moral law. It is thought that now with the arrival of the Messiah, that only the moral law remains to be followed by God's people. (My own family, with mixed Presbyterian and Methodist roots, comes from a heritage which emphasized the "moral law" of God remaining valid for God's people.)

Within today's broad Messianic movement, different perspectives are witnessed as they involve the ongoing relevance of the Torah or Moses' Teaching for God's people. For sure, it is agreed that the Torah composes the ethnic and cultural heritage of today's Jewish people, to which they should be faithful. Yet, how do we approach the Torah as our spiritual heritage?

---

[5] Jon D. Levenson, "Torah," in Adele Berlin and Marc Zvi Brettler, eds., *The Jewish Study Bible* (Oxford: Oxford University Press, 2004), 1.

[6] W.D. Davies, "Law in the NT," in George Buttrick, ed. et. al., *The Interpreter's Dictionary of the Bible*, 4 vols. (Nashville: Abingdon, 1962), 3:96.

A Torah Foundation

As far as it involves the continuity of the Torah for the Body of Messiah, there are those who believe, often following dispensational theology, that the Law of Moses was for a previous era. There are others—perhaps or perhaps not influenced by theological traditions that have emphasized the so-called "moral law" as continuing—which have thought that a review of practices believed abolished such as the seventh-day Sabbath/*Shabbat*, appointed times or *moedim* of Leviticus 23, and the kosher dietary laws, is important. Those who believe in a widespread continuity of Torah practices in the post-resurrection era, tend to focus on the themes of the prophesied New Covenant of Jeremiah 31:31-34 and Ezekiel 36:25-27, and how God's commandments are to be written on the heart, **and is a decisive work of the Holy Spirit.** Concurrent with this would be the necessity for God's people today to recapture a proper understanding of how "sin is lawlessness" (1 John 3:4), the need to be holy (Deuteronomy 14:2; 28:9), and how blessings are given to those who obey the Lord (Deuteronomy 30:9-10). Unfortunately, given the great importance of a Torah foundation for those in Messiah, there are those who we will encounter, who can be very legalistic and inflexible.

Does the New Testament Really Do Away With the Law?

Today's broad Messianic movement does adhere to some form of post-resurrection era validity to the Torah of Moses. At the very least, today's Messianic people believe that the weekly Torah portions should be read and contemplated, as we let its accounts inform our understanding of how God works in history, and how we need the salvation of Yeshua the Messiah. By virtue of holding its main worship services on *Shabbat* or the seventh-day Sabbath, observing holidays and festivals not adhered to by most of today's Messiah followers, and being concerned about clean and unclean meats—today's Messianic people do inevitably have some conflict with a great deal of contemporary Christian thought and theology, which teaches that the Torah or Law of Moses has been abolished. In the minds of many Messianics, the idea that the Law has been abolished, has not only been a significant cause of many (claiming) Christians today being engrossed in great sins—ranging from abortion, pre-marital sex, and homosexuality—but has also caused many to be *utterly anemic* in their approach to the Scriptures, and how relevant the Bible is for their lives.

What did Yeshua the Messiah say about the Torah? In His famed words of the Sermon on the Mount, our Lord communicated, "Do not think that I came to abolish the Torah or the Prophets! I did not come to abolish, but to fulfill. Amen, I tell you, until heaven and earth pass away, not the smallest letter or serif shall ever pass away from the Torah until all things come to pass. Therefore, whoever breaks one of the least of these commandments, and teaches others the same, shall be called least in the kingdom of heaven. But whoever keeps and teaches them, this one shall be called great in the kingdom of heaven" (Matthew 5:17-19, TLV). Many people in

The Messianic Walk

today's Messianic community, either Jewish Believers who originally came to faith via an evangelical Christian experience—and especially non-Jewish Believers who have been drawn into Messianic things—can testify to being convicted by these words. Yeshua the Messiah says that the Torah or Law of Moses remains in effect until our present universe passes away. And, the venerable Apostle Paul, whose writings are often purported to say that the Torah has been abolished, notably did say that proper doctrine must "agree with sound words, those of our Lord Yeshua the Messiah, and with the instruction in keeping with godliness" (1 Timothy 6:3, TLV).

If Yeshua says that the Torah is to be regarded as valid instruction for His followers, and if Paul says that proper doctrine must be in alignment with the Messiah's words—then some necessary reevaluation of many Bible passages is in order. Today's Messianic movement, in addition to simply wanting to have a *fully Biblical and holistically Scriptural view*, has to have a high view of the Torah of Moses for God's people today, given its mission involving Jewish outreach and evangelism. Deuteronomy 13:1-5 specifically warned Ancient Israel against any figure who would come and perform signs and wonders for the people, and then teach against God's commandments. Such a person was to be regarded as a false prophet. Unfortunately, this is precisely how much of Christianity has historically presented Yeshua the Messiah:

"Whatever I command you, you must take care to do—you are not to add to it or take away from it. Suppose a prophet or a dreamer of dreams rises up among you and gives you a sign or wonder, and the sign or wonder he spoke to you comes true, while saying, 'Let's follow other gods'—that you have not known, and—'Let's serve them!' You must not listen to the words of that prophet or that dreamer of dreams—for *ADONAI* your God is testing you, to find out whether you love *ADONAI* your God with all your heart and with all your soul. *ADONAI* your God you will follow and Him you will fear. His *mitzvot* you will keep, to His voice you will listen, Him you will serve and to Him you will cling" (Deuteronomy 13:1-5, TLV).

Many of us, whether we be Jewish or non-Jewish Believers, can testify to how when we informed various friends, acquaintances, or even family members *that we were simply attending a Messianic congregation that held its worship service on Saturday*, that we were in danger of falling from grace, committed some kind of sacrilege, or at the very least were trying to earn our salvation via works. We have each been confronted with a barrage of accusations, mainly quoting texts from the Apostolic Scriptures or New Testament, about why the Torah or significant aspects of it, are no longer relevant for today's Messiah followers. Few are aware of how debated the issue of the Law of Moses has been, for the holiness and sanctification of born again Believers, in Protestant theology over the past three centuries.[7] But more importantly, too many people have been subjected to sub-standard interpretations and approaches to Bible passages, which were issued in a specific ancient context, and to which there might be various transmission debates from the source text into English.

Does the New Testament really do away with the Law? Our ministry has actually produced a substantial book (over 750 pages) on this issue, **The New Testament Validates Torah MAXIMUM EDITION**. The bulk of this resource examines fifty Bible passages, mainly from the Apostolic Scriptures, which are frequently invoked to claim that the Torah of Moses is no longer relevant for God's people today. Certainly, while we do stress that we live in a post-resurrection era with new realities that have been inaugurated by the sacrifice of the Messiah,[8] a widescale dismissal of the Torah is untenable—not only given Yeshua's own words about the matter (Matthew 5:17-19), but also the steadfast reality that the New Covenant He has brought about (Luke 22:20) involves the supernatural writing of the commandments onto the new hearts of those cleansed by His work (Jeremiah 31:31-34; Ezekiel 36:25-27).

The following is an abbreviated synopsis of the fifty Bible passages examined in *The New Testament Validates Torah MAXIMUM EDITION*, addressing common Christian approaches which see the Torah as something for a previous time:

Isaiah 1:13-14:
"God hates the Jewish feasts of the Old Testament"
The Lord actually says that He hates people who sacrifice and pray to Him, whose hands are covered with the blood of the innocent (Isaiah 1:15-17). The festivals and observances in view are notably labeled as "yours," which places a huge burden of proof on the human people observing them inappropriately, not that they have all of a sudden been rejected by God as having value as instructions given by Him. Going through external religious motions, while at the same time facilitating injustice, is the problem.

Ezekiel 20:12-26:
"God actually gave His people bad laws that they could not follow"
The Prophet Ezekiel describes the challenges that existed with the Israelites delivered from Egypt via the Exodus, and their children, in their difficulties with obeying God's Instruction to them (Ezekiel 20:12-24). Their descendants, being

---

[7] Consult the varied perspectives presented in Wayne G. Strickland, ed., *Five Views on Law and Gospel* (Grand Rapids: Zondervan, 1996).

[8] Consult the article "The Significance of the Messiah Event" by Margaret McKee Huey and J.K. McKee, appearing in the *Messianic Torah Helper*.

engrossed by sin and rebellion against God, were turned over to bad laws (Ezekiel 20:25) such as child sacrifice (Ezekiel 20:26). Such bad laws involved either outright paganism, or a perversion of a good Biblical commandment, such as the dedication of the firstborn (Exodus 22:9).

Hosea 2:11:
"God has put an end to the Old Testament Sabbath and feast days"

The Northern Kingdom of Israel practiced syncretism, where Biblical practices such as the Sabbath were kept in conjunction with the worship of pagan deities. Its disloyalty to God is depicted as an act of harlotry (Hosea 2:1-7), with the people not realizing how their prosperity came from the Lord and not Baal (Hosea 2:12-13). The religious observances that will cease are notably labeled as "her new moons, her Sabbaths" (Hosea 2:11), an indication how they had been taken up into the idolatry of the Northern Kingdom.

Matthew 5:17:
"Jesus fulfilled every jot and tittle of the Law"

The Messiah's expressed purpose in association with the Torah of Moses was precisely not "to destroy but to fulfill" (Matthew 5:17, NKJV). Whether Yeshua's fulfillment of the Torah be viewed as His proper interpretation of Moses' Teaching, and/or His fulfillment of Messianic prophecies, our Lord says that "not the smallest letter or serif shall ever pass away from the Torah until all things come to pass" (Matthew 5:18, TLV), and that the present Heaven and Earth must disappear in order for the Torah to be regarded as unimportant.

Matthew 11:13:
"The Law of Moses was only in effect until John the Baptist"

What is actually said is, "For all the prophets and the Torah prophesied until John" (Matthew 11:13, author's rendering). With the arrival of John the Immerser, a shift in salvation history was taking place. The arrival of John was prophesied, and subsequently the Messiah and the new realities He would inaugurate would follow (Matthew 11:12). No disparagement of the Tanach Scriptures or Torah of Moses is intended here, but what is intended is that they are incomplete without the Messiah they anticipate.

Mark 7:1-23:
"Jesus Christ declared the dietary laws to be obsolete"

There was a controversy present because Yeshua's Disciples did not ritually wash their hands before eating, as did various Pharisees (Mark 7:1-5). Yeshua highlights some significant hypocrisy present here (Mark 7:6-13), and then addresses how what enters into a person does not defile him (Mark 7:14-15), as what is spoken by someone is what truly defiles (Mark 7:20-23). In informing His Disciples that what proceeds from a person is what truly defiles (Mark 7:18), Yeshua said, as is properly translated from the Greek of Mark 7:19, "because it does not go into his heart, but into his stomach, and goes out into the latrine, purging all the foods [*katharizōn panta ta brōmata*]" (author's rendering). Ultimately, what is eaten is excreted from the human body.

John 1:17:
"The Law was given through Moses; grace and truth realized through Christ"

Speaking of the arrival of the Messiah on the scene of history, John 1:16 narrates, "For of His fullness we have all received, and grace upon grace" (NASU). It is then stated, "Torah was given through Moses; grace and truth came through Yeshua the Messiah" (John 1:17, TLV). The Torah of Moses is actually to be regarded as a revelation of God's grace, but its grace has now been surpassed—as God's grace is continuous—with the grace available in the work of the Messiah. This does not abrogate the Torah of Moses, but does reveal its incompleteness without the presence of Yeshua.

John 13:34:
"Jesus Christ gave us a new law of love to replace the laws of the Old Testament"

Responsible Bible readers are aware that the commands to love God and neighbor are actually a part of the Tanach or Old Testament (Deuteronomy 6:5; Leviticus 19:18). When Yeshua directed, "I give you a new commandment, that you love one another. Just as I have loved you, so also you must love one another" (John 13:34, TLV), this can be taken as either (a) a new quality of demonstrating love for others, as seen in the Messiah's own ministry, or (b) a love manifested via the power of the prophesied New Covenant (Jeremiah 31:31-34; Ezekiel 36:25-27).

Acts 10:1-48:
"Peter was shown a vision nullifying the dietary laws"

Peter did see a vision of a sheet of unclean animals, which he was commanded to eat (Acts 10:9-13). God told Peter not to regard as unholy that which He cleansed (Acts 10:14-15). Following this, Peter goes to declare the good news to the Roman centurion Cornelius, informing him, per his vision, that "God has shown me that I should not call any person common or unclean" (Acts 10:28, ESV). The main intention of Peter's vision was to communicate how all human beings have been made clean by the sacrifice of Israel's Messiah, and that as a Jew Peter should not fear interacting with those of the nations.

Acts 15:19-21:
"The Apostolic decree says nothing about new Christians observing the Mosaic Law"

The Jerusalem Council specifically met to answer the claim of some hyper-conservative Jewish Believers, that the new, non-Jewish Believers had to be circumcised and keep the Torah of Moses to be saved (Acts 15:1, 5). Peter made it clear that all are saved by God's grace (Acts 15:7-9, 11), and that a heavy yoke or burden was being unnecessarily imposed (Acts 15:10). James the Just testified that the salvation of the nations was prophesied in the Tanach, per the restoration of the Tabernacle of David (Acts 15:14-18; Amos 9:11-12). The Apostolic decree mandated only four things, which could have been construed as a "burden" (Acts 15:28), requiring immediate changes from those turning to the Messiah of Israel (Acts 15:20). When followed, these new Believers would be cut off from their spheres of social and religious influence in Greco-Roman paganism. Far from these people being "order[ed]...to keep the law of Moses" (Acts 15:5, ESV) by demanding mortals, Tanach prophecy and the plan of God were to instead be facilitated (Acts 15:15). This would necessarily involve the nations coming to Zion to be taught God's Instruction (Micah 4:1-3; Isaiah 2:2-4), a work that could only take place at the prompting of the Holy Spirit per the Jeremiah 31:31-34 and Ezekiel 36:25-27 New Covenant.

Acts 20:7:
"The early Christians met on the first day of the week, a clear abolishment of the Jewish Sabbath"

Scholars debate what is intended by "first of the week" (Acts 20:7), as to whether this was a meeting "on Sunday to worship" (The Message) or "On the Saturday night" (NEB/REB) after the Sabbath or *Shabbat* had closed. This could make the meeting in Troas "*Motza'ei-Shabbat*" (CJB/CJSB), a get together of the Believers remembering the departure of the Sabbath.

Romans 3:19-22:
"Through the works of the Law no one will be justified."

Traditionally, Romans 3:19-22 has been interpreted as meaning that human action in association with the Law of Moses will not bring one a status of redemption. Alternatively, various scholars have proposed that "works of the Law" involves ancient Jewish *halachah*, and that "justification" here primarily involves membership among God's people. The actual purpose of the Torah is not justification; instead "through the Torah *comes* the knowledge of sin" (Romans 3:20b, author's rendering).

Romans 3:28:
"Justified by faith apart from works of the Law"

Even with components of "justification" likely involving membership among God's people, the purpose of the Torah is not to provide justification. Justification is to take place via faith, for both Jewish people and those of the nations (Romans 3:29-30). Yet as Paul also asserts, "Do we then overthrow the law by this faith? By no means! On the contrary, we uphold the law" (Romans 3:31, RSV).

A Torah Foundation

Romans 4:5:
"God justifies those who do not work"
A bad interpretation of Romans 4:5 would conclude that God is not concerned about born again Believers demonstrating good works resultant of their faith. The issue instead is people thinking that their human actions will merit some kind of justification, forgiveness, and a declaration of innocence before God—like a laborer would receive his wages (Romans 4:4).

Romans 6:14:
"We are not under law, but under grace"
Born again Believers not being "under the law" is commonly interpreted as meaning that they should not concern themselves with the commandments of God's Torah. The actual status of "under the law" is something contrary to being "under grace," meaning being forgiven and remitted of sins. Many Protestant theologians throughout history have advocated that being "under the law" is a status possessed by non-Believers, who stand condemned as unrighteous sinners by God's Torah—a clear antithesis to being "under grace."

Romans 6:23:
"Eternal life is a free gift"
Salvation is a free gift that human actions cannot earn. Debates always ensue about the behavior and obedience required of those who receive salvation—activities which are to result because of the supernatural action of God's Spirit on the hearts of the redeemed.

Romans 7:1-25:
"We were made to die to the Law through the body of Christ"
The main bulk of the discussion in Romans 7:7-25 describes the status of someone who recognizes the high value of God's Torah, but cannot quite seem to keep it due to innate human limitations. Paul says that born again Believers have been "made dead to the Torah through the body of Messiah" (Romans 7:4, author's rendering), which is like how a widow "is discharged from the law concerning the husband" (Romans 7:2, author's rendering; cf. Numbers 5:20, 29). The relationship of the unredeemed person is like the law of marriage being applicable to a wife. When the husband dies the law or instruction pertaining to marriage is no longer applicable to the wife—but this hardly means a widescale abandonment of the Torah's code in other matters. Just like the law of marriage is not applicable to a widow, so is the Torah's condemnation of sinners no longer applicable to the redeemed, and what Believers are actually "made dead" to is the Torah's condemnation, which was taken upon Yeshua the Messiah.

The Messianic Walk

Romans 8:1-4:
"The law of the Spirit of life has set us free from the law of sin and death"

"The law of the Spirit of life in Messiah Yeshua" is a spiritual law or constant demonstrated within a person, who recognizes Yeshua as Lord, is declared free of guilt and condemnation from Torah disobedience, is spiritually regenerated, and receives the gift of the Holy Spirit. A second spiritual law or constant, "the law of sin and death," is that once a person commits sin, he or she will die spiritually and experience a condition of exile from the Creator, and exist in a permanent state of condemnation and punishment if never rectified. A definite purpose of being saved and set free from sin is "that the righteous requirements of the law might be fully met in us" (Romans 8:4, NIV).

Romans 10:4:
"Christ is the end of the law for righteousness to everyone who believes"

Longstanding theological debates have ensued over the word *telos* (τέλος) in Romans 10:4, a term which can also mean aim, purpose, or goal, as witnessed in various alternative translations: "Christ is the goal of the Law, which leads to righteousness for all who have faith in God" (Common English Bible).

Romans 11:6:
"Grace is no longer on the basis of works"

It is a common misunderstanding among many contemporary evangelical people that grace was not present in the period of the "Old Testament." Paul actually references a number of Tanach passages (1 Kings 19:10, 14, 18; cf. Romans 11:1-5) in emphasizing how God's gracious choice has always allowed for a remnant of righteous. The statement, "But if it is by grace, it is no longer on the basis of works, otherwise grace is no longer grace" (NASU) should be taken as a logical argument, demonstrating how God's grace has always been present in all time periods, not that there was once a time when grace could be actually earned from human works.

Romans 14:
"God does not care about what days people celebrate or what food they eat"

The information in Romans ch. 14 is often applied to matters of *adiaphora* in contemporary religious settings today, such as the music people listen to or the movies people watch. In all probability, Paul's instruction to the Romans about eating and sacred days (Romans 14:2-6) involved unnecessary criticism of those who would only eat vegetables at fellowship meal times, and not "common" (Romans 14:14, LITV) meat that others would eat, Biblically clean but not ceremonially acceptable to some. These people were not to be looked down upon.

A Torah Foundation

There is a long-standing alternative opinion that the religious "days" in view (Romans 14:5-6) were times of traditional Jewish fasting. If one should not be criticized for fasting on a particular day—likely remembering or memorializing a tragic event in Israel's history—then one should surely not be criticized for not eating certain things at a communal fellowship meal.

1 Corinthians 6:12-20:
"All things are now lawful"

A correct translation of *Panta mou exestin* in 1 Corinthians 6:12 would be "Everything is permitted for me" (TLV). Numerous versions place this clause in quotation marks " ", reflecting the opinion of most scholars that this was a slogan used by a particular group in the Corinthian assembly. When Paul says, "'Everything is permitted for me'—but not everything is helpful. 'Everything is permitted for me'—but I will not be controlled by anything" (1 Corinthians 6:12, TLV), he is actually cross-examining and refuting something said by a group of Corinthians; this is not reflective of his own personal beliefs.

1 Corinthians 8:
"Paul permitted Gentile Christians to eat idol food, a clear violation of the Mosaic Law"

Paul did not permit any of the Corinthians to knowingly eat meat sacrificed to idols, and was critical toward those who thought that they had the freedom to do so (1 Corinthians 8:9). He focused his admonitions heavily toward those who thought that given the supremacy of the One God, that it did not matter if they ate meat sacrificed to idols, given how idols were dead objects (1 Corinthians 8:4). Their actions could have had grossly negative consequences, as there were new Believers who once ate their meals as an act of reverence or worship to idols (1 Corinthians 8:7), and eating meat sacrificed to idols could cause them to relapse back into paganism (1 Corinthians 8:10).

1 Corinthians 9:19-23:
"It is only necessary to keep
the Old Testament law to convert Jews to Christ"

If Paul only taught that some adherence to the Torah or Law of Moses was necessary for Jewish evangelism, then Paul could rightly be accused of violating his own words about not bringing the good news in a manner of craftiness (2 Corinthians 4:1-2). When Paul communicates "To the Jews I became as a Jew, so that I might win Jews" (1 Corinthians 9:20a, NASU), among the other groups he lists (1 Corinthians 9:20b-23), this is best taken as a statement of rhetoric. Paul self-identifies with the position of the diverse groups in the First Century Mediterranean, in order to best communicate the good news of salvation to them. Paul never stopped being a Jew after coming to Messiah faith. But, there were certainly aspects of the First Century Jewish experience and recent history—

among other groups' experiences—that he had to be quite conscious of, in going to synagogues and declaring that Yeshua was the Messiah of Israel.

1 Corinthians 10:14-33:
"Paul says to eat whatever is set before you"

The specific context of Paul saying to eat what is set before you, involves the acceptance of an invitation to eat at a non-Believer's home (1 Corinthians 10:27). What is set before a Believer on his or her plate, is to be graciously received as a matter of the host's hospitality. Should it become public knowledge that any meat had been offered to idols, then it is to not be eaten (1 Corinthians 10:28), as it would be a bad witness of one's faith in the One God of Israel.

1 Corinthians 16:2:
"The early Christians met on the first day of the week, a clear abolishment of the Jewish Sabbath."

The reference to the Corinthians meeting "on the first of the week" has been traditionally approached as Sunday worship services replacing the seventh-day Sabbath. There have, at times, been some dissenting opinions from this, given how this meeting on the first of the week was specifically for collecting monies. This would not be a permissible activity for the Sabbath. Also, in view of the Biblical day beginning in the evening, it has been usefully proposed that what is in view is *Motza'ei-Shabbat* (CJB/CJSB), or a special time closing off the Sabbath on Saturday evening.

2 Corinthians 3:
"The veil of the old covenant has been removed."

The Old Covenant is specifically labeled by Paul to be "the ministry of death" (2 Corinthians 3:7) or "condemnation" (2 Corinthians 3:9). It involves the Torah, at most, being delivered on lifeless stones, only able to condemn people as sinners. The supernatural work of "the ministry of righteousness" (2 Corinthians 3:9) involves activity of Divine principles being written onto human hearts and manifest to others (2 Corinthians 3:3). This is language taken from the New Covenant promises of Jeremiah 31:31-34 and Ezekiel 36:25-27, which speak of the commandments of God written by His Spirit onto new hearts of flesh. The reading of the Old Covenant ministry of condemnation (2 Corinthians 3:14), the Torah operative for a non-Believer, should convict people of their sins. Unfortunately, a veil lies over the heart of many, especially Jewish non-Believers, when the Torah can only operate as Old Covenant (2 Corinthians 3:15-16). The veil that separated Moses' face from Ancient Israel (Exodus 34:34) was not unlike the curtain separating out the Holy of Holies in the Temple complex—which was split in two at the Messiah's death (Mark 15:38; Matthew 27:51; Luke 23:45). The veil over a non-Believer's heart, prohibiting God's salvation and sanctification to take place, is what is removed. The Torah no longer functions in a condemnatory fashion, but in principles imbued on a redeemed psyche by the Spirit.

Galatians 2:11-21:
"By the works of the Law shall no flesh be justified."
Whether "works of the law" is approached from its traditional vantage point of being "observing the law" (Galatians 2:16, NIV)—or "works of the law" is approached in association with various sectarian deeds involving formal proselyte conversion to Judaism (cf. 4QMMT)—justification comes only through belief in Yeshua the Messiah and what He has accomplished. Who we are as redeemed human beings is to be focused around the work of Yeshua, and not any human action. We are to obey the Lord's Instructions as a result of the Divine work of Yeshua in our lives.

Galatians 3:12-14:
"Christ redeemed us from the curse of the Law."
Those who disobey God's Instruction are cursed, and the Messiah's death on the tree (Deuteronomy 21:23) is what merits those who believe in Him a redemption from the effects of sin. Obedience to God's Instruction, however, is to bring with it a high quality of life lived on Earth (Leviticus 18:5).

Galatians 3:23-25:
"The Law is our tutor to lead us to Christ."
It is said, "Therefore the Torah became our guardian to lead us to Messiah, so that we might be made right based on trusting" (Galatians 3:24, TLV). Salvation does not come by any human actions involving the Torah. But, the Torah's Instruction is to convict people of their sins, so that they might come to a point of realizing that only the work of Yeshua can provide salvation. The Torah's pre-salvation role is one of instruction and harsh discipline, revealing the human limitations and faults of people

Galatians 4:8-11:
"The Sabbath and Old Testament feast days are weak and worthless principles."
Paul specifically told the Galatians, "but now that you have come to know God, or rather to be known by God, how can you turn back again to the weak and beggarly elemental spirits?" (Galatians 4:9, RSV). The non-Jewish Galatians, in being errantly influenced to be circumcised as proselytes to Judaism to be truly reckoned as God's own, were returning to practices they left behind in Greco-Roman paganism. Has Paul associated Biblical commandments in God's Torah, such as those involved with the appointed times, and paganism, as being quantitatively indifferent? Or, in becoming formal converts to Judaism, did the Galatians feel that they could still participate in the Roman Emperor cult as good citizens? Alternatively, were the Judaizers/Influencers who had been persuading the Galatians, practitioners of any proto-Gnostic or mystical errors, with superstitions infused into their observance of their appointed times? A variety of

The Messianic Walk

interpretations are available at a reader's disposal, all of which have been proposed in Galatians scholarship over the past few decades.

Galatians 5:1-4:
"Those who try to keep the Law of Moses have fallen from grace."

It is actually stated by Paul, "You have been severed from Messiah, you who would be justified by the Torah; you have fallen away from grace" (Galatians 5:4, author's rendering). This specifically involved non-Jewish Believers seeking some kind of right-status before God, originating in the Torah and not the Messiah. It also involved whatever commitments they made in undergoing formal proselyte circumcision, where one would make himself "a debtor to do the whole law" (Galatians 5:3, YLT), a negative condition to be sure. Born again Believers, reliant upon the work of Yeshua of Nazareth, are not to be debtors of any kind to perform the Torah, but are rather to fulfill its righteous requirements via the supernatural work of the Holy Spirit inside of them (Romans 8:4), something resultant of the justification they have experienced.

Ephesians 2:8-10:
"We are saved by grace, not as a result of works."

No one true to the Scriptures can deny the clear imperative, "For it is by grace you have been saved, through faith—and this not from yourselves, it is the gift of God—not by works, so that no one can boast" (Ephesians 2:8-9, NIV). Eternal salvation does not result from any human activity—be that activity general works, or actions in association with the Torah of Moses. Yet, it is also absolutely true, that "we are His workmanship—created in Messiah Yeshua for good deeds, which God prepared beforehand so we might walk in them" (Ephesians 2:10, TLV). Those who have received the salvation of Yeshua, are to walk in good works of obedience, serving as definite external proof of the internal change which has occurred within them.

Ephesians 2:14-15:
"The Law was abolished in the flesh of Christ."

The breaking down of the barrier wall (Ephesians 2:14) has frequently been interpreted by Christians, as meaning that the Torah of Moses had to be abolished in order to bring unity to Jewish and non-Jewish Believers. While there was a dividing wall present in the Second Temple, designed to keep pagans and non-proselytes out on threat of death (Josephus *Antiquities of the Jews* 15.417; *Wars of the Jews* 5.194), such a wall is nowhere specified in the Torah itself. Some Protestant traditions, favorable to the moral instructions of the Law, conclude that Ephesians 2:15 is only speaking of ceremonial instructions of the Law, and not the Torah as a whole. The Greek clause *ton nomon tōn entolōn en dogmasin* specifies a kind of direction that has been abolished: *dogma*. This term appears nowhere in the Septuagint translation of the Tanach in regard to any Biblical commandments, but instead in regard to regal decrees of the Babylonians and

A Torah Foundation

Persians (Daniel 2:13; 6:8; Esther 3:9) or Jewish ancestral traditions (3 Maccabees 1:3; 4 Maccabees 10:2). What was abolished by Yeshua were various extra-Biblical dogmas or decrees responsible for erecting the barrier of the dividing wall in the Temple complex—passing themselves off as "Torah"—and resulted in an inappropriate spiritual culture where people from the nations were being kept out of God's Kingdom, rather than being welcomed into it.

Philippians 3:2-11:
"Righteousness is not derived by the Law."

In spite of Paul's significant Jewish pedigree (Philippians 3:5), he recognized that his human achievements were meaningless in view of Yeshua (Philippians 3:7-8). He emphasizes how as a Believer, that he be "found in Him, not having a righteousness of my own from the Torah, but that which is through the faithfulness of Messiah, the righteousness which is from God on the basis of faith" (Philippians 3:9, author's rendering). Paul's identity is centered and focused around placing his faith or trust in what Yeshua the Messiah has accomplished in being sacrificed for human sin. Messianic Believers today, who place a high emphasis on following the Torah, do so because they want to emulate the Messiah who followed the Torah—while steadfastly recognizing that their righteousness is to be found in His atoning work.

Colossians 2:14:
"The Law of Moses was nailed to the cross of Christ."

That something was nailed to the execution-stake or wooden scaffold of the Messiah, is clear enough from Colossians 2:14: "He wiped away the bill of charges against us. Because of the regulations, it stood as a testimony against us; but he removed it by nailing it to the execution-stake" (CJB/CJSB). Many have interpreted what was nailed to the execution-stake of Yeshua as the Torah of Moses in its entirety. Throughout Protestant history, though, many others have been more tempered in their conclusions. Instead of the Torah as a whole being "nailed to the cross," the most frequent alternative has been to conclude that the capital penalties and condemnation of the Torah were absorbed onto Yeshua.

Colossians 2:16-23:
"Christians are not to be judged
for not keeping the Sabbath and Old Testament feast days."

Unnecessary or unfair judgment of people, for what they do or do not do, is certainly not warranted from mature Believers. However, the statement "Therefore no one is to act as your judge in regard to food or drink or in respect to a festival or a new moon or a Sabbath day" (Colossians 2:16, NASU), is directly connected to a false philosophy that denigrated the Divinity of Yeshua (Colossians 2:8-9), and involved self-abasement and asceticism (Colossians 2:18, 20-22). Torah instructions involving *Shabbat* or the appointed times are supposed to reveal a significant Messianic substance to them (Colossians 2:17), something which adherents of the Colossian false teaching were not able to comprehend. Frequently, Colossians 2:16 is read out of context with what the judging actually involved per the situation being faced: What did various Torah practices mean, when caught up in association with the false teaching or false philosophy?

1 Timothy 1:8-9:
"The Law is not made for a righteous man."
The verb *keimai* correctly means "to lie upon," and appears in Yeshua's teaching about the ax that is laid at the root of the trees (Matthew 3:10; Luke 3:9). 1 Timothy 1:9 is correctly translated with "the law is not laid down for the just but for the lawless and disobedient, for the ungodly and sinners" (RSV). This is speaking of the penalties and condemnation of the Torah being used against those who violate it. Those who are redeemed in the Messiah do not have such harsh condemnation used against them.

1 Timothy 4:1-5:
"Those who observe the dietary laws have committed apostasy against Jesus."
The false teaching encountered in 1&2 Timothy, not only involved some kind of abstinence from eating meat, but also sexual relations (1 Timothy 4:3), as well as the errant belief that the general resurrection of the dead had already taken place (2 Timothy 2:18). True spirituality for initiates was believed to involve a return to a pre-Fall condition, where humans only ate a vegetarian diet and presumably did not engage in intercourse. The issue in 1 Timothy 4:3 involves a total abstention from eating all forms of meat, not the kosher dietary laws separating out clean and unclean meats.

2 Timothy 1:9:
"Salvation is not according to works."
"He has saved us and called us with a holy calling—not because of our deeds but because of His own purpose and grace. This grace was given to us in Messiah Yeshua before time began" (2 Timothy 1:9, TLV). People in today's Messianic community who give an importance to the Torah for God's people in the post-resurrection era, do so because of the need to live a life in accordance with His holiness *resultant of* their salvation—because human actions, deeds, or works cannot merit one eternal salvation.

2 Timothy 2:15:
"The Word of God is to be rightly divided between the Old and New Testaments, Israel and the Church."
While one needs to understand Holy Scripture in its ancient context(s) for sure, and recognize that Biblical books were not written directly to Twentieth and Twenty-First Century people, the KJV rendering of 2 Timothy 2:15 has led to

some bad conclusions: "Study to shew thyself approved unto God, a workman that needeth not to be ashamed, rightly dividing the word of truth." The idea that Holy Scripture needs to be rigidly split up, as it were, between the Tanach and Messianic Writings, is not sustainable. More modern versions correctly render the verb *orthotomeō* as "rightly handling" (RSV), "accurately handling" (NASU), "correctly handles" (NIV), or even "keep strictly" (REB).

Titus 1:14:
"The Old Testament law is to be regarded as nothing more than Jewish myth"
The troublemakers on Crete are said to have been pushing "Jewish myths or...merely human commands" (Titus 1:14, TNIV). Is this actually to be regarded as the Tanach Scriptures, or instead something outside the mainstream? Given the later reference to "genealogies" (Titus 3:9; cf. 1 Timothy 1:4), various exaggerations and embellishments on various minor characters in the Tanach, for which fringe branches of Ancient Judaism offered much speculation and lore, is more likely in view.

Titus 3:5-8:
"He did not save us according to our deeds, but according to His mercy"
God indeed does save people according to His mercy, and not according to their deeds or works. This takes place "by the washing of regeneration and renewing by the Holy Spirit" (Titus 3:5, NASU). Yet, it is also true that the promise of the New Covenant is that God will cleanse His people from their sins, and by His Spirit supernaturally empower them to keep His commandments (Ezekiel 36:25-27).

Titus 3:9:
"We are not to be concerned about obedience to Jewish laws"
Titus 3:9 actually says, "avoid foolish controversies and genealogies and strife and disputes about Torah, for they are unprofitable and useless" (TLV). For the circumstances addressed in Crete, this involved an irresponsible usage of the Torah, as a responsible usage is to reveal and condemn sin (1 Timothy 1:8-11).

Hebrews 4:1-10:
"Jesus is our Sabbath rest now"
There is little doubting that for those who have received salvation in the Messiah, that they do experience a rest from the guilt incurred by sin. Surely, however, given the future realities to be anticipated in salvation history, the institution and significance of the seventh-day Sabbath should not be haphazardly dismissed. The complete Sabbath rest that is to be experienced by born again Believers involves nothing less than the complete establishment of the Kingdom of God in eternity. Some Protestant theological traditions, while errantly thinking that the Sabbath

was transferred to Sunday, have rightly emphasized that the Messianic rest of the future cannot be properly understood unless a Believer partakes of a day of rest once a week. The weekly Sabbath or *Shabbat* is to teach God's people important principles about the rest of the Messiah—which we already partake of now via our salvation from sins, but which we are to anticipate more of at the culmination of the age.

Hebrews 7:11-12, 18-19:
"A change of law has taken place, because it was weak and worthless"

Due to the sacrifice and resurrection of the Messiah, "a change of the Torah" has taken place, but this is specified to involve "the priesthood being changed" (Hebrews 7:12, author's rendering). The overall context of Hebrews 7:11-12 and 18-19 makes it clear that it is not the ethical code of the Torah, or even institutions such as the appointed times or *moedim*, which are in view of being affected some sort of change or alteration. Changes which have been affected to the Torah involve the Levitical priesthood and animal sacrifices. The animal sacrifices could not provide permanent atonement and forgiveness for human sin, whereas Yeshua's sacrifice could. Yeshua's priestly service before the Father in Heaven is not Levitical, but instead is after the order of Melchizedek (Hebrews 7:11).

Hebrews 8:
"The New Covenant makes the Old Covenant obsolete"

No one denies that the work of Yeshua the Messiah has inaugurated the New Covenant. However, Hebrews 8:8-12, includes the longest quotation in the Messianic Scriptures from the Tanach, that of the New Covenant or *b'rit chadashah* from Jeremiah 31:31-34. It is a mistake to think that the New Covenant has nothing to do with the Torah, when the promise includes the explicit word, "I will put my laws into their minds, and write them on their hearts" (Hebrews 8:10, ESV). The transcription of the Torah's commandments onto the hearts and minds of God's people, for sure, can only come about because they have received Yeshua into their lives. It is also a supernatural work that can only take place via the sanctifying activity of the Holy Spirit.

Hebrews 10:1:
"The Law was only a shadow of good things to come"

A Bible version like the New American Standard Update, which employs *italics* for words added, indicates how "*only*" has been added: "For the Law, since it has *only* a shadow of the good things to come *and* not the very form of things, can never, by the same sacrifices which they offer continually year by year, make perfect those who draw near." The source text of Hebrews 10:1 says *Skian gar echōn ho nomos tōn mellontōn agathōn*, "For the law having a shadow of the coming good things" (YLT). While it is true that the Torah and its ordinances do include types and shadows of the substantive reality of the Messiah, the addition of "*only*" is intended to downplay the importance of those types and shadows. The Torah is incomplete without the revelation of Yeshua of Nazareth, but none of us can have confirmation of who He is, without knowledge of the Torah's Instruction and expectations.

Hebrews 10:9:
"God takes away the first covenant to establish the second"

The overall context of Hebrews 10:2-8 makes it clear that the issue in view is the limitation of the animal sacrifices of the Levitical priesthood, compared and contrasted to the final sacrifice of Yeshua the Messiah. As the author of Hebrews inquires, "The Torah has a shadow of the good things to come—not the form itself of the realities. For this reason it can never, by means of the same sacrifices they offer constantly year after year, make perfect those who draw near. Otherwise, would they not have ceased to be offered, since the worshipers—cleansed once and for all—would no longer have consciousness of sins? But in these sacrifices is a reminder of sins year after year—for it is impossible for the blood of bulls and goats to take away sins" (Hebrews 10:1-4, TLV). The issue in Hebrews 10:9, "He does away with the first in order to establish the second" (ESV), is restricted to the role of animal sacrifices in the atonement of sin.

Revelation 1:10:
"The Sabbath has now been replaced with the Lord's Day"

Various theologians have made the case, that per the subject matter of the Book of Revelation, that John did not receive his visions on "the Lord's Day" or Sunday, as would be seen in the emerging Christianity of the Second Century. Instead, John received his visions on "the Day of the Lord" (CJB/CJSB, TLV).

Serving the Lord as a Messianic Believer

Today's Messianic Believers, who are convinced of the validity of the Torah from the Apostolic Scriptures or New Testament, need to be consciously aware of how many of today's Christians will look at their lives rather critically. Whether you are a Messianic Jew or non-Jew does not matter here: such people will try to find what they perceive to be weaknesses in your life or faith practice, specifically as to whether or not Yeshua the Messiah (Jesus Christ) is the central focus of your faith. *Is the Messiah the focus of your faith?* We have just examined many of the common verses that contemporary Christians will direct toward Messianic Believers, as self-justification for them not having to keep most, if any, of the Mosaic Law.

While we have offered some fair-minded answers for you to provide such critics, keep in mind that Messianic examination and teaching on the Apostolic Scriptures need to go *far beyond* just having answers to passages that are commonly read as being anti-Torah. Many Messianics do not spend a great deal of time considering the important message and theology that the New Testament

The Messianic Walk

conveys to us. We have the definite responsibility as a Messianic faith community to truly regard the Apostolic Writings as being a part of "all Scripture" (2 Timothy 3:16) too, and not *exclusively* spend our time focusing on the Torah and Tanach, as can be commonplace in some sectors. If we do not have a high regard for the value and integrity of the Messianic Scriptures, then today's Messianic community will be neutered not only from understanding the continuing plan of salvation history—but most of all from accomplishing the Heavenly Father's objectives in restoring a sense of sanctified obedience to the Body of Messiah.

STUDY QUESTIONS FOR UNIT ONE

1. What are some of the reasons why you are involved in today's Messianic movement?

2. In considering some of the history of the First Century Believers, to the emergence of the modern Messianic movement—what biggest shift in your thinking has had to take place? (Note: While you cannot change the past, you can affect the future.)

3. What are some useful ways that the Messianic movement can be viewed as an "end-time move of God"?

4. Are you fully committed to being a part of the Messianic walk, even if it takes you right to the cusp of the return of Yeshua? Or, is being a part of the Messianic movement just a spiritual novelty for you, perhaps only for a limited season?

5. How important do you think it is to follow the weekly Torah reading cycle? Have you ever followed the Torah cycle through in a single year?

6. What do you think about the broad Messianic conviction that the Torah or Law of Moses bears relevance in the post-resurrection era? How much customary evangelical theology do you think needs to be reevaluated or jettisoned? What issues or passages do you need to more thoroughly review?

THE MESSIANIC EXPERIENCE
FOR FURTHER READING AND EXPLORATION

Brown, Michael L. *Our Hands Are Stained With Blood: The Tragic Story of the "Church" and the Jewish People* (Shippensburg, PA: Destiny Image 1992).

Chernoff, David. *An Introduction to Messianic Judaism* (Havertown, PA: MMI Publishing, 2012).

Chernoff, Yohanna, with Jimi Miller. *Born a Jew, Die a Jew: The Story of Martin Chernoff A Pioneer in Messianic Judaism* (Hagerstown, MD: EBED Publications, 1996).

Goldberg, Louis, ed. *How Jewish is Christianity? 2 Views on the Messianic Movement* (Grand Rapids: Zondervan, 2003).

Juster, Daniel C. *Jewish Roots: A Foundation of Biblical Theology* (Shippensburg, PA: Destiny Image, 1995).

Liberman, Paul. *The Fig Tree Blossoms: The Emerging of Messianic Judaism* (Kudu Publishing, 2012).

McKee, J.K. *Introduction to Things Messianic: An Introduction for Newcomers to the Messianic Movement* (Messianic Apologetics, 2012).

McKee, J.K. *The New Testament Validates Torah MAXIMUM EDITION: The New Testament Does Not Abolish the Law of Moses* (Richardson, TX: Messianic Apologetics, 2017).

Stern, David. H. *Messianic Judaism: A Modern Movement With an Ancient Past* (Clarksville, MD: Messianic Jewish Publishers, 2007).

Strickland, Wayne G., ed. *Five Views on Law and Gospel* (Grand Rapids: Zondervan, 1996).

SHABBAT, THE APPOINTED TIMES, JEWISH HOLIDAYS

UNIT TWO

Introducing the Biblical Appointments

Why are holidays important?[1] A holiday, as we call it in English, is defined by *The American Heritage Dictionary* as "A day on which custom or the law dictates a halt to ordinary business to commemorate or celebrate a particular event." Another definition is very simply, "A holy day," meaning a day set aside to remember something religious.[2] The holidays that we find in the Holy Scriptures give us a great opportunity as Believers to commemorate Biblical history and the work of our Messiah.

In the opening verses of Leviticus 23, we are told, "The LORD spoke again to Moses, saying, 'Speak to the sons of Israel and say to them, "the LORD's appointed times which you shall proclaim as holy convocations—My appointed times are these"'" (vs. 1-2, NASU). The Hebrew word for "appointed time" or "appointed festival" (ATS) is *moed*, and its plural form is *moedim*. It has a variety of meanings, including: "appointed time, place, meeting," and "*sacred season*," "*set feast*," or "*appointed season*" (*BDB*).[3] It is to be a special time between God's people and Him. The *ArtScroll Chumash* tells us,

". . .*Moadim* are the days which stand out from the other days of the year. They summon us from our everyday life to halt and to dedicate all our spiritual activities to them. . ..The *Moadim* interrupt the ordinary activities of our life and give us the spirit, power, and consecration for the future by revivifying those ideals upon which our whole life is based, or they eradicate such evil consequences of

---

[1] This has been adapted from a previous edition, appearing in J.K. McKee, *Introduction to Things Messianic* (Kissimmee, FL: TNN Press, 2009).

[2] William Morris, ed., *The American Heritage Dictionary of the English Language* (New York: American Heritage Publishing, 1969), 628.

[3] Francis Brown, S.R. Driver, and Charles A. Briggs, *Hebrew and English Lexicon of the Old Testament* (Oxford: Clarendon Press, 1979), 417.

past activity as are deadly to body and spirit and thus restore us to lost purity and the hope of blessing."[4]

It is important that the "Tent of Meeting," where Moses and Aaron and the elders of Israel met the Lord in the wilderness, is called the *ohel moed*. It could be understood as the "Tent of Appointment." Numbers 20:6 says, "Then Moses and Aaron came in from the presence of the assembly to the doorway of the tent of meeting and fell on their faces. Then the glory of the LORD appeared to them" (NASU). Using this as a frame of reference, if we truly want the glory of God to appear before us, then the importance of meeting Him when *He wants* cannot be overstated.

The term for "convocation" (Leviticus 23:1-2), also often used to describe the appointed times, is the Hebrew *miqra*. It specifically means "convocation, convoking, reading," in reference to a "religious gathering on Sabbath and certain sacred days" (*BDB*).[5] It is derived from the verb *qara*, to "*call, cry, utter a loud sound*," "*make proclamation*," and "*summon*" (*BDB*).[6] The appointed times call us together to rejoice in the Lord, focusing on Him, and make mention to one another of the work that He has done for us.

Many Messianic Believers, especially those who place a high prophetic emphasis on the pattern of the Biblical appointments, define the festivals of the Lord as *rehearsals*. Certainly, when we celebrate the Biblical holidays we not only remember the historical events in the life of Ancient Israel such as the Passover and Exodus, or the giving of the Ten Commandments, but we also recognize the prophetic fulfillment, both past and future, of Messiah Yeshua in them (Colossians 2:17). We essentially "rehearse" what is to come, in preparation for the Messiah's return, and we learn important lessons about God's ongoing plan of salvation history.

Another Hebrew term that is often used in Scripture to describe the Biblical feasts is *chag*, which *AMG* defines as "a feast, a festival."[7] It is derived from the verb *chagag*, "to hold a feast, a pilgrim feast, to celebrate a holy day. . .It is usually used in the context of rejoicing and describes festive attitudes and actions, often while on the way to worship or when celebrating a feast."[8] One of the clear elements of the appointed times is *celebration*. The *moedim* are to be times of great rejoicing in the Lord.

---

[4] Nosson Scherman, ed., et. al., *The ArtScroll Chumash, Stone Edition*, 5th ed. (Brooklyn: Mesorah Publications, 2000), 682.

[5] *BDB*, 896.

[6] Ibid., 895.

[7] Warren Baker and Eugene Carpenter, eds., *The Complete Word Study Dictionary: Old Testament* (Chattanooga: AMG Publishers, 2003), 312.

[8] Ibid., 313.

Introducing the Biblical Appointments

The Biblical holidays as outlined in Leviticus 23 may be divided up into three general seasons: Passover, Pentecost, and Tabernacles. Thus, when someone refers to Passover, he or she may not just be referring to Passover, but also the Festival of Unleavened Bread that occurs immediately thereafter. The listing below provides a brief reference of each of the Biblical holidays in Leviticus 23, and various extra-Torah and extra-Biblical celebrations that are beneficial and edifying to the Body of Messiah.

The Sabbath

Shabbat: *Shabbat* is the first appointed time given, although there are those who do not reckon it among the *moedim*, instead considering it to be its own unique institution.

Shabbat (or *Shabbos* in the Ashkenazic pronunciation) is the seventh-day Sabbath. Remembering the Sabbath is considered to be a sign of holiness (Exodus 31:16), where no work is conducted. The institution of the Sabbath is inclusive to all strata of society, including animals (Exodus 20:8-11), and welcomes in strangers and foreigners from outside the community of Israel (Isaiah 56:6-7). *Shabbat* is regarded as a memorial of both the Creation (Genesis 2:3) as well as the Exodus (Deuteronomy 5:15). *Shabbat* is a time where there is to be no buying or selling (Nehemiah 13:15), kindling of a fire (Exodus 35:3)—but most especially be a time of delighting in the Lord (Isaiah 58:13-14).

Yeshua the Messiah said that "The sabbath was made for humankind, and not humankind for the Sabbath" (Mark 2:27, NRSV), indicating how its rest is open for all people. However, as Lord of the Sabbath (Matthew 12:7-8), rather than *Shabbat* being legalistically burdensome through undue regulations, Yeshua emphasized that performing acts of goodness were permitted on the Sabbath (Matthew 12:1-5, 9-11; Luke 13:15).

The weekly Sabbath is a holy convocation (Leviticus 23:3), and by Second Temple times was often focused around synagogue worship and study. *Shabbat* is to be a weekly outward sign that is to distinguish God's people as they rest from all their work sundown Friday evening to sundown Saturday evening. Messianic congregations usually hold their weekly worship and teaching services on either Friday evening or Saturday morning, often attended with either a fellowship meal (or *oneg*) and other activities. The Sabbath is often closed with a traditional service known as *Havdalah*, preparing those who kept it for the next working week. *Shabbat* will be observed by the entire world in the future Millennium (Isaiah 66:23).

The Messianic Walk

The Spring Holidays

Pesach: *Pesach* or Passover commemorates God's deliverance of the Ancient Israelites from slavery and His subsequent judgment on the Egyptians (Leviticus 23:5-8). The prime element of Passover is the lamb (Exodus 12:3, 6-7), and how the blood of the lamb protected the Israelites from the death of the firstborn (Exodus 12:12-13, 29-33). The account of the Passover and Ancient Israel's deliverance from Egyptian servitude, is a theme which is carried on throughout the Holy Scriptures

Customary observance of the Passover in Jewish tradition extending back to Second Temple times focuses one's attention on the *seder* meal, a time of retelling the Passover story in the home, by incorporating the elements of unleavened bread, green herbs, bitter herbs, and *charoset*. Those involved in the *seder* will follow an *haggadah*, a basic order of service, which incorporates four cups of wine. The *seder* plate will be the centerpiece of the Passover evening, where the different elements of the meal will be represented. Throughout the *seder* meal, green herbs will be dipped into saltwater, remembering the bitterness of Israel's slavery, *charoset* represents the mortar used by the slaves to build for the Egyptians, and unleavened bread reminds one of the hasty departure the Israelites had to make from Egypt.

For Believers in Israel's Messiah, Yeshua, He is the Passover Lamb who was sacrificed for our sins (1 Corinthians 5:7; John 1:29). Passover and the Exodus story are vital to the understanding of one's salvation! Yeshua's sacrifice at Golgotha (Calvary) as *our* Passover Lamb, delivers us from slavery to sin and into eternal life in Him. Yeshua's Last Supper held with His Disciples (Matthew 26:17-35; Mark 14:1-31; Luke 22:1-23; John 13:1-20), was actually a Passover *seder* meal. The plagues issued by the God of Israel upon Egypt, not only serve as clear indicators of the judgments of the One True God over the false gods of Egypt—but also speak to the judgments of the Book of Revelation. The Pharaoh of Egypt, is certainly representative of the future antimessiah/antichrist.

Chag HaMatzah: *Chag HaMatzah* is the Festival of Unleavened Bread (Leviticus 23:5-6). It occurs for one week following Passover, in remembrance of the Ancient Israelites leaving Egypt and having to eat *matzah* or unleavened bread, the bread of haste (Exodus 12:39). Items without leavening or yeast are to be eaten during this time. Since *matzah* is without leaven, for Believers in Yeshua it represents His sinless nature for us and how we must remove the sin from our lives (1 Corinthians 5:8; Galatians 5:9). Since Unleavened Bread occurs in conjunction with Passover, it is often not distinguished as a separate holiday (see Scripture references for *Pesach*).

Shavuot: *Shavuot* (or *Shavuos* in the Ashkenazic pronunciation) or the Feast of Weeks is more commonly called Pentecost, a Greek-derived name meaning "fiftieth" (Grk. *pentēkostē*). The Feast of Weeks was originally established as an

Introducing the Biblical Appointments

agricultural festival where the first of the wheat harvest would be presented to God as an offering (Leviticus 23:15-21). *Shavuot* is also the time when it is traditionally believed that the Torah was given to Moses on Mount Sinai. Following the giving of the Torah, the Ancient Israelites worshipped the golden calf and Moses destroyed the two tablets of the Ten Commandments (cf. Exodus 19-33). *Shavuot* or Pentecost is the traditional time when the Holy Spirit was poured out on the Believers at the Upper Room in Jerusalem following Yeshua's ascension into Heaven (Acts 2:1-4). Messianic people can often associate *Shavuot* with the formal giving of the New Covenant (Jeremiah 31:31-34; Ezekiel 36:25-27), concurrent with the giving of the Torah at Mount Sinai 1,300 (or 1,500) years earlier.

The Fall Holidays

Yom Teruah: *Yom Teruah* is the Day of Blowing, as specified in the Torah (Leviticus 23:23-25). It is remembered as *Rosh HaShanah* or the Civil New Year in Judaism today, although it is hardly remembered as a January 1 new year. *Yom Teruah* or *Rosh HaShanah* was established to be a holy convocation celebrated by the blowing of trumpets, and involves special blowings of the *shofar* or ram's horn. This convocation is intended to prepare the people for the ten Days of Awe before *Yom Kippur*, where unresolved conflicts between others in the community are repented of. *Rosh HaShanah* has special significance to us as Believers in the Messiah as we will be caught up in the air to meet Him at the blast of the trumpet at His Second Coming (cf. 1 Corinthians 15:51-52; 1 Thessalonians 4:16-17).

Yom Kippur: *Yom Kippur* is the Day of Atonement (Leviticus 23:26-32). In the past, this was the only time when the high priest was permitted to enter into the Holy of Holies and spread the sacrificial blood upon the Ark of the Covenant (Leviticus 16:2; cf. Hebrews 9:3-5). The releasing of the scapegoat is also featured prominently on *Yom Kippur* (Leviticus 16:5-9, 10, 21-22). On the Day of Atonement we are commanded to afflict ourselves by fasting (cf. Acts 27:9), and reflect on our sin. Within the Messianic community, while the final atonement for sin has been offered by Yeshua the Messiah, *Yom Kippur* is still a time of prayer and intercession, resolving corporate conflicts and sins, and entreating for the salvation of the Jewish people and the world. *Yom Kippur* has special prophetic significance to us who know Yeshua, because it is likely that a future *Yom Kippur* will be when the Day of the LORD occurs, when His judgment is poured out upon humanity at the Battle of Armageddon.

Sukkot: *Sukkot* (or *Succos* in the Ashkenazic pronunciation) is the Feast of Tabernacles, also called the Feast of Booths. The Israelites were to dwell in a temporary house known as a *sukkah*, or a hut covered by leafy branches for seven days (Leviticus 23:33-44; Numbers 29:12). The Feast of Tabernacles commemorates

The Messianic Walk

the Ancient Israelites' journey in the wilderness and how God wanted earnestly to tabernacle or dwell with them. It involves the waving of branches (Leviticus 23:40), and is to be a family affair (Deuteronomy 16). Many think that the American holiday of Thanksgiving has its roots in the Feast of Tabernacles. *Sukkot* is also a likely time when Yeshua the Messiah was born (John 1:14), and it will be celebrated by all after His return. Tabernacles will be a critical holiday for all the nations to celebrate during the Millennium (Zechariah 14:1-21).

Shemini Atzeret: *Shemini Atzeret* (or *Shemini Atzeres* in the Ashkenazic pronunciation) or the Eighth Day of Assembly is often overlooked as its own separate holiday, coming after the seven days of *Sukkot* (Leviticus 23:36b-37a). *Shemini Atzeret* represents the desire of our Heavenly Father to stay with us for one more day, as we reflect back on the tabernacling during *Sukkot*. It symbolizes how we will live with Him forever in the New Jerusalem (Revelation 21:3-4).

Other Holidays In and Out of the Bible

Chanukah: *Chanukah* (or *Channukah*, *Hanukah*, *Hanukkah*, etc.) or the Feast of Dedication is an eight day holiday commemorating the work of the Maccabees and their defeat over the Syrian Greeks in 165 B.C.E. The Syrian Greeks or Seleucids had conquered the Land of Israel and desecrated the Temple (cf. Daniel 8:21-25), sacrificing a pig and erecting an altar to the god Zeus in it. It was illegal on the threat of death for the Jewish people to circumcise their sons, observe the Sabbath, observe the Torah-prescribed festivals, and eat kosher food. The Syrian Greeks promoted forced assimilation of the Jewish people to Hellenistic paganism. *Chanukah* celebrates how the Maccabean resistance fought off the Seleucids, restoring Jewish independence, and how the Temple was rededicated (1&2 Maccabees in the Apocrypha). There was only enough consecrated oil to light the candelabra or *menorah* in the Temple for one day, but instead it lasted for eight days (b.*Shabbat* 12a in the Talmud). Yeshua the Messiah is witnessed to remember *Chanukah*, most often appearing in English Bibles as "the Feast of the Dedication" (John 10:22, NASU).

Purim: *Purim* or the Feast of Lots commemorates the story of Esther, the events of which occur after the Persian Empire conquers the Babylonian Empire, which has a large population of Jews dispersed from the Land of Israel. *Purim* celebrates the defeat of the evil Haman, who had planned to kill all the Jews, and how God's sovereignty and protecting hand prevailed through the Jewess Esther, wife of the Persian emperor, and her cousin Mordechai. The name *Purim* comes from the *pur* or lot that was to be cast to determine when the mass executions were to take place (Esther 3:13). Frequently in the Jewish community, *Purim* is a time when a customary retelling of the story of Esther is delivered in dramatic

Introducing the Biblical Appointments

form, a tradition which is carried out to various degrees in the Messianic movement as well.

Tishah b'Av: *Tishah b'Av* or the Ninth of Av is an extra-Biblical fast day when the destruction of the First and Second Temples in Jerusalem is remembered. Historically, the Ninth of Av has also been a day when terrible, tragic events have occurred to the Jewish people, such as their eviction from Spain in 1492. It has been a time to remember the past and terrible events like the Crusades or the Holocaust.

Simchat Torah: *Simchat Torah* (or *Simchas Torah*) or Joy of the Torah occurs on the same day as *Shemini Atzeret*. It was added by the Jewish Rabbis to celebrate the ending of the reading of the yearly Torah cycle, and to rejoice in the forthcoming reading of the next Torah cycle.

Modern-Day Israeli Holidays

Yom HaShoah: *Yom HaShoah* or Holocaust Memorial Day is when the 6 million Jews who died in the Holocaust are formally remembered. It specifically commemorates the 1943 Warsaw Ghetto uprising.

Yom HaZikaron: *Yom HaZikaron* or Israel's Remembrance Day commemorates the war heroes of the State of Israel, those who have fought and died for the preservation of the Jewish people and the Jewish state.

Yom HaAtzmaut: *Yom HaAtzmaut* is Israel Independence Day when the State of Israel was established as an independent country in 1948. The Zionist cause and early pioneers of the State of Israel are remembered, as are those who have fought and died to maintain Israel's freedom and independence.

Yom Yerushalayim: *Yom Yerushalayim* or Jerusalem Day commemorates the recapturing of the Old City of Jerusalem in the 1967 Six Day War.

The Messianic Walk

Remembering Biblical and Jewish Holidays as a Messianic Believer

Each of us tends to be a person of habit, and there are ongoing daily, weekly, and annual cycles which tend to give focus and meaning to our lives. Certain days appear on the calendar which have importance to us. We may look forward on a certain day each week, to eat at a particular restaurant having a special. We may look forward to the weekend, to simply relax and not work. We may look forward to a birthday, an anniversary, or a day when something extremely important took place in our individual or family's lives.

People in today's Messianic movement have a different life cycle, than those many others who claim faith in Israel's Messiah. While we have our birthdays and anniversaries like other people—the Jewish and non-Jewish Believers who compose today's Messianic community, follow a different cycle throughout the week and throughout the year. For many Jewish Believers in Yeshua, being a part of the Messianic movement has been **a significant lifeline,** especially given the past history of many Jewish Believers who had become part of Christianity. Only until the past century or so, it was normative for Jewish Believers to assimilate into non-Jewish Christianity, its religious holidays, its customs, and for the children of Jewish Believers to quickly forget about their Jewish heritage. *After all, it was thought that being Jewish and receiving Jesus meant that one became a Christian and stopped being a Jew.* Today, with the Messianic Jewish movement, this is thankfully no longer the case. Not only it is a very Jewish thing to believe in Yeshua as Israel's Messiah—but it is entirely acceptable to do Jewish things like remembering *Shabbat*, the festivals of the Torah, and the historical commemorations of the Jewish people.

The Messianic Walk

A significant number of the non-Jewish Believers, whom God has specially called into the Messianic movement at this point in time, have often been led by Him to remember Yeshua in the Biblical feasts. A passage like Colossians 2:17, which speaks of how the appointed times have shadows of the substance of the Messiah, and how various Torah instructions portray elements of His redemptive work, really speak to the hearts and minds of non-Jewish Believers. These are people who want to live more like Yeshua and His Disciples, recognizing themselves as "fellow-citizens with God's people and members of God's family" (Ephesians 2:19, CJB/CJSB). As followers of Israel's God and Israel's Messiah, *and* as a part of the Commonwealth of Israel (Ephesians 2:11-13), what God has specified for His people and what He has done in the history of Israel, bears supernatural importance.

What does it mean for today's Messianic people to regularly remember the Biblical appointed times and holidays in Scripture, as well as various commemorations from Jewish history and tradition? Many Jewish Believers see a magnanimous fulfillment of these things, wondering how their ancestors and family members continue to miss the Messiah. Many non-Jewish Believers feel that they had been robbed from past spiritual experiences, which did not include the appointed times of Leviticus 23 and other remembrances, and they can run into significant conflicts with their family and friends over why they are not necessarily observing previous engagements any more.

The Weekly Shabbat

For many Jewish homes, especially more religiously observant ones, the work week culminates in the remembrance of the weekly Sabbath or *Shabbat*. The *Erev Shabbat* family dinner is a huge centerpiece in the Jewish community, so much so that many non-religious Jews still think it is important to light candles, break *challah*, recite blessings, sing songs, and gather around the table together. For those who are followers of Israel's God, the *Erev Shabbat* meal is important for maintaining the relationship between not only family members, but also with the larger Jewish community and with its God. This of course is carried over into the actual Sabbath day, frequently with morning services held at one's local synagogue or temple, including traditional liturgy, Hebrew canting from the Torah, and a message that is typically delivered from the weekly Torah portion.

The Messianic Jewish *Shabbat* experience, while varied, does rightly incorporate a great number of the edifying traditions witnessed in the Synagogue. It is important that families get together once a week, and share a meal. It is vital that we all come together corporately in worship. And as Messianic Jews remember traditional prayers and customs, sometimes from their own childhood—Yeshua the Messiah being the center of the *Shabbat* rest, and identifying a number

Remembering Biblical and Jewish Holidays as a Messianic Believer

of the Jewish Sabbath traditions originating during Second Temple times, brings great joy and elation to them.

Non-Jewish Believers in the Messianic movement, observing *Shabbat*, is frequently a sight to behold. Many eagerly embrace *Shabbat* and its theme of rest—**because they know that all human beings need rest!** Admittedly for some, attending *Shabbat* services is little more than going to "Saturday church." Yet, for many others, their introduction to *Shabbat* may have begun when a Messianic Jewish friend invited them into their homes for an *Erev Shabbat* dinner, and then they got hooked. Others, per the theological traditions of their Protestant heritage, may have looked at Sunday as a proper Sabbath day, including a prohibition on conducting in commerce, but appreciate that they now have embraced *Shabbat* with the fullness and richness that is seen in Judaism.

The Fall High Holidays

Jewish people of generally all varieties, take some notice of the high holidays of *Rosh HaShanah* and *Yom Kippur*. For the observant, the time period leading up to and around these days is most vital, to make sure that any sins or errors of the previous year, and faults committed against others, are resolved. *Rosh HaShanah* and *Yom Kippur* are times, for religious Jews, where they believe that God is indeed looking at their hearts, and actively determining where they stand before Him. It is a very serious time for prayer, contemplation, and entreating the Lord for His mercy. Jewish people, who are nominally or non-religious, still tend to make an effort to attend some synagogue service for one or both holidays.

People in the Messianic community, because of affirming Yeshua of Nazareth as the prophesied Redeemer of Israel—while surely admiring customary Jewish approaches to *Rosh HaShanah* and *Yom Kippur*—have a much different orientation toward these two high holidays, **precisely because we believe that He has been sacrificed for our sins.** While it is useful and appropriate that we all try to make amends for the errors we have committed toward our neighbors, and come in corporate confession and repentance as congregations and assemblies—we do not sit in a service, with some angst hanging over us about our sins not being fully taken care of. Instead, we come together in praise of what the Lord has done for us, and we entreat Him for the salvation of Israel and the world. This is especially appropriate, given how many conclude that on a future Feast of Trumpets and Day of Atonement significant events will take place in association with the return of the Messiah to Planet Earth, and the defeat of His enemies.

Following the high holidays of *Rosh HaShanah* and *Yom Kippur* is the eight-day Feast of Tabernacles or *Sukkot*. Traditionally in the Diaspora Jewish community, a *sukkah* or tabernacle is constructed in one's back yard or at one's synagogue, where families will often spend time for meals, and invite their friends for socializing. This is also the frequent way *Sukkot* is observed in the Diaspora

The Messianic Walk

Messianic Jewish community, although congregations can make *Sukkot* a time where there are special teachings or special functions to attract a larger audience. In North America, at least, the Feast of Tabernacles does tend to take place within the Fall, corresponding to various harvest themed activities that one may encounter in the local community.

The Fall holidays of the Feast of Trumpets, Day of Atonement, and the Feast of Tabernacles tend to be a major season when Messianic Jewish congregations make a considerable effort to reach out to the larger Jewish community with the good news. Messianic Jewish congregations often advertise to the Jewish people in their city—especially those who may only tend to visit a synagogue once or twice a year—that their congregation not only has *Rosh HaShanah* or *Yom Kippur* services, but that they are free! In many Jewish synagogues, members have to actually *pay* for their seats—yet Messianic congregations have been especially set up for Jewish non-Believers to come, visit, and be presented with the good news of Israel's Messiah.

Non-Jewish Believers, whom God has directed into the Messianic movement, tend to have different approaches, or even reactions, to the Fall holidays. Many simply appreciate the reverence, traditional prayers and liturgy, and overall seriousness of *Rosh HaShanah* and *Yom Kippur*. Focusing on one's individual and corporate standing before God and others is actually therapeutic. And certainly, praying that the Jewish people come to faith in Yeshua, and that the world can experience *shalom*, is also most vital. At the same time, just as Messianic congregations can have a "flood" of Jewish visitors for *Rosh HaShanah* and *Yom Kippur*, there can also be many Christian visitors. But, rather than focus on some of the holy themes and prayers of these high holidays, these people tend to rather be focused on being present for what they think might be the season for "the rapture." Unfortunately, their interest is not so much on entreating the Lord for His mercy toward the unsaved, and His concern that His people be accomplishing His Kingdom purposes.

Most Messianic Jewish congregations holding *Sukkot* activities do something similar to what is witnessed in the mainstream Synagogue. They are likely to have a *sukkah* on the congregational property, and they may have some event or major gathering open to the public—which more than anything else gives the congregation significant exposure. A number of congregations and/or Messianic ministries will hold various week-long retreats at a rural campground. (More frequently than not, this is a feature of the independent Hebrew/Hebraic Roots movement.) It can be witnessed that attendance at one's Messianic congregation might be down, because people are off attending some *Sukkot* function. Regardless of how *Sukkot* is remembered by your local assembly, make sure that it is a welcoming time, where people notice the presence of the *sukkah*, they can fellowship, worship the Lord, and truly experience community.

Remembering Biblical and Jewish Holidays as a Messianic Believer

The Winter Holidays

The Winter holiday season is frequently a very tense time of the year, for people within the broad Messianic movement. A definite feature of the Jewish experience, during the month of December, is remembering the holiday of *Chanukah*, the Feast of Dedication. The events involving *Chanukah* are mainly recorded in the Apocryphal Books of 1-2 Maccabees, as it involved the resistance of the Jewish people against the Seleucid Greeks—who wanted to see them give up their Torah way of life and assimilate into Greek polytheism—and the subsequent rededication of the Temple after their defeat. In much of the Jewish tradition, the festival of *Chanukah* is a time when families gather to light the *menorah*, they eat special foods (often fried), and it is a time to demonstrate good will and happiness toward one another, often with the giving of gifts.

Messianic Jewish congregations observing *Chanukah*, often transfer over much of the Synagogue communal experience, although as the *menorah* is lit, Yeshua the Messiah will be emphasized to be the Light of the Word. Messianic teachings during *Chanukah* do appreciably tend to focus more on the historical record of the Second Century B.C.E. Maccabean crisis, the Books of Maccabees, various prophecies of Daniel, and actually what can be learned from the Maccabees' resistance not only to apostasy from the God of Israel—but how there are vital connections to be made to the end-times, the future rise of the beast, and how Believers in Yeshua need to resist apostasy. And, for our overall Biblical Studies, it does tend to be discussed how the First Century Jewish Believers were affected by the social fallout of the Maccabean crisis, as it did play a role in some of the tensions that erupted between the Jewish, Greek, and Roman Believers, as the good news spread out into the Mediterranean. Overall, Messianic Believers tend to learn new things about how relevant the story of *Chanukah* actually is for our contemporary lives as Messiah followers today.

Huge controversies can and do erupt during the month of December, regarding how Messianic people are to approach the Christian holiday of Christmas, on December 25. Many Messianic Jews simply do not see Christmas as something Jewish, they do not see it as something for them, but if Christians observe it, they are not going to oppose them. Many Messianic people, particularly intermarried couples, often keep both *Chanukah* and Christmas. Many other Messianic people, oppose Christmas, although for different reasons and with different levels of opposition. Some of this may simply come from December 25 not being a specified holiday in the Bible, or established by the Apostles. Others see Christmas on December 25 as a clear result of syncretism practiced by Christians of the Second-Fourth Centuries, where pagan holidays were reinterpreted and "Christianized" with Biblical themes. Many see Christmas on December 25 as outright paganism, Christmas trees directly prohibited in Scripture (i.e., Jeremiah 10:2-5), and most

The Messianic Walk

Christians serving the Kingdom of Darkness. And, a few others, noting some early opposition to Christmas by a number of the Protestant Reformers, see Christmas on December 25 as a symbol of corrupt Roman popery. *Those who hold to all of these positions are likely to be found at your local Messianic congregation during the month of December.*

All of us should be mature enough as adults to recognize that during the month of December, due to all of the nativity scenes and different Christmas carols, that more people are going to be presented with hearing about Jesus and some form of the gospel, than at any other time during the year. In spite of many of the questionable practices and origins surrounding Christmas, God has brought people to Himself during this time of year. Yet Messianic people should also be wise enough to recognize that the Savior declared today during the month of December, is broadly not the Messiah of Israel, who is returning to reign over Planet Earth from Jerusalem—but is instead a universal Christ of tolerance (for human sin). While many sincere Christian people have honored God in ignorance on December 25, Christmas on December 25 is not a God-honoring activity. Still, Messianic Believers who may observe *Chanukah*, do not need to be odious to Christian people during this time, creating unnecessary scenes. Wishing "Happy Holidays" when being told "Merry Christmas," is entirely legitimate.

The Spring Holidays

Usually as the Winter is closing, or as early Spring begins, in North America, the Jewish community remembers *Purim* or the Feast of Lots. The main focus of *Purim* is to recall the events of the Book of Esther, and how God used individuals like Esther and Mordechai, to bring about His deliverance of the Jewish people from certain annihilation. The Messianic Jewish movement remembers *Purim* via many of the same customs and traditions as the Synagogue, and tends to rightfully use it as a time to focus on not only the necessary deliverance of the Jews—for without the Jews there would be no Messiah Yeshua—but also how we can stand against anti-Semitism in our own day.

Passover and the Festival of Unleavened Bread, where the deliverance from Ancient Israel from Egypt, the ten plagues, and the centerpiece of the lamb are recalled—**is one of the most important features of anyone's reading of the Bible.** The significance that the Exodus story has had, not just in controlling redemptive and salvation themes throughout Holy Scripture, the self-identity of the Jewish people throughout history, but also many political and reforming movements in history, *is quite staggering.* Without appreciating the Passover and the Exodus, one is very much likely to not understand salvation history.

Within the broad Jewish tradition, extending back to Second Temple times, the story of the Passover has been remembered via the Passover *seder* meal. This mainly involves a retelling of the Exodus, the ten plagues upon Egypt, and incorporates the elements of unleavened bread, wine, and bitter herbs. The Passover *seder* has definitely been adapted throughout many centuries of Jewish history, often for the unique needs of diverse Jewish communities throughout the Diaspora. **The Passover account alone should be compelling for all followers of the God of Israel.** Yet, today's Messianic Jewish movement has extended considerable efforts from its beginning, to make clear connections between the ancient Passover *seder* and the Last Supper meal held between Yeshua and His Disciples, before His sacrifice as the Lamb of God. The Last Supper was a Passover *seder*, although a very unique one, as the Disciples were being prepared to see their Lord executed in atonement for the sins of Israel, and indeed, all of humanity.

The Passover season is a significant time for the broad Messianic community, not only because of the critical need for us to rejoice in the sacrifice and resurrection of the Messiah—**but because more people get exposed to the Messianic movement during Passover, than at any other time.** While Messianic families, or groups of families, tend to often hold home Passover *seder* meals—inviting many guests—Messianic congregations tend to especially be keen on having a large communal Passover meal, sometime during the week of Unleavened Bread. This is often used as a dual-outreach, first to the Jewish community, as there are many non-religious Jewish people who can especially be reached with the good news during this time—knowing that Passover is, at least, a part of their cultural heritage. Secondly, evangelical Protestant interest in the Passover, has also been quite high over the past few decades. Wanting to understand the Last Supper as an actual Passover *seder*, as something that Yeshua did and should still be remembered (cf. 1 Corinthians 5:7), has drawn many evangelical people into the Messianic movement, embracing their Hebraic and Jewish Roots.

Some tension can erupt in the Spring, over the approach that the Messianic movement has regarding the Christian Easter Sunday. **Messianic people absolutely must affirm the centrality of the death, burial, and resurrection of Yeshua the Messiah to our faith!** Yet, there is considerable discussion and debate, even among evangelical Protestants, regarding the origins of the term "Easter." Some think it comes from the Babylonian goddess Ishtar, others from the Teutonic Eostre. This is why in some churches, the terminology Resurrection Sunday has been employed. And thankfully for many evangelical Believers, their Resurrection Sunday is precisely about the resurrection of Yeshua, and not about the Easter Bunny or Easter eggs. Some people in the Messianic community can cause a scene with various Christian people, over their observance of Easter. At the same time, other Messianic people properly integrate a remembrance of Yeshua's death, burial, and resurrection into their home and congregational Passover activities.

During the season of Unleavened Bread, a seven-week or fifty-day period called the Counting of the Omer begins, which leads up to *Shavuot* or the Feast of Weeks,

The Messianic Walk

Pentecost. For Ancient Israel in the Torah, the Feast of Weeks was originally an early harvest festival, but became quickly associated with the giving of the Law at Mount Sinai. It was a key pilgrimage festival, noted in the First Century as being the time when the Holy Spirit was poured out (Acts 2). There are varied customs and traditions regarding how *Shavuot* is remembered, which can involve all-night readings of the Book of Ruth, and special teachings from the Mishnah tractate *Pirkei Avot* or Sayings of the Fathers. In the Synagogue today, *Shavuot* is a relatively minor festival, but in Messianic settings, the equal giving of both God's Torah and God's Holy Spirit, tends to be the focus of one's commemoration.

Indeed, when one factors in the storyline from Passover to *Shavuot*, today's Messianic Believers are presented with all of the key components of a person's salvation. (1) Men and women are saved from their bondage to slavery via the blood of Yeshua the Lamb, just as Ancient Israel was saved from its bondage to Egyptian servitude via the original Passover lambs. (2) Believers in Israel's Messiah are immersed in water, reminiscent of the Israelites led through the parting of the Red Sea. (3) Believers in Israel's Messiah are to receive His charge for living lives of holiness and obedience, just as Ancient Israel was brought to Mount Sinai to be formally given the Torah. And (4) followers of Israel's Messiah are to enter into His purpose, accomplishing the tasks of the Kingdom of Heaven, similar to how the Israelites were being prepared to enter into the Promised Land.

Remembering Biblical and Jewish Holidays

To any Messianic Jewish family, it is essential and imperative that the Biblical and Jewish holidays be observed. History is replete with too many examples, that when Torah institutions such as *Shabbat*, Passover, or *Yom Kippur* are overlooked or not remembered, among others, that Jewish people have a tendency to quickly forget their identity. The Hebrew Christian movement of the early Twentieth Century did not do a good job at emphasizing both the cultural *and* Biblical responsibility that Jewish Believers have to remember the appointed times. Even today, when Messianic Believers, think that it is acceptable to keep both *Chanukah* and Christmas, two opposing messages are affirmed. The Festival of Dedication has a theme of resisting assimilation to the world and its ways, whereas the syncretistic holiday of Christmas communicates that it is acceptable to take the ways of the world and "reinvent" them with Biblical themes.

Non-Jewish Believers have been entering into the Messianic community, in substantial numbers, since the 1990s—with the Biblical and Jewish holidays a significant magnet for them doing so. They often conclude that a short Sunday Church service, Christmas on December 25, and Easter Sunday, are spiritually anemic and not able to fulfill all of their needs. A weekly *Shabbat* rest, the appointed times of Leviticus 23, and edifying extra-Biblical commemorations from Jewish history are found to be very inviting! While there might be some good

Remembering Biblical and Jewish Holidays as a Messianic Believer

memories which linger, at times, of past family experiences—the future is embraced as one which not only ministers to the human soul on many more levels, but where one can have the genuine assurance of knowing that you are doing something that Yeshua (Jesus) did!

People being who they are, it has to be recognized that there can be a tendency to think of oneself as being a bit superior, as a Messianic Believer, involved with *more Biblical* things on a weekly and annual basis—whereas most of the worldwide Body of Messiah, at present, could not care that much about them. Proverbs 16:18 does need to remind some of us, "Pride *goeth* before destruction, and an haughty spirit before a fall" (KJV). Many who should be considering the value of the Biblical and Jewish holidays—be it Jewish Believers who have come to faith in Israel's Messiah, perhaps rediscovering lost or forgotten parts of their family heritage, and non-Jewish Believers just now considering their spiritual heritage in the Tanach (Old Testament)—can find themselves turned off or even repelled, **if we do not have the right attitude.**

All of us can, for certain, have an edifying orientation when it comes to either the Sabbath, appointed times, or various extra-Biblical Jewish holidays. When Jewish people who need Yeshua, or evangelical Believers who need to grasp a hold of their Hebraic and Jewish Roots, **see us**—are they attracted to us, because they want to be a part of a loving and Spirit-filled community of Messiah followers fulfilling God's tasks in the Earth? Do they feel genuinely welcomed and accepted by us, as they are wooed by the Lord to join with us, experiencing great blessings, and being part of the great things that He has in store for the Messianic movement in the days ahead? Do we, in our remembrance of these various holidays, actually live forth their substance in our lives of faith in Israel's Messiah?

The Messianic Walk

Controversies Involving Biblical and Jewish Holidays as a Messianic Believer

For people throughout the broad Messianic movement, the appointed times or *moedim* of the Torah, and the various traditional Jewish holidays and commemorations, are significant moments of celebration, enrichment, and enlightenment. Jewish Believers in Israel's Messiah are often reconnecting with deeply significant traditions and customs, practiced not only by their ancestors, but by their immediate family which has yet to recognize Yeshua. Non-Jewish Believers called by God, into the Messianic movement, are embracing things which were practiced by Yeshua and His first followers. When the Biblical and Jewish holidays take place, these are supposed to be seasons of great personal, familial, and congregational unity and spiritual growth. As we reflect upon what the Lord has done in the past, we are to all embody the Psalmist's grand word, "How very good and pleasant it is when kindred live together in unity!" (Psalm 133:1, NRSV).

A majority of you who commemorate the Biblical and Jewish holidays experience precisely this: a sense of spiritual fulfillment and unity when they appear in the annual cycle. Yet, it would be entirely inappropriate to introduce you to the appointed times, without also letting you know that these can be periods of division and discord within the Messianic community. Many of you already know this to be the case, if for any other reason because you have volunteered at your local Messianic congregation or fellowship to help, in some capacity, during the Fall high holidays or with the congregational Passover *seder*. You probably got a quick lesson in how it is one thing to remember the Biblical and Jewish holidays within

The Messianic Walk

the privacy of your own home; it is another thing to remember the Biblical and Jewish holidays in a much larger venue of people *who have opinions about the "right way" things are to be done.*

Unnecessary divisions and tensions are a part of human living, and whenever you have to help out, usually behind the scenes, with a large group of people remembering something important—it is inevitable that an incident of some kind will take place. This especially involves gatherings where large quantities of food have to be prepared and served, different people have been asked to cook the same item, but each has probably altered a recipe here or there to his or her liking. For a great number of you remembering the Biblical and Jewish holidays at a congregational level, the controversies you will encounter are likely to be involved with the logistical details of how a larger gathering of people can get the most out of them.

I wish all of the controversies involving the Biblical and Jewish holidays in today's Messianic movement solely concerned "the menu" of traditional foods and recipes offered at congregational gatherings. Most of the controversies involving the holidays actually tend to concern individual people investigating particular aspects or components of a season, either on their own *or* usually via some Internet source, which challenges a traditional Jewish understanding. While the Messianic Jewish movement, because of its affirmation of Yeshua as Israel's Messiah, has certainly challenged traditional views of the Synagogue—a wide array of traditional Jewish practices and customs are still observed. In our information age, though, it is very easy for those involved in a Messianic congregation to see the appointed times observed according to a philo-traditional model, but then have such a model either criticized or condemned, by encountering some online media. While not always offered by those within the independent Hebrew/Hebraic Roots movement—and sometimes even presented by evangelical Christians opposed to Messianic Judaism—those who tend to challenge Messianic Jewish employment of mainline Jewish traditions and approaches to the appointed times, are not too concerned with the Messianic movement's original vision of Jewish outreach, evangelism, and Israel solidarity.

Titus 3:9 does astutely communicate, "avoid foolish controversies and genealogies and strife and disputes about Torah, for they are unprofitable and useless" (TLV). Yet at the same time, whether it be the weekly *Shabbat* service, or seasons such as the Fall high holidays or the Passover—the appointed times tend to be *the major periods* when one's local Messianic Jewish congregation is able to reach out to the Jewish community with the good news of Yeshua. You need to know what a number of the common controversies associated with the Biblical and Jewish holidays are, so when you encounter them, you can not only not be disturbed—but you can help stop potential problems before they start. Our list is

Controversies Involving Biblical and Jewish Holidays as a Messianic Believer

by no means extensive, but will highlight some of the most common problems you are likely to witness.

The Sabbath Debate

Whether various leaders and teachers want to publicly admit it or not, the fact that today's Messianic movement holds its main worship services on Saturday, in observance of the seventh-day Sabbath as prescribed in the Fourth Commandment (Exodus 20:8-11; Deuteronomy 5:12-15), immediately places it in conflict with most of the worldwide Body of Messiah.

An honest reading of the Gospels and Book of Acts will reveal that Yeshua the Messiah and His first followers, observed the seventh-day Sabbath or *Shabbat*—although Yeshua did come into conflict from time to time with how various Jewish religious leaders and Pharisees applied various Sabbath regulations. As Yeshua poignantly asked, "Is it permitted on Shabbat to do good or to do evil, to save a life or to kill?" (Mark 3:4, TLV). The Sabbath keeping of Yeshua of Nazareth was one where it was permitted to perform the good deeds of the Kingdom of Heaven, and the Messiah is indeed witnessed performing significant acts of healing and restoration to people on *Shabbat*. Later, it is said of a figure like the Apostle Paul, "As was his custom, Paul went into the synagogue, and on three Sabbath days he reasoned with them from the Scriptures" (Acts 17:2, 2011 NIV). Rather than abandon the institution of the Sabbath as a result of his Messiah faith, Paul used the weekly *Shabbat* service as a venue by which he could go to a Jewish synagogue, and declare Yeshua as Israel's Messiah from the Tanach Scriptures.

While there are varied reasons given by modern evangelical Protestants, the most common claims issued for why the seventh-day Sabbath is not observed by most Christians any more are either: (1) The discovery of the empty tomb of Yeshua by Sunday morning necessitates a Divinely-approved transfer of the seventh-day Sabbath to the first day of the week, Sunday. Or, (2) the seventh-day Sabbath has been abolished for the post-resurrection era. Non-Jewish Believers in today's Messianic movement, as well as many Messianic Jewish leaders trained in Protestant institutions, have been exposed enough to both of these points of view. More frequently than not, Christian people who are supportive of the Messianic movement as a means for Jewish evangelism, will come from a (dispensational) theological framework which approaches the seventh-day Sabbath as an institution which was only intended for Ancient Israel of the past, and not for the worldwide Body of Messiah in the present. Still, even though thinking that the seventh-day Sabbath was a thing of the past, such people will pragmatically recognize that Messianic congregations holding their services on Saturday is an appropriate way to attract Jewish non-Believers to the gospel—certainly in a way that a church which holds its services on Sunday will broadly be incapable of doing.

The Messianic Walk

While it is doubtlessly true that Messianic congregations holding their services on Saturday should attract Jewish people who need to hear the good news of Israel's Messiah—today's Messianic community broadly does not think that the only reason why *Shabbat* is to be observed, is for matters of Jewish outreach. In the future Millennium, the seventh-day Sabbath is unambiguously to be enforced as a mandatory, worldwide observance (Isaiah 66:23), and today we are to largely represent such future realities in our present conduct, as we are able. *Shabbat* is a time to rest from our labors, commune with God and with one another, and to truly enter into a period of intimacy and union with our Creator. And for many Messianic people, *Shabbat* truly is a time of physical rest and spiritual refreshment. Attending one's *Shabbat* service on Saturday becomes something that many Messianic people look forward to—not just because it is a significant time for worshipping the Lord and for studying the Scriptures—but often because it is the social highlight of the week, where we get to fellowship with fellow brothers and sisters in the Messiah.

Many Messianic people have learned how to carefully interact with Christian people who do not keep the seventh-day Sabbath. They recognize that the focus of our common faith is to be the atoning sacrifice of Yeshua of Nazareth, and rather than condemn those who disregard *Shabbat* or think it was changed to Sunday—they prefer to invite Christian friends and colleagues to their Messianic congregation on *Shabbat*, so they can see what makes the *Shabbat* experience much different than Sunday church. For many, the close community of a Messianic congregation, centered around its weekly service on Saturday, can do more to get people to see the value of *Shabbat* than any theological argument.

There are scores of Internet teachings out there which over-emphasize how the first day of the week was used in ancient paganism as a religious day—but most Protestants think that Sunday church originated much earlier, in the time of the Apostles (cf. Acts 20:7; 1 Corinthians 16:2). Yet, few are informed enough from either study of the Scripture or contemporary examinations, that it has been challenged as to whether or not some sporadic references to the "first of the week" seen in the Apostolic Writings (New Testament) are actually the beginnings of what would become "Sunday church." What if various "first of the week" gatherings actually took place on Saturday evening, per ancient Jewish reckoning of time where the new day would begin in the evening—and such gatherings were more reminiscent of *havdallah*, the ceremony that closes out the Sabbath?

While it is true that by the early-to-mid Second Century C.E., with the death of the Jewish apostles and their major successors, that the *ekklēsia* largely abandoned the seventh-day Sabbath in favor of Sunday activities—pockets of Christians over many centuries are witnessed to have observed the seventh-day Sabbath as a Creation institution (cf. Genesis 2:2-3). As the shackles of Catholicism were being thrown off, the issue of Sabbatarianism arose in the Protestant Reformation, although most Protestants believing in the continuance of a Sabbath-principle from the Fourth Commandment were actually seen to practice semi-Sabbatarianism—with the Sabbath believed to be changed from Saturday to Sunday. Still, various groups ranging from the Seventh-Day Baptists to the Seventh-Day Adventists have kept the discussion of the validity of the seventh-day Sabbath alive and well in the world of theology. Various resources of note have been released over the past several decades, in favor of, and against, the continuance of the seventh-day Sabbath.[1]

In our external relations, today's Messianic movement is going to have debates with others about the seventh-day Sabbath. And, there are certainly some significant discussions which have taken place in theological quarters about the ongoing importance of *Shabbat*. Yet for many of us, we see the Sabbath as a great gift given to people by our Creator, *a gift that far too many have dismissed or rejected.* So, in our keeping of *Shabbat*, let us be forever mindful of the famed admonition of Isaiah 58:13-14,

"'If you turn back your foot from Shabbat, from doing your pleasure on My holy day, and call Shabbat a delight, the holy day of *ADONAI* honorable, if you honor it, not going your own ways, not seeking your own pleasure, nor speaking your usual speech, then You will delight yourself in *ADONAI*, and I will let you ride over the heights of the earth, I will feed you with the heritage of your father Jacob.' For the mouth of *ADONAI* has spoken" (TLV).

The Calendar Debate

One of the biggest controversies—which always tends to erupt at the most inconvenient time for Messianic congregational leaders and teachers—involves the Biblical calendar. The appointed times of the Torah are obviously observed on a different calendrical cycle than the Gregorian calendar used by secular society today. In the Creation account it is specified, "Let lights in the expanse of the sky be for separating the day from the night. They will be for signs and for seasons and for days and years" (Genesis 1:14, TLV). The common Hebrew word for month, *chodesh*, also means "moon," a sure testament to the Hebrew calendar being lunar based.

---

[1] Two books that have widely framed the debate are Samuele Bacchiocchi, *From Sabbath to Sunday* (Rome: Pontifical Gregorian University Press, 1977), defending the validity of the seventh-day Sabbath from a Seventh-Day Adventist perspective, and D.A. Carson, ed., *From Sabbath to Lord's Day* (Eugene, OR: Wipf and Stock, 1999 [1982 actual publication]), cross-examining Bacchiocchi and defending Sunday as "the Lord's Day" from a broadly evangelical viewpoint.

A more recent analysis from a Seventh-Day Adventist standpoint is Sigve K. Tonstad, *The Lost Meaning of the Seventh Day* (Berrien Springs, MI: Andrews University Press, 2009). More general is Christopher John Donato, ed., *Perspectives on the Sabbath: Four Views* (Nashville: B&H Academic, 2011).

The Messianic Walk

During Second Temple times, the Jewish religious council known as the Sanhedrin would have been able to determine and agree when a new month had started, by the visible sighting of the New Moon. When the New Moon was sighted in the vicinity of Jerusalem, and the Sanhedrin could agree, then signal fires were lit, and passed on over many hundreds of miles, signaling to the wider Jewish community that a new month had begun. This system was not exact, but it was what was employed until several centuries after the fall of Jerusalem. In 358 C.E., Rabbi Hillell II introduced a pre-calculated calendrical system for the worldwide Jewish community, now in a broad worldwide Diaspora. A pre-calculated calendar is what is employed by the mainstream Jewish community today.

For today's Messianic Jewish movement, the issue of what calendar to use for the Biblical holidays is a simple one; the Messianic Jewish movement uses the same calendar as the mainstream Jewish community. When the Jewish community meets for *Yom Kippur*, so does the Messianic Jewish community. If the Messianic Jewish movement uses a completely different calendar for the Biblical and Jewish holidays, how is it going to best fulfill its mandate of reaching out to Jewish people with the good news of Israel's Messiah? Attendance at Messianic Jewish congregations peaks during any of the holidays, after all!

While today's Messianic Jewish movement follows the pre-calculated calendar of the wider Jewish community, it is widely observed that the independent Hebrew/Hebraic Roots movement does not tend to follow the mainstream Jewish calendar. A number of fellowships and groups within the Hebrew/Hebraic Roots movement may be seen to follow the mainstream Jewish calendar, for most of the dates of the Biblical holidays, with a number of exceptions like following the Saddusaical rather than Pharisaical determination of counting the *omer* to *Shavuot*. The Saddusaical method of counting the *omer* reckons "the day after the sabbath" (Leviticus 23:11, NASU) to be the weekly Sabbath during the Festival of Unleavened Bread, whereas the Pharisaical method interprets the Sabbath here as being the High Sabbath of the Festival of Unleavened Bread. It is historically documented though that the Pharisaical method was followed in Second Temple times (Josephus *Antiquities of the Jews* 3.250-251; Philo *Special Laws* 2.162), and it is what is observed in the Jewish community today.[2]

Unlike Messianic Judaism, the independent and mostly non-Jewish Hebrew/Hebraic Roots movement will widely follow various calendars of its own invention. Some of these calendars will follow the determination of the New Moon as offered by the Karaite movement in Israel, a Jewish sect which rejects all forms of Rabbinical authority and the commentary of the Oral Torah. At the same time, other fellowships and groups are witnessed to formulate their own calendar on the

---

[2] For a further evaluation of technical details, consult the FAQ, "Omer Count" (appearing in the *Messianic Spring Holiday Helper*).

basis of their own sighting of the New Moon, at a place outside of Jerusalem and the Land of Israel, which is usually where they meet. Further complications are witnessed when various groups' presumed "restored Biblical calendar" interjects speculations on the actual year since the Creation of the universe, but most especially prognostications about the time of the Messiah's return.

Ultimately, the issue involving the calendar followed by today's Messianics does concern our approach to Jewish tradition and the authority of the Rabbis. Many people are of the opinion that Jewish religious authorities which have rejected Yeshua of Nazareth, are to be rejected as having any legitimate things to say about any Biblical matters. Others, per Yeshua's words about the Pharisaical authorities sitting in the seat of Moses (Matthew 23:2-3), would conclude that the Jewish religious authorities should be followed in major matters such as what calendar should be followed for the Biblical holidays. Spiritual hypocrisy is actually what is to be dismissed (Matthew 23:4-35), not the dates on which the religious community remembers the Passover or other holidays. For Messianic Jews, and non-Jewish Believers in the Messianic movement, following the mainstream Jewish calendar for all of the dates of the appointed times, is as much about Jewish outreach and evangelism, as it is about recognizing that the Jewish religious leaders do have an authority to not be easily disregarded. What kind of testimony is it to Jewish non-Believers, to not stand in solidarity with them during the appointed times—because a completely different calendar may be followed?[3]

Traditional Jewish Liturgy

There is little doubting the fact that liturgy is an important part of traditional Jewish worship, which the Messianic Jewish community is significantly affected by. Any Messianic Jewish service, on *Shabbat* or otherwise, is going to employ traditional and customary Jewish prayers and hymns. The significant majority of the liturgical prayers found in the *siddur* are taken either directly from Tanach Scripture, or from the prayers and hymns offered up to God in the worship of the First and Second Temples.

While it might be said that in the Orthodox Jewish tradition, liturgy and traditional prayers make up the bulk of one's worship activities—a moderate amount of mixed Hebrew and English liturgy is what one tends to find in the Messianic Jewish community, concurrent with what is seen in Conservative or Reform Judaism. For many Messianic Jews, employing liturgy in congregational worship services is not just a vital part of being connected to one's Jewish heritage and the prayers issued to God from one's ancestors; it is also a critical part of providing structure and reverence to corporate worship. Many non-Jewish

---

[3] For a further discussion, consult the FAQ, "Biblical Calendar" (appearing in the *Messianic Torah Helper*).

The Messianic Walk

Believers, from various Protestant backgrounds, greatly appreciate the value of liturgy, particularly in its ability to instill a sense of holiness.

Not everyone who comes into the Messianic movement likes liturgy. Some Messianic Jews, who were perhaps raised in Orthodox settings, would prefer that little or no traditional Hebrew liturgy be used by today's Messianic movement. Those from Pentecostal or charismatic backgrounds, are those who especially frown or oppose any usage of liturgy, as it is believed that only spontaneous forms of prayer are acceptable to God. Statements by Yeshua the Messiah, are typically invoked to dismiss any place for liturgy. Did He not say, "And when you are praying, do not babble on and on like the pagans; for they think they will be heard because of their many words" (Matthew 6:7, TLV)? Did He not also criticize the Pharisees of His day, in how they "make long prayers as a show" (Luke 20:47, TLV)? Frequently, there are those who conclude that liturgy only facilitates dead, rigid religion.

Yeshua the Messiah certainly opposed prayers which were repeated over and over by the religious leaders of His day, for the sole purpose of others observing them and being seemingly impressed by false, outward piety. However, how many of us in our spontaneous prayers to God, have ever been led to open our Bibles and read the Lord's Prayer (Matthew 6:9-13), or perhaps recite a Psalm? If you have ever done this, you have employed a liturgical style of worship.

Today's Messianic congregations should not unnecessarily bore people with endless Hebrew liturgy, where one's worship activities become stale and manufactured. At the same time, liturgical worship does have a place in one's remembrance of *Shabbat* and the appointed times. When employed properly, it is something that can be edifying, spiritually enlightening, and above all cause each of us to stand in awe of the holiness of Israel's God.

Extra-Torah and Extra-Biblical Jewish Remembrances

Within the annual cycle of the Messianic Jewish community, there are various holidays beyond those of the appointed times of Leviticus 23 which are observed. These holidays commemorate events which post-date the Exodus. Within Holy Scripture, *Purim* commemorates the deliverance of the Jewish people from the schemes of Haman to annihilate them. Mordechai saw to it that an annual remembrance be founded (Esther 9:20-22). Messianic Jewish Believers and most non-Jewish Believers in the Messianic movement recognize that without the deliverance of *Purim*, there would have been no Jewish people into which the Messiah Yeshua would be born. They recognize the value of *Purim*, although from time to time one will find people in the independent Hebrew/Hebraic Roots movement who (significantly) frown on it. It is their opinion that commemorating historical events in the life of Israel, subsequent to the giving of the Torah, is "adding" to the commandments.

Controversies Involving Biblical and Jewish Holidays as a Messianic Believer

Chanukah, or the Feast of Dedication, is an extra-Biblical holiday commemorating the defeat of the Syrian Greeks and cleansing of the Temple (1 Maccabees 4:59). In the Jewish community today, *Chanukah* is remembered for eight days, where families and synagogues light the *menorah*, eat traditional foods such as potato latkes, and give gifts to one another. In Biblical Studies, the events surrounding the Second Century B.C.E. Maccabean crisis are imperative to understanding some of the complicated relations between Jews, Greeks, and Romans in the time of Yeshua and His early followers. The Jewish people faced forced assimilation into Hellenistic paganism, and rightly resisted. Today's Messianic Jewish community appropriately celebrates *Chanukah*, as did Israel's Messiah (John 10:22). People in the independent Hebrew/Hebraic Roots movement will, at times, be found dismissive of *Chanukah*, thinking that its remembrance is in violation of the Torah—when the celebration of *Chanukah* is technically similar to American Independence Day or any holiday remembering an important victory over evil.

Your Further Education in the Appointed Times

Whether you are a Jewish Believer in Yeshua, who is reconnecting with his or her heritage as a result of your Messiah faith, or a non-Jewish Believer first connecting with his or her Hebrew and Jewish Roots—every year the appointed times are remembered, is going to be a year of learning something new and important. This might involve further Bible studies, a greater appreciation for ancient histories, or admiring various Jewish traditions and customs. The appointed times possess a significant Messianic substance to them (Colossians 2:17), and as such we should learn more about the salvation history work of Yeshua when we observe them. Given the fact that we are all limited human beings on a steady path toward greater spiritual maturity, we also have the responsibility to learn to act and behave more like Yeshua, and focus on "whatever is true, whatever is honorable, whatever is just, whatever is pure, whatever is lovely, whatever is commendable" (Philippians 4:8, TLV).

The Messianic Walk

STUDY QUESTIONS FOR UNIT TWO

1. What do you think there is to learn about the work of Yeshua the Messiah, in both studying and honoring, the appointed times or *moedim*?

2. Which one of the appointed times are you most familiar with? Which one of the appointed times do you need to look into further?

3. What are some of the conflicts and misunderstandings that can erupt when today's Messianic people keep the appointed times?

4. What are some of the major conflicts that can take place as they involve today's Messianic movement, and traditional Christian holidays like Christmas and Easter? How do you intend to reduce tensions?

5. Are you aware of some of the problems and challenges that can erupt when the appointed times are observed with a Messianic congregation? If so, fairly describe your experience.

6. What might be some of the distinct challenges present in a Messianic Jewish congregation, when there has been insufficient attention given to understanding mainline Jewish traditions and customs associated with the appointed times?

SHABBAT, THE APPOINTED TIMES, JEWISH HOLIDAYS
FOR FURTHER READING AND EXPLORATION

Donato, Christopher John, ed. *Perspectives on the Sabbath: Four Views* (Nashville: B&H Academic, 2011).

Huey, Margaret McKee, ed. *Messianic Sabbath Helper* (Richardson, TX: Messianic Apologetics, 2015).

Huey, Margaret McKee, ed. *Messianic Fall Holiday Helper* (Richardson, TX: Messianic Apologetics, 2017).

Huey, Margaret McKee, ed. *Messianic Winter Holiday Helper* (Richardson, TX: Messianic Apologetics, 2017).

Huey, Margaret McKee, ed. *Messianic Spring Holiday Helper* (Richardson, TX: Messianic Apologetics, 2018).

Huey, William Mark. *Counting the Omer: A Daily Devotional Toward Shavuot* (Messianic Apologetics, 2012).

Kasdan, Barney. *God's Appointed Times: A Practical Guide for Understanding and Celebrating the Biblical Holidays* (Baltimore: Lederer, 1993).

Lancaster, D. Thomas. *From Sabbath to Sabbath: Returning the Holy Sabbath to the Disciples of Jesus* (Marshfield, MO: First Fruits of Zion, 2016).

Nadler, Sam. *The Feasts of Israel: God's Appointed Times in History & Prophecy* (Charlotte, NC: Word of Messiah Ministries, 2002).

Richardson, Susan E. *Holidays & Holy Days* (Ann Arbor, MI: Servant Publications, 2001).

Shannon, Jill. *A Prophetic Calendar: The Feasts of Israel* (Shippensburg, PA: Destiny Image, 2009).

KOSHER

TORAH-BASED "MEANS OF GRACE"

UNIT THREE

Kosher and Torah-Based "Means of Grace"

A major historical difference, that has been witnessed between Judaism and Christianity, has been how Christianity has often been responsible for promoting a dualism, where one's inward heart condition is so important, that external actions of spirituality can be disparaged. Judaism, in stark contrast to this, emphasizes the wholistic unity of one's being, where internal heart attitude *and* external deeds, are carefully balanced.[1]

Within the Hebrew Tanach, external activities such as work, sexual intercourse, or eating and drinking, are all lauded as having value. Qohelet says, "Behold, this is what I myself have seen. It is beneficial and good for one to eat and drink, and to enjoy all of his toil that he labors under the sun during the few days of his life that God has given him—for this is his reward" (Ecclesiastes 5:17[18], TLV). Given the certain fact that human beings cannot earn favor before God for their salvation (Ephesians 2:8-9), Christian people throughout history have especially struggled with the fact that while works or deeds are not the *cause* of salvation, works or deeds are to *result* from salvation. James 3:13 directs, "Who among you is wise and understanding? By his good conduct let him show his deeds in the gentleness of wisdom" (TLV). And, as James 1:27 specifies, "Pure and undefiled religion before our God and Father is this: to care for orphans and widows in their distress, and to keep oneself unstained by the world" (TLV).

Certainly throughout history, there have been faithful Jews and Protestants who have recognized the significance of the external good works that God requires of His own. The famed word of Micah 6:8 states, "He has told you, O mortal, what is good; and what does the LORD require of you but to do justice, and to love kindness, and to walk humbly with your God?" (NRSV). It should not be

---

[1] Consult some of the relevant points appearing in the FAQ, "Dualism" (appearing in *To Be Absent From the Body*).

The Messianic Walk

unreasonable to note that those who are best able to live forth such an imperative, are men and women who are disciplined in their relationship with the Creator. These are people who pray, they read and study the Holy Scriptures, they fellowship with those of the local faith community—and consequently they do look out for the needs of others.

Today's Messianic community, because of its undeniable connection to its Jewish theological and spiritual heritage, will emphasize various physical actions of God's people, that today's evangelical Protestantism not only considers unnecessary, but will backhandedly dismiss. Yet, once you start attending a Messianic congregation or fellowship on *Shabbat*, it is not difficult to be exposed to questions about eating what is considered clean or unclean, and various tactile objects such as prayer shawls or the *mezuzah*, which obviously have importance for not just the Torah or Law of Moses, but also Jewish heritage.

Many Bible readers are conditioned to take Yeshua's words of Matthew 23:28 to the Pharisaical leaders, and then see them applied to anyone who takes seriously outward forms of Biblical expression: "Even so you too outwardly appear righteous to people, but inwardly you are full of hypocrisy and lawlessness" (author's rendering). So, whether it be Messianic Jews who were raised in a nominally religious home, (re)claiming a definite part of their heritage, or non-Jewish Believers integrating into the Messianic community and actually wanting to live in a similar manner to Yeshua and His early followers—such people can find themselves criticized for apparently being inwardly decrepit and bankrupt. However, such Messianic people would not be alone, as those in various holiness and piety movements in Protestantism since the Reformation have had similar accusations issued to them. It was thought that their significant commitment to doing good deeds, was apparently trying to compensate for a lack of salvation assurance.

While only our Heavenly Father knows the true intent of any man or woman trying to obey Him *internally and externally*, there is a strong spiritual value in performing external actions of faith. How one eats, and how one employs ritual objects such as *tzitzityot* or a *kippah*, can be spiritually edifying. Certainly in much Christian thought, the process of being immersed in water (baptized) as an outward sign of one's redemption, is critical not only for identifying with Yeshua's own death and resurrection (Romans 6:4), but also as a time for publicly declaring before the world of one's salvation. Various external instructions, appearing in the Scriptures, were called by John Wesley to be a "means of grace," whereby Believers can physically partake of deeper, internal spiritual realities. When Messianic people do anything that is external, whether it is specified by commandments in the Torah, or derived from Torah commandments, how are they partaking of deeper, internal spiritual realities? 1 Thessalonians 5:23 astutely admonishes,

Kosher and Torah-Based "Means of Grace"

"Now may the God of *shalom* Himself make you completely holy; and may your whole spirit and soul and body be kept complete, blameless at the coming of our Lord Yeshua the Messiah" (TLV).

Kosher (Kashrut)

The term *kosher* does not appear in the Hebrew Bible, but is instead derived from the verb *kasheir*, "to be suitable, fit to use" (*HALOT*).[2] A term used throughout Judaism is *kashrut*, "fitness, worthiness, legitimacy" (*Jastrow*).[3] In most of the common usage that Messianic people will encounter—kosher, *kasheir*, and kashrut—will almost always be employed in reference to the Torah's dietary instructions, and the list of clean and unclean meats in Leviticus 11 and Deuteronomy 14. However, in Jewish usage, the term kosher will be employed in a much wider array of applications, involving not only food and diet, but also the condition of various ritual objects, as well as one's moral and ethical behavior.[4]

Today's Messianic people often find various reasons for considering the kosher dietary laws important. Many Jewish people, who have come to faith in Yeshua, were raised in Reform Jewish homes which did not bother to keep kosher, but ate unclean meats, and so many of today's Messianic Jews have actually reclaimed an important part of their ancestral heritage. Many non-Jewish Believers, often starting with the prohibitions of the Apostolic Decree (Acts 15:19-21, 28-29), find that adopting a kosher-style of diet is useful in emulating the Torah obedience of Yeshua the Messiah and/or for various health considerations. The workbook *Messianic Judaism Class* recognizes these significant reasons for today's Messianic Believers and kosher, first noting how,

"[T]he animals that are forbidden to eat are predators and scavengers. You don't know what a predator or scavenger has just eaten. It could be something diseased. Also some of the animals are high in fat and cholesterol."[5]

It is then further stated,

"It is obedience to God. If the Ruakh HaKodesh (Holy Spirit) is leading you to be grafted in and you have been changing your lifestyle to identify more with Israel and with how Yeshua lived on this earth, then this is one more way to do that."[6]

Principally within the Torah, one turns to Leviticus 11 and Deuteronomy 14 for the list of clean and unclean meats, to begin one's review of the dietary laws.

---

[2] Ludwig Koehler and Walter Baumgartner, eds., *The Hebrew & Aramaic Lexicon of the Old Testament*, 2 vols. (Leiden, the Netherlands: Brill, 2001), 1:503.

[3] Marcus Jastrow, *Dictionary of the Targumim, Talmud Bavli, Talmud Yerushalmi, and Midrashic Literature* (New York: Judaica Treasury, 2004), 677.

[4] Consult the many useful thoughts offered by Ron Isaacs, *Kosher Living: It's More Than Just the Food* (San Francisco: Jossey-Bass, 2005).

[5] *Messianic Judaism Class*, Teacher Book, 53.

[6] Ibid.

The Messianic Walk

Kosher land animals (Leviticus 11:2-8; Deuteronomy 14:3-8) must have a split hoof and chew a cud. Clean land animals would include cattle, sheep, goats, deer, and various other sorts of wild game. Unclean land animals would include the camel, and most especially the pig. **Kosher fish** (Leviticus 11:9-12; Deuteronomy 14:9-10) must have fins and scales, which would automatically disqualify all popular shellfish such as shrimp, crabs, lobsters, and oysters as being kosher. **Non-kosher birds** (Leviticus 11:13-19; Deuteronomy 14:11-18) are mainly birds of prey or carrion eaters, with **kosher birds** determined entirely by Jewish tradition (i.e., chicken, duck, goose, and turkey). **Kosher insects** (Leviticus 11:20-23; Deuteronomy 14:19) mainly involve locusts, crickets, and grasshoppers.

Biblically Kosher and Traditional Jewish Kosher

In much of today's Messianic movement, Messianic people are seen witnessed following a dietary regimen which they label as **"Biblically kosher."** This is a level of kosher which mainly avoids unclean meats such as pork and shellfish. Traditional Jewish kosher, as particularly witnessed in the Orthodox Jewish community, is much more strict. Traditional Jewish **kashrut** involves explicit details concerning the slaughter of animals, the removal of blood, separation of meat and dairy (based on Deuteronomy 14:21), as well as dishes and utensils intended for meat or for dairy. There are Jewish regulatory agencies which inspect the factories and equipment where processed foods are produced, to ensure their kosher status, and that no non-kosher items were used in their manufacture.

It is safe to say that today's kosher-friendly Messianic people do appreciate the higher level of standard observed by the Orthodox Jewish community, and like to see that various food products they purchase may have a stamp of approval. However, the higher cost of kosher-certified meat, for example, is prohibitive to many Messianic families who are not willing to completely eliminate meat from their diet. So, the meat of clean animals is usually purchased from the supermarket, but with various steps taken, such as soaking in water or broiling, to see that any remaining blood is removed.

Observance of kosher can, at times, become tense in various congregations' fellowship meal times. Some have "Biblically kosher" policies where only pork and shellfish need to be avoided, but where meat and dairy can be mixed. Others have stricter policies where all meat must have a kosher certification, and where meat and dairy cannot be mixed. Yet others follow a policy of *parve* (neutral), where meat is not served, but fish is served because those observing a strict level of kosher can mix fish with dairy. These are all areas where it is appropriate for each of us to be flexible and tolerant of others' opinions.

Kosher and Torah-Based "Means of Grace"

Eating Controversies in the Messianic Scriptures

While any emphasis on the importance of the kosher dietary laws, is likely to immediately upset or confuse many Christian people who look at the Messianic movement, it cannot go overlooked how many Jewish people were raised not keeping kosher. Reform Judaism dismissed the kosher dietary laws in the late Nineteenth Century as not only being antiquated, but as instructions which would unnecessarily impede Jewish integration into modern society. So, while non-Jewish Believers led by God into the Messianic movement might have more obvious challenges when considering the value of a kosher style of diet, many Messianic Jewish Believers have a few challenges as well, as they were not raised with kosher being a part of their background. And, many of these same Messianic Jewish Believers may have come to faith in an evangelical Protestant setting, which was dismissive of the kosher dietary laws.

There are a number of significant objections that are raised, as they involve the ongoing validity and relevance of the kosher dietary laws. **Peter's vision of the sheet** in Acts 10, where he is shown a diverse array of unclean animals, and the declaration "What God has made clean, you must not consider unholy" (Acts 10:15, TLV), is commonly interpreted to mean that the distinctions of clean and unclean meats have been abrogated. While there are details to be evaluated, as to what "four-footed animals and reptiles and birds of the air" (Acts 10:12, TLV) may represent in regard to ancient paganism, Peter's own interpretation of his vision, as he met with the Roman centurion Cornelius, cannot go overlooked: "You yourselves know that it is not permitted for a Jewish man to associate with a non-Jew or to visit him. Yet God has shown me that I should call no one unholy or unclean" (Acts 10:28, TLV). The main issue communicated to Peter, by the vision, was the overturning of non-Biblical injunctions which prohibited Jewish people from interacting with outsiders, particularly in terms of sharing a common meal (*Jubilees* 22:16; m.*Ohalot* 19:7).[7]

Also frequently referred to by many people who are dismissive of the kosher dietary laws, is **the statement of Mark 7:19.** In most English Bibles it appears as "Thus he declared all foods clean" (RSV), and many will conclude that Yeshua the Messiah not only canceled the Torah's dietary code, but all forms of external ritual purity. Surely, it is absolutely true that "There is nothing outside the man that can make him unholy by going into him. Rather, it is what comes out of the man that makes the man unholy" (Mark 7:15, TLV), as internal purity of the heart is more imperative than external purity. However, the actual issue in view was not the kosher dietary instructions, but instead a ritual handwashing practiced by many First Century Jews (Mark 7:1-13), but not necessarily by Yeshua's disciples. Bread

---

[7] For a further evaluation of details, consult the analysis on Acts 10:1-48 in the *Messianic Kosher Helper* by Messianic Apologetics.

The Messianic Walk

eaten with unwashed hands does not defile someone, "For it does not enter into the heart but into the stomach, and then goes out into the sewer, cleansing all foods" (Mark 7:19, TLV). It has been widely recognized among commentators how the clause *katharizōn panta ta brōmata* can be rendered as continuing the sentence, with "purging all the foods" (author's rendering) speaking of the process of excretion.[8]

Kosher continuance is something detected in the Apostolic decree issued by the Jerusalem Council, to the new Greek and Roman Believers coming to faith in Israel's Messiah. While they were not mandated or coerced to keep the Torah (Acts 15:1, 5), there were various stipulations that they had to observe for proper fellowship with Jewish Believers, and hence also interaction with the Jewish community. These included prohibitions on things strangled and blood (Acts 15:20, 29), which would surely limit the number of places where meat could be procured. *Were they to keep kosher?* A resource like the workbook *Messianic Judaism Class* concludes, "They are not required for Gentiles according to Acts 15, but Gentiles may keep them if they are led by God to do so."[9] Frequently, it is thought that non-Jews in today's Messianic movement are likened unto the *gerim* or sojourners in Ancient Israel, who were notably not permitted to catch unclean wild game (Leviticus 17:13), by necessity implying that the domesticated animals they would have eaten would be clean.

Problems in the Messianic movement tend to erupt when people are completely inflexible about the issue of kosher—especially from those whose faith tends to rise or fall on what people eat, rather than on internal heart cleanliness. If you keep a kosher style of diet on the outside, but do not take care that you are *internally clean* in your heart and mind, what have you achieved?

For fellowship meals at various Messianic congregations, one generally finds that pork and shellfish are off limits. The guidelines prescribed by the workbook *Messianic Judaism Class* are, "No Biblically un-kosher foods, please: no pork, no shellfish, no hunted meat."[10] Your Messianic congregation or fellowship might be a little more strict in some areas, as it may look for a *hechsher* or an authorized symbol from one of the various Jewish kosher certification agencies. Some fellowship meal times do not permit the mixing of meat and dairy, they might be *parve* and permit fish and dairy, or they might be vegetarian. Other fellowship meal times might, in stark contrast, allow for meat and dairy to be served together, and one might even see fried chicken from a KFC or pizza from a local establishment, available for general consumption.

---

[8] For a further evaluation of details, consult the analysis on Mark 7:1-23 in the *Messianic Kosher Helper* by Messianic Apologetics.

[9] *Messianic Judaism Class*, Teacher Book, 53.

[10] Ibid., 54.

Kosher and Torah-Based "Means of Grace"

There are issues that do arise in the Messianic movement, as they concern the implementation of the dietary laws in modern settings, recognizing some of the more specific details of blood and fat, being sensitive to the diversity of opinions—but also recognizing various exceptions due to life circumstances. In the context of ancient missionary evangelism, Paul instructed the Corinthians, "If an unbeliever invites you over and you want to go, eat whatever is set before you, without raising questions of conscience" (1 Corinthians 10:27, TLV). There are going to be times when one might be served unclean things, and as a matter of being gracious to one's host, they should be eaten (without taking seconds). As the workbook *Messianic Judaism Class* properly directs, "'Go and preach the Gospel' is a higher law than the dietary laws."[11]

Tzitzits and Tallits

An important Torah instruction is witnessed in Numbers 15:38, "Speak to the Israelite people and instruct them to make for themselves fringes on the corners of their garments throughout the ages; let them attach a cord of blue to the fringe at each corner" (NJPS). The fringe, tassel, or *tzitzit* was originally to have a cord of *tekheilet* or blue, although the traditional dye employed for the *tekheilet* from the *chilazon* sea snail was lost for many centuries, with most *tzitzit* today being all white. Fringes or tassels were worn by Yeshua the Messiah, as witnessed throughout the Gospels. The general statement made in Mark 6:56 is, "And wherever He entered villages, towns, or countryside, people were placing the sick in the marketplaces and begging Him to let them touch even the *tzitzit* of His garment—and all who touched it were being healed" (TLV; cf. Malachi 4:2).

In Judaism today, the fringes or *tzitzityot* are to be attached to a four-corned garment, with the *tallit* having developed in the post-Second Temple period. Orthodox Jewish males will often wear an undergarment called a *tallit katan* at all times, whereas other Jews will employ the *tallit* for traditional morning prayers and daytime *Shabbat* services. Traditionally, the *tallit* is to be worn only during the daytime, with the exception of the evening services of *Rosh HaShanah* and *Yom Kippur*. Given how the command is issued to *b'nei Yisrael* or the "children of Israel," Conservative and Reform Judaism permits females to employ the *tallit*. There is a wide degree of variance witnessed in the Messianic movement regarding *tzitzityot* and the *tallit*, some of it sitting outside the general bounds of Jewish tradition. It is safe to say, though, that homemade *tzitzits* tied to one's beltloops,

---

[11] Ibid., 54.

For a further evaluation of details, consult the analysis on 1 Corinthians 10:14-33 in the *Messianic Kosher Helper* by Messianic Apologetics.

The Messianic Walk

which one will frequently encounter in the independent Hebrew/Hebraic Roots movement, sit well outside of what is traditionally witnessed.[12]

Tefillin (Phylacteries) and Mezuzah

Within the *Shema* of Deuteronomy 6, where God's supremacy and exclusiveness is declared, it is explicitly stated, "These words, which I am commanding you today, are to be on your heart. You are to teach them diligently to your children, and speak of them when you sit in your house, when you walk by the way, when you lie down and when you rise up. Bind them as a sign on your hand, they are to be as frontlets between your eyes, and write them on the doorposts of your house and on your gates" (Deuteronomy 6:6-9, TLV). There is a definite need to see the Instruction of God impressed onto the human heart, and to convey the significance of His commandments to one's offspring.

In Jewish practice, certainly from Second Temple times, it is seen how the direction to bind the Word on one's hand and forehead is taken literally, via the tradition of wrapping *tefillin* or phylacteries (derived from *phulaktērion*). The *tefillin* are a set of two leather boxes, one for the arm and hand (the opposite of whether the user is right or left handed), and one for the head, containing four Torah passages written on parchment (Exodus 13:1-10; 13:11-16; Deuteronomy 6:4-9; 11:13-21). Wrapping *tefillin* is something that takes place at traditional times of prayer. Various people in today's Messianic movement are seen to wrap *tefillin*, whereas others interpret the commandment to bind God's Word as something metaphorical. There are some who do not wrap *tefillin* because a pair of *tefillin* can frequently be very expensive, although they do not frown on the value of the tradition.[13]

When one walks into a Jewish synagogue, or the home of an observant Jew—and certainly many Messianic congregations and Messianic homes—a *mezuzah* will be seen at the entry. The term *mezuzah* is today frequently taken to apply to the small case and parchment attached to the doorpost, which includes the Deuteronomy 4:6-9 and 11:13-21 instructions. Just as touching the Torah scroll during the *Shabbat* service is intended to honor it, the *mezuzah* will be touched as a sign of honor by those entering or exiting a doorway that has one attached.[14]

---

[12] For a further evaluation of details, consult the FAQ, "Tzitzits."

[13] For a further evaluation of details, consult the FAQ, "Tefillin."

[14] For a further discussion, consult Chapter 13 of *Torah In the Balance, Volume II*, "Messianic Believers and Religious Symbols."

Kippah (Yarmulke)

One of the most obvious elements of modern Jewish identity witnessed in the world today, is men wearing the *kippah* (or *yarmulke*) or skullcap. The main idea behind wearing this small skullcap is that it shows submission to God. Other ideas are that wearing the *kippah* is a sign of mourning the destruction of the Second Temple, or that it is a symbol of how human beings have a Divine authority over them. Still, wearing a head garment like the *kippah* may simply be rooted in Ancient Near Eastern customs of people wearing things on their head keeping the Sun off them. In various Jewish communities, and in modern Israel, wearing a particular style of *kippah* may identify you with a particular religious or even political sect.

Issues do arise in some Messianic congregations, particularly when non-Jewish Believers can be witnessed to be insensitive to the Jewish tradition of wearing the *kippah* or *yarmulke*. Many recognize that wearing the *kippah*, while not a Biblical commandment, is appropriate for synagogue protocol. Others, based on some statements appearing in 1 Corinthians 11, conclude that men wearing the *kippah* is prohibited. While a complicated passage for sure, when it is recognized that there were ancient First Century Corinthian issues in view, then 1 Corinthians 11:4 cannot be seen as prohibiting the *kippah*. As the Brown and Comfort interlinear renders *pas anēr proseuchomenos ē prophēteuōn kata kephalēs*, "every man praying or prophesying down over [his] head."[15] What was considered dishonorable as something hanging down from the head (*kata kephalēs*) for the men in Corinth is stated in the text as long hair: "Doesn't the natural order of things teach you—if a man has long hair, it is a disgrace for him?" (1 Corinthians 11:14, TLV).[16]

---

[15] Robert K. Brown and Philip W. Comfort, trans., *The New Greek-English Interlinear New Testament* (Carol Stream, IL: Tyndale House, 1990), 603.

[16] For a further evaluation of details, including "covered" and "uncovered" in 1 Corinthians 11:1-16 involving ancient hairstyles, consult the relevant sections of the author's commentary *1 Corinthians for the Practical Messianic*.

The Messianic Walk

Our Family Experiences Going Kosher

Margaret McKee Huey

I was born into a very typical American Southern Protestant family in the 1950s in the town of Annapolis, Maryland.[1] My parents, Bill and Mary Ruth, were both from the Deep South (Alabama and Georgia, respectively), where food has always been an important part of daily living and family gatherings. I grew up to love this Southern cuisine from my childhood that always seemed to include pork or pork drippings in it!

We ate pork chops, pork loins, ham steaks, ham hocks, pork sausage links, pork sausage patties, pork rolls, and, of course, pork bacon. We had green beans with bacon drippings (also known as bacon grease), fried chicken with bacon drippings, fried corn with bacon drippings, corn bread with bacon drippings—just about everything my mother or grandmother cooked was flavored with bacon drippings!

Since I was born in Annapolis, on the shores of the Chesapeake Bay, I was also raised to eat and appreciate the finer fare of shellfish. We feasted on Maryland steamed crabs, boiled crabs, crab cakes, soft-shelled crabs, crab gumbo, crab dip and crab soup. We delighted in boiled shrimp, fried shrimp, shrimp cocktail, shrimp gumbo, shrimp scampi and barbequed shrimp. We ate steamed clams, fried clams, clam chowder and clam dip. We had raw oysters, fried oysters, oyster stew, smoked oysters and smoked oyster dip. *I could go on and on!* When we visited my grandmother at her beach house in Gulf Shores, Alabama every summer, she made sure that every meal contained crab or shrimp. She was known for her amazing crab gumbo that everyone raved about. As a child, I thought it tasted pretty good, but she did have a lot of scary looking creatures in her gumbo pot!

---

[1] This chapter has been reproduced from the *Messianic Kosher Helper* (Richardson, TX: TNN Press, 2014).

The Messianic Walk

However, the Southern cuisine that I was especially brought up to appreciate, and even revere, was Southern pork barbeque with all of its distinct regional barbeque sauces.

If you are Southern, it is just understood that you will not only eat pork, but you will love pork—especially barbeque. Most families will have their own special rubs and sauces that they prefer, with family recipes being passed down and perfected generation to generation. My family had its favorite restaurants we would frequent when visiting our grandmother in Alabama. She would also bring jars of sauce from these places when she came to visit us in Annapolis. My father would smoke his own pork butt, always hoping that it would be at least close to the meat from Birmingham. We were all raised to believe that Southern pork barbeque was the quintessential food of the South! As a child, I was such a lover of all things pork, that my older brother gave me the nickname of "Porka" even though I was a very skinny little girl! Our devotion to Southern pork barbeque cuisine was never so evident as on the day of my father's funeral in 1989 in Birmingham. We ate at one of his favorite restaurants before his funeral, and at another one after his funeral, so we could have a barbeque "taste-off" in honor of our daddy before we all flew back to our homes across the country.

I went to college in Tennessee where I was able to continue to embrace my Southern roots in cuisine. There I was able to branch out into other regional taste treats that all included pork. The Tennessee barbeque was a bit different from the Alabama version my father raised us on. However, the Memphis style barbeque was also greatly appreciated by this girl named Porka. Never did I ever consider that pork was not considered an acceptable meat in the Bible!

I was married after college and moved to the Greater Cincinnati-Northern Kentucky area, where I was introduced to a great deal of German cuisine. One of Cincinnati's nicknames is actually "Porkopolis"! Brats and goetta were new pork dishes that I had never known about. Pork brats were cooked instead of hotdogs, and everyone served them. We lived in Northern Kentucky which was firmly in the Southern food region, so I felt right at home there while enjoying the new German cuisine of Cincinnati. However, in Cincinnati, I had my first taste of beef brisket barbeque. It was very good, but different from the pork version I had been raised on. Little did I know that many years later, my own son would become quite the beef brisket barbeque smoker as a Messianic Kosher Believer!

In 1992, I lost my husband, Kimball McKee, who was the father of my three children, to malignant melanoma. With his death, my life seemed to have come to an end, but my faith in the Lord and my belief that He had not forgotten me, or my children, never failed me. By God's grace, within two years of Kim's death, I was remarried to an old college boyfriend, Mark Huey, and was relocated with my three children to Dallas, Texas. However, with this move and brand new life, I would

Testimonial Our Family Experiences Going Kosher

never have believed that the Lord would also have us start on a new adventure in our quest to know Him better and to walk in His ways like never before.

Becoming Messianic

In December 1994, after six months of marriage to Mark, we went to Israel on a Zola Levitt tour. By being on a tour led by Messianic Jews, we were able to see and understand places, customs and events in a unique First Century Biblical way that we had really not been introduced to in our evangelical Christian upbringing. Mark and I had amazing times with the Lord all over the Holy Land, as He led us to seek more and more of what He is doing at this time with people of faith. After an amazing two weeks in Israel, we returned to Dallas with a supernatural desire to walk like Jesus walked and to at least start to celebrate the Biblical feasts of the Lord in a Messianic way. I have to confess that we did not immediately start seeking this direction, for it took more than nine months for us to finally attend a Messianic congregation.

During the Fall High Holidays of 1995, our family started attending a Messianic Jewish congregation in Dallas. We were immediately blessed by all the new things that we were learning; things that were not only in the Hebrew Scriptures—but also in the New Testament. To finally start being taught Scripture from an Hebraic perspective, both historically and ethnically, had amazing results within our new blended family. We were singing songs with words that came directly from the Psalms. We were taught that Yeshua (Jesus' Hebrew name) and His Second Coming will be beautifully and prophetically fulfilled at the Fall festival time during *Rosh HaShanah* (Trumpets) and *Yom Kippur* (the Day of the Lord).[2] We were taught that Yeshua's First Coming had already been prophetically fulfilled at the Spring festival time during *Pesach* (Passover) and *Shavuot* (Pentecost).[3] Our daughters learned to not only praise the Lord through singing Messianic songs, but to also learn to praise Him through Davidic dance to these same tunes. Every worship service was a joy to us all, as we learned more and more about the Jewish Roots of our Christian faith, which had been washed out of traditional Christian teaching for centuries. We very much felt and believed that we were experiencing worship and teaching much like the early non-Jewish Messianic Believers were doing in the First Century, as we stood side by side with Messianic Jewish Believers as Jew and non-Jew yet one in Messiah Yeshua!

In the Spring of 1996, Mark and I started to attend the new members class. After its completion, we were able to feel more and more accepted into the Messianic fellowship. We started to learn all that we could about the Messianic walk, and what we needed to "tweak," so we could feel that we were fitting in the

---

[2] Consult the *Messianic Fall Holiday Helper* by Messianic Apologetics.

[3] Consult the *Messianic Spring Holiday Helper* by Messianic Apologetics.

The Messianic Walk

best we could as a new, non-Jewish Messianic family, which had grown up in the Church and not in the Synagogue! We changed Sunday worship to *Shabbat* worship and rest. We changed Church holidays to the Biblical feasts of the Lord. And last, but not least, we changed our eating habits!

The one thing that really got us to find out how our eating needed to be changed, came when the congregational leader would remind us all to only bring "Bibilically kosher" food items to meal gatherings. I knew that Jews did not eat pork, but I had no idea about anything else. So, to be careful not to offend our new Messianic Jewish friends, I began to investigate what "Biblically kosher" really meant for them. I had no idea that I would be finding out what it also would mean for me and my family!

I can remember it as though it were yesterday! I had picked up a Messianic magazine that was given freely at the congregation, which had teachings for the weekly Torah Portions, as well as other pertinent topics that were certainly new to me. One issue had a nice long article about kosher eating, so I was not only relieved, but eager to read it! I quickly found out that about seventy-five percent of the fare that I was raised with, was not considered kosher: not only all the pork, but the shellfish, too. And pork barbeque?—*totally on the naughty list.* My heartfelt desire in reading and learning about kosher eating had originally been to be sensitive to the request to only bring Biblically kosher food to any congregational gathering. I was not prepared for the conviction that this article would have on my own heart...

Becoming Kosher

The very loving and concise Messianic article I had read, laid out verse after verse from the Torah, about what God considered food. It also laid out corresponding verses from the Apostolic Scriptures (New Testament) which indicated what was also considered food—and what was not! Needless to say, I had never been taught any of this growing up as a Christian. I was so completely taken aback by this article, that I even remember exclaiming out loud for my whole family to hear that "This is for us, too!" Of course, my husband and children wanted to know what in the world I was reading, and why in the world I was so worked up about it. We were in the car going on a trip, and I did have a captive audience, so I proceeded to read the whole article on eating Biblically kosher to them. Since we were now being taught at our Messianic congregation that the Torah forms the bedrock, where we get our original information, which is further explained in the Apostolic Scriptures—it was hard for any of us to negate the list of what was considered fit to eat from Leviticus. Yeshua and the Disciples did not teach that those meats which were not considered food in the Torah could now be acceptable to eat. Yeshua and Paul never gave explicit permission to eat a meat that was not considered fit food to eat.

Testimonial Our Family Experiences Going Kosher

I was completely overwhelmed with the truth of Scripture! I, with my childhood nickname of Porka, became totally convicted, since the diet I had been raised on probably consisted of almost seventy-five percent unclean meat that was not Biblical to eat. I did not overreact by condemning my parents or upbringing, now that I had an overwhelming example of how far away from our Jewish Roots Christianity had gone concerning the dietary laws in God's Word. I made the announcement on our trip to my family, that as soon as we got home, I would get rid of all the unclean things we had in our pantry, refrigerator and freezer! *You can imagine the mixed reactions I received.* My husband Mark was totally on board with the new regime. He had also been cut to the quick by the Leviticus Scriptures I had read out loud. My daughter Jane, who did not like any of the unclean meats I had been trying to teach her to eat her whole life, was thrilled and finally felt vindicated that she had been "right" all along. My youngest daughter Maggie did not really eat much of what we were now cutting out of our diet, so she did not have much of an adjustment. However, my son John, who was 15 and had been excellently trained in my Southern family recipes and traditions, really balked! He started to question our new family food direction, and even declared that he **did not plan to comply** with it when he was away from home.

I will not tell you that it was an easy transition, especially since we were still learning what was kosher and what was not. We had to wade through what was Biblical and what was tradition. We had to discern from the traditions—what was good and what was excess. We had just greatly diminished what we had been eating from generations past, so we had to start using new recipes and ideas for the food that we could still eat. It was a challenge at first, and John did come around to the new kosher ideas as the Holy Spirit convicted him! After a while, John actually became more aware of the meat we needed to stay away from than I did, and the proper *halachah* for moving forward. He was also very involved in helping us try new dishes and new family traditions. His true claim to fame had been his love of pork barbeque, which he turned into perfecting the smoking of beef brisket. He has since perfected his own barbeque sauces, as well as smoking chicken, turkey, lamb, beef ribs and turkey sausage. He is an expert now on what type of wood to use with each type of meat. All his friends consider it a real honor to be asked to one of John's barbeque dinners with all the fixings![4]

During those early years of the mid-to-late 1990s, it was something of a stumbling block to some of our family and friends who did not really understand why we would want to be living a Messianic lifestyle. The summer of 1996, when we all started to eat Biblically kosher, I had to announce to my five siblings and their families, who we vacation with every year in Gulf Shores, Alabama, that we would no longer be eating the pork and shellfish that was so abundantly served by

---

[4] Some time in the future, Messianic Apologetics will be releasing a BBQ cookbook by J.K. McKee.

The Messianic Walk

them all. We were all very nice about it, and did not suggest that they were in the wrong—but only that *we* had changed our eating habits. For the most part, our request was well received, yet the relatives who had the biggest problem with accepting our eating change, were actually the ones who present themselves as being the most committed evangelical Christians. By our considering Scripture from the Tanach, that they had cast aside, was something very challenging to them. They belonged to a particular Protestant denomination which tends to claim that it follows the Bible the best—and their pastor said we were all wrong to be doing "Old Testament things."

It has been over two decades since our family has "gone kosher," and my extended family has been able to see that we are *still* Messianic Believers and are *still* trying to walk like Yeshua walked—and **eat** like Yeshua ate. We still get sarcastic comments now and then from one particular relative, who has gotten rather unhealthy—and almost morbidly obese—during these same years as we have gotten fitter. By us wanting to follow Scripture in all areas of our lives, I know that we are doing what is right for us both spiritually and physically.

In our family's observance of eating a Biblical kosher (or some might say kosher-style) diet, we have been willing to put aside some very meaningful and special recipes and cuisine styles, because of our commitment to living Biblically. Yet we know from our experience in Messianic ministry, that giving up the pork and shellfish from our Christian background, is actually comparatively little, when many Messianic Jews who come to faith in Yeshua, have their families turn on them and treat them as being deceased. Yeshua the Messiah, however, was the One who gave up His exalted glory in Heaven, to be humiliated and executed as a human being—for the sins of us all!

Controversies Involving Torah-Based "Means of Grace"

While it is unfortunate to have to say this, some of the biggest controversies which face the contemporary Messianic movement today, involve misunderstandings of various outward actions and activities—which are intended to bless, and **not divide**—the people of God. Whether we want to admit it or not, as an emerging faith community, today's Messianic movement has areas of its theology and practice which are under-developed, or which involve applications limited to a local congregation or assembly, dependent on a group's circumstances. People can inappropriately assume, at times, that "one size fits all," when in fact, some things might instead need to be examined on a case-by-case basis.

In my own life, I have been personally involved in planning the funeral of my father (1992) and the wedding of my sister (2015). It is fairly easy to recognize that in planning a funeral or a wedding, that the needs of the immediate family, the larger extended family, and the friends involved, need to be taken into consideration. While the basic rituals of remembering the deceased and burying the remains, *and* the recitation of marriage vows and a celebration of a new couple joining together, remain consistent for a funeral or for a wedding—every funeral and every wedding have things requested by the family, which the spiritual leader officiating has to take into consideration. Consequently, a number of the divisive issues involving Torah-based means of grace, are those which precisely concern a consultation between families and their local Messianic congregational leader. And if necessary, we should be honest enough as people who compose a still-developing Messianic movement, to recognize those areas where further study and investigation are required.

The Messianic Walk

Bar/Bat Mitzvah

How many people really know what the discipline of going through *bar mitzvah* or *bat mitzvah*, truly is? Many have the impression, based on portrayals in popular culture, that a *bar mitzvah* is just an opportunity to have a party, showering a thirteen year old boy or girl with endless gifts, somehow intended for their future. While various festivities may be involved with the commemoration of a *bar mitzvah*, the discipline and procedures of going through a *bar mitzvah*—especially within today's Jewish community—are quite serious and even rigorous.

The term *bar mitzvah* means "son of the commandments," with *bat mitzvah* meaning "daughter of the commandments." The exact origins of the more modern process of a Jewish youth going through *bar mitzvah* are unclear. The workbook *Messianic Judaism Class*, in answering the question "Is this custom a Biblical command?", answers, "It's a part of Jewish tradition since the 13th century. It's an extra-Biblical tradition that is not forbidden by Biblical teaching."[1] Among the different reasons it lists for the significance of *bar* or *bat mitzvah*, include: a rite of passage, boyhood to manhood and girlhood to womanhood, acceptance of personal responsibility of oneself before God, learning Hebrew, learning to be a leader, identification with Judaism and the faith community. The *bar/bat mitzvah* process typically involves a recognition, for a young man or woman (usually 13 for boys, 12 for girls), that he or she is about to enter into adulthood.

Within the Jewish community, the process of going through *bar/bat mitzvah* involves Hebrew education, study of Jewish history and culture, and a review of the responsibilities that a Jewish man or woman will have as he or she enters into adulthood, and takes up some place within congregational life. At the *bar/bat mitzvah* ceremony, the young person who has completed his or her required classes, will often cant from the Hebrew Torah portion, and give a short teaching. As the young man or young woman is formally recognized as an adult before the assembly, he or she not only is to be committed to a life of service to God and the Jewish people, but the corporate body too has a responsibility of being there to support these young people. While it is traditional for those going through *bar/bat mitzvah* to be teenagers, adults well into their seventies and eighties have gone through *bar/bat mitzvah*.

While many of the traditions and procedures associated with *bar/bat mitzvah* originate from post-Second Temple times, Jewish history does record the need for young people to be trained in the Scriptures, and be recognized as members of the spiritual community. The First Century historian Josephus recorded, "when I was a child, and about fourteen years of age, I was commended by all for the love I had to learning; on which account the high priests and principal men of the city came

---

[1] *Messianic Judaism Class*, Teacher Book, 56.

Controversies Involving Torah-Based "Means of Grace"

then frequently to me together, in order to know my opinion about the accurate understanding of points of the law" (*Life* 1.9).[2] The authors of *Messianic Judaism Class*, referencing Yeshua's encounter at the Temple in Luke 2:41-43, 46-49, conclude, "Yeshua is doing what we do at a Bar Mitzvah. The boy or girl reads that week's passage and then they do a little teaching from it."[3] As it was recorded of the young Yeshua:

> "Now His parents were going every year to Jerusalem for the Passover feast. When He became twelve years old, they were going up according to festival custom. As they headed home after completing the days, the boy Yeshua remained in Jerusalem, but His parents didn't know...After three days they found Him in the Temple, sitting in the center of the teachers, listening to them and asking them questions. And all those hearing Him were astonished at His understanding and His answers. When His parents saw Yeshua, they were overwhelmed. And His mother said to Him, 'Child, why did you do this to us? Look! Your father and I were searching for You frantically!' He said to them, 'Why were you searching for Me? Didn't you know that I must be about the things of My Father?'" (Luke 2:41-43, 46-49, TLV).

Each Messianic congregation will have some kind of *bar/bat mitzvah* education regimen, involving Hebrew study, Bible study, a review of Jewish history and culture, some likely review of Christian history, a review of the modern Messianic movement, and likely also discipleship instruction for young adults experiencing puberty. In Messianic *bar/bat mitzvah*, the young adult is honored before the congregation, as the corporate Body of Messiah does have to recognize its responsibility in seeing young people welcomed and mentored. (As it is noted in *Messianic Judaism Class*, "It has been copied by the church in confirmation."[4] Protestant denominations which offer confirmation classes to young adults, usually offer classes on what it means for young people to be responsible Christians, church members, Bible readers, and they address the challenges facing teenagers going through many life changes, as they face adulthood.)

The *bar/bat mitzvah* process does bear spiritual importance for young people not only being recognized as adults, but for evaluating their present standing before God. Galatians 3:24 communicates how "the Torah became our guardian to lead us to Messiah, so that we might be made right based on trusting" (TLV), meaning that our common human violation of the Torah's instruction is to show us our need for a Redeemer. An ideal time to confirm that this has indeed happened, is when a young man or young woman is going through the process of *bar* or *bat mitzvah*.

---

[2] *The Works of Josephus: Complete and Unabridged*, 1.
[3] *Messianic Judaism Class*, Teacher Book, 56.
[4] Ibid.

The Messianic Walk

Certainly Messianic Jewish children, and the children of intermarried couples in the Messianic movement, would be naturally anticipated to be those who go through *bar/bat mitzvah*. But what about non-Jewish children in the Messianic movement? This is where it has to be recognized that there is variance of approach in the Messianic community. More often than not, though, your local Messianic congregation will have its *bar/bat mitzvah* classes open to the children of both its Jewish and non-Jewish members. In fact, it is likely that there might be grown adults in attendance at its *bar/bat mitzvah* classes! If you are a non-Jewish parent, your local Messianic congregational leadership might recommend some modifications of the different blessings which are offered in the *bar/bat mitzvah* service, for your son or daughter. And, whether you are Jewish or non-Jewish, if your son or daughter is going through *bar/bat mitzvah*, you might want to suggest that some things be incorporated into their service, in order to honor their lives thus far. Much of this is dependent on the venue of your local Messianic congregation, and for an accounting of the needs of one's family, extended family, and guests in attendance.

Circumcision

At the close of the 2010s, our faith community does not have a coherent theology of circumcision, even though its physical and spiritual components do make up a critical part of the Biblical narrative. The Ancient Israelites were admonished in Deuteronomy 10:16, "circumcise your heart, and stiffen your neck no longer" (NASU; cf. Colossians 2:11), speaking to the important lesson of circumcision: removing an outer barrier placed between a human being and God. Yet, the physical rite of male circumcision, is something we seldom address—mainly because it is a sexual issue. However, anyone knowing about the standard basics of the Jewish life cycle, should be familiar enough with how by ancient convention, male Jews are circumcised on the eighth day. Furthermore, anyone with a cursory understanding of some of the controversies which arose in the First Century *ekklēsia*, should be aware of how circumcision was a huge debate involving the inclusion of Greek and Roman Believers into the Body of Messiah.

Male circumcision, as a medical practice, was something which pre-dated the Patriarch Abraham, even though it is correctly recognized that male circumcision is the memorial sign of the Abrahamic covenant:

"God also said to Abraham, 'As for you, My covenant you must keep, you and your seed after you throughout their generations. This is My covenant that you must keep between Me and you and your seed after you: all your males must be circumcised. You must be circumcised in the flesh of your foreskin, and this will become a sign of the covenant between Me and you. Also your eight-day-olds must be circumcised, every male, throughout your generations, including a house-born slave or a slave bought with money from any foreigner who is not of your seed.

Controversies Involving Torah-Based "Means of Grace"

Your house-born slave and your purchased slave must surely be circumcised. So My covenant will be in your flesh for an everlasting covenant' (Genesis 17:9-13, TLV).

So severe was male circumcision, it was said, "But the uncircumcised male who is not circumcised in the flesh of his foreskin—that person will be cut off from his people; he has broken My covenant" (Genesis 17:14, TLV). Leviticus 12:3 would further codify for native born males, born into Ancient Israel, "In the eighth day the flesh of his foreskin is to be circumcised" (TLV). Sojourners, entering into Ancient Israel, would have to be circumcised in order to eat of the Passover sacrifice, but as a result would be considered as natives: "But if an outsider dwells with you, who would keep the Passover for ADONAI, all his males must be circumcised. Then let him draw near and keep it. He will be like one who is native to the land. But no uncircumcised person may eat from it" (Exodus 12:48, TLV). Israel's enemies in the Tanach, in particular the Philistines, were often taunted for being "uncircumcised" (i.e., 1 Samuel 17:26, 36; 2 Samuel 1:20).

During the Maccabean crisis of the Second Century B.C.E., the Seleucid Greeks made it illegal for Jewish mothers to circumcise their infant sons, on the threat of death (1 Maccabees 1:48). The right for Jews to circumcise, was something that the Maccabees properly fought and gave their lives for. So, it should not be surprising that by the First Century C.E., as the good news or gospel was going out into the Mediterranean, that it was definitely believed, that in order for non-Jews to be fully admitted into the people of God, that they needed to be circumcised as Jewish proselytes. While there were ancient Jewish discussions involving what it meant for a non-Jew to become a proselyte, circumcision was widely agreed to be necessary. Debates are witnessed throughout Paul's letter to the Galatians whether circumcision was necessary of Greek and Roman Believers for them to be fully received into the Body of Messiah, and the Jerusalem Council of Acts 15 met to decisively address the issue: "It is necessary to circumcise them and to order them to keep the law of Moses" (Acts 15:5, ESV). Circumcision was not deemed necessary for non-Jewish Believers to be fully welcomed in as equal brothers and sisters of the Jewish Believers (Galatians 3:28).

There is little doubting the importance that male circumcision continues to have for Jewish Believers in Israel's Messiah. Yeshua the Messiah Himself, was circumcised (Luke 1:57-66). The Apostle Paul was circumcised (Philippians 3:5), and he definitely says, "Then what is the advantage of being Jewish? Or what is the benefit of circumcision? Much in every way. First of all, they were entrusted with the sayings of God" (Romans 3:1-2, TLV). Paul had his disciple Timothy, who was born of a Jewish mother but had a Greek father, circumcised (Acts 16:1-3). Yet, Paul also warns against any over-inflated self-opinions about circumcision that First Century Jews might have had, as he also says, "Circumcision is indeed worthwhile if you keep the Torah; but if you break the Torah, your circumcision has become uncircumcision. Therefore, if the uncircumcised keeps the righteous decrees of the Torah, will not his uncircumcision be counted as circumcision?" (Romans 2:25-26, TLV).

Most of us are not fully informed as to all the details regarding the circumcision of infant males in our various Messianic congregations and assemblies. At most, we are probably aware of how a Messianic Jewish couple or intermarried couple, will make sure that a newborn male is circumcised on the eighth day. Sometimes, a Jewish *mohel*, who has been specially trained in circumcision, will circumcise a Messianic Jewish male infant. Involved with this will be various traditions and customs involving the naming of the male child (cf. Luke 1:59), and blessings issued upon him. When a Jewish *mohel* is not available, then if there is a doctor in your local congregation, he or she will usually be consulted for the options that are available, which may then result in the infant male being circumcised in a hospital setting. At a later time, some kind of infant dedication, perhaps involving Jewish circumcision blessings, will take place.

Beyond the Jewish community, male circumcision has been a widescale medical practice in much of the West, for well over a century. Although its medical benefits have been debated in recent times, the authors of *Messianic Judaism Class* address the question "Are there any physical benefits to circumcision?" with, "There might be. They have discovered in Africa that the tribes that circumcise their males have a lower rate of HIV/AIDS infection."[5] Because male circumcision is a common medical practice, questions inevitably arise regarding what non-Jewish families in the Messianic movement should do, when having a male child. **All agree that physical circumcision is not required for salvation.** There are those in the Messianic movement, approaching a passage like 1 Corinthians 7:17-24 as it addressing a vocational calling, who think that non-Jewish infant males should not be circumcised.[6] There are others, who think that physical circumcision as a medical practice, is hardly prohibited, but that some of the traditional Jewish ceremonies and blessings involving the naming of a male child, should be reserved for infant males of Messianic Jewish and intermarried couples. Another sort of ceremony or child dedication should be practiced to bless a non-Jewish infant male. Significant questions are posed for the future, given how in the Millennial Kingdom,

---

[5] *Messianic Judaism Class*, Teacher Book, 56.

[6] There is no agreement among examiners whether 1 Corinthians 7:17-24, and its reference to "Let each man abide in that calling wherein he was called" (1 Corinthians 7:20, American Standard Version), relates to a vocational calling or a calling into salvation and sanctification.

The latter position is what the author ascribes to, based on the Greek source text and related statements in the Pauline letters (Ephesians 4:1; 2 Timothy 1:9). Consult the author's commentary *1 Corinthians for the Practical Messianic*.

no one uncircumcised of heart or flesh can enter into the Lord's sanctuary (Ezekiel 44:9).[7]

Water Immersion

Within the broad Christian tradition, to be sure, some significance is placed on what is customarily called "baptism." Baptism as an English term is widely derived from the Greek verb *baptizō* and Greek noun *baptisma*. The verb *baptizō* appears in not just the Greek New Testament or Apostolic Scriptures, but also the Septuagint, or ancient Greek translation of the Hebrew Tanach. As is noted by the *Thayer* lexicon, *baptizō* can mean "*to cleanse by dipping or submerging, to wash, to make clean with water.*"[8] Due to much of the socio-religious associations that can go along with the English term "baptism," the Messianic community tends to employ the more neutral term "immersion." It is also quite common to hear the term *mikveh* employed, representative of a "*gathering of water, esp. the ritual bath of purification*" (*Jastrow*).[9] Many of the debates that take place in Protestantism, to be sure, involving "baptism," do not need to be repeated in today's Messianic congregations.

While Believers in Israel's Messiah can often conclude that water immersion is something which is only witnessed in the Messianic Scriptures (New Testament), water immersion for Believers is rooted in the purification rituals of the Tanach (cf. Exodus 29:1, 4; Leviticus 17:15-16; Psalm 51:2). Individuals, and certainly members of the Levitical priesthood, had to typically go through a ritual purification in water, before approaching God in the Tabernacle or Temple. In Second Temple times, water immersion was required of new proselytes to Judaism, who would often be regarded as "born again" (b.*Yevamot* 48b). Yet, Jewish persons would often go through ritual immersion in water for other reasons in life, namely to denote a significant status change. When John, the precursor of Yeshua of Nazareth, arrived on the scene immersing people in water, it was precisely so that they could be called to repentance and be readied to recognize the coming Messiah (Matthew 3:4-6; John 1:24-25; cf. Matthew 3:13-17).

Water immersion following salvation (cf. Matthew 28:19-20), was deemed quite critical for new Believers in the First Century C.E. Those who were saved on the day of *Shavuot*/Pentecost were immersed in water (Acts 2:38), as were Cornelius and his companions when the good news was declared to them by Peter (Acts 10:45-48). The total immersion of a human person into water following a

---

[7] For a further review, consult the author's article "Is Circumcision for Everyone?", appearing in *Torah in the Balance, Volume II*.

[8] Joseph H. Thayer, *Thayer's Greek-English Lexicon of the New Testament* (Peabody, MA: Hendrickson, 2003), 94.

[9] *Jastrow*, 829.

The Messianic Walk

declaration of faith in Israel's Messiah, is to not only signify a status change (Romans 6:6-7), but also for one to be identified with His death, burial, and resurrection: "Or do you not know that all of us who were immersed into Messiah Yeshua were immersed into His death? Therefore we were buried together with Him through immersion into death—in order that just as Messiah was raised from the dead by the glory of the Father, so we too might walk in newness of life. For if we have become joined together in the likeness of His death, certainly we also will be joined together in His resurrection" (Romans 6:3-5, TLV).

Messianic Jewish Believers can, at times, have some initial difficulty with water immersion as a part of coming to faith, because of *forced baptisms* enacted during the Middle Ages by Roman Catholicism. Frequently, European Jews were forced to convert and be baptized, or they could face seizure of property, deportation, or even death.[10] Non-Jewish Believers from evangelical Protestant backgrounds—particularly where "Believer's baptism" was practiced—can have difficulty with not necessarily seeing how water immersion is rooted within Tanach purification rituals, but how the Jewish *mikveh* is something which has a wider range of applications. While the most important status change for a man or woman, is when he or she receives the salvation of Yeshua—there are likely other times when going through water immersion may be something useful. In Orthodox Judaism, women are immersed in water following their menstrual cycle. People in today's Messianic community, may decide to go through a *mikveh* when a significant status change in their life is about to take place. Your congregational leadership should be consulted, before you go through any water immersion. As obvious as it might be, while Messianic congregations frequently do not require one to be re-immersed for congregational membership—going through a *mikveh* might be something you find useful, should you enter into a new community of Messiah followers.[11]

Communion

Significant questions can be raised by various people entering into the Messianic movement, from evangelical backgrounds, particularly regarding what is done regarding the common practice of communion. In diverse Christian traditions, remembering the Last Supper of Yeshua can take place any number of ways and any number of times. Sometimes communion is weekly, sometimes it is monthly; sometimes communion is offered to all in church attendance, and sometimes it is only offered to members of a particular denomination or assembly. Sometimes

---

[10] *Messianic Judaism Class*, Teacher Book, 63.

[11] For a further review, consult the article "The Waters of Immersion," appearing in *Torah in the Balance, Volume II*.

Controversies Involving Torah-Based "Means of Grace"

Christian communion uses leavened bread and grape juice, and sometimes Christian communion uses an unleavened wafer and wine.[12]

Messianic people are of the broad conviction that what is commonly called the Last Supper, held between Yeshua and His Disciples before His execution, was actually a Passover *seder* meal. Yeshua's establishment of the New Covenant, by referencing the elements of bread and wine, were conducted in association with the unleavened bread and wine of the traditional *seder* meal (Luke 22:19-20; 1 Corinthians 11:23-25). While many Christians remember the Lord's Supper via a weekly or annual communion, Messianic practice tends to be far more infrequent.

How do Messianic people approach "For as often as you eat this bread and drink this cup" (1 Corinthians 11:26, TLV)? As indicated by the workbook *Messianic Judaism Class*, "Some interpret this to mean, 'as often as you celebrate Pesakh, once per year. Some interpret this as every time you gather together. Some interpret this as one per week, month, quarter. Some interpret this as whenever you are guided by the Spirit.'"[13] On the whole, within the broad Messianic community, the Lord's Supper will be remembered within the context of the Passover *seder*, making it an annual **serious** occurrence. If the Lord's Supper is at all honored a bit more regularly, it will likely be observed at some kind of a private prayer meeting, employing unleavened bread and grape juice.

Consult Your Rabbi

The four areas we have just covered: *bar/bat mitzvah*, circumcision, water immersion, and communion, are areas where today's Messianic movement is admittedly still developing and exploring. The way that these practices are observed and applied in one congregation, is not likely to be the same as they are observed in another congregation. In the customary packaging for items labeled as "Kosher for Passover," one also frequently finds "Consult your Rabbi." This means that there might be some questions that need to be asked of one's local, spiritual leader. And indeed, when it involves *bar/bat mitzvah*, circumcision, water immersion, communion, or some other significant practice witnessed in today's Body of Messiah—your local, spiritual leader(s) will likely need to be consulted. And, such leader(s) should be honest enough with you, to indicate those areas where the Messianic movement as a whole is in need of some further theological refinement.

The admonition of Hebrews 13:17 directs Messiah followers to "Obey your leaders and submit to them, for they keep watch over your souls as ones who must give an account. Let them do this with joy and not with groaning, for that would be

---

[12] For a further review, consult Paul E. Engle, ed., *Understanding Four Views on the Lord's Supper* (Grand Rapids: Zondervan, 2007).

[13] *Messianic Judaism Class*, Teacher Book, 67.

The Messianic Walk

of no benefit to you" (TLV). Yet, all of us—recognizing a few of the present difficulties of our still-emerging and developing Messianic faith community—have at times been in (strong) disagreement with congregational leadership, over a particular issue or two. We need to each recognize how **there is only one Messianic movement,** and it is very small. None of the subjects we have just talked about, should merit one leaving a congregation or assembly, if you have a disagreement with your congregational leadership—or more likely some (outspoken) people within your congregation—over their implementation and application. Instead, we should each learn to give one another the space that we need to live out a Messianic walk of faith, and also respect the individual and familial needs of other people.

STUDY QUESTIONS FOR UNIT THREE

1. Have you ever been taught that it is only one's internal heart condition that is important, and that external actions or deeds do not matter? Describe some of your experiences.

2. What external areas of Torah adherence are you most familiar with? What external areas of Torah adherence will you need to study and investigate further?

3. What are some of the challenges that today's Messianic people often have with eating a kosher style of diet? How many of them are theological, and how many of them involve deep family traditions?

4. What is some of the variance one may witness at a Messianic congregation, in terms of how the Torah's dietary laws are honored?

5. Why can there be various controversies associated with external forms of Torah adherence? How much do they relate to an individual's or family's interpretation and application of various instructions?

6. What are the kinds of Torah-based practices that you think require an individual or family to consult with congregational leadership? Why do you think some people are more divisive than others, in matters of Torah keeping?

KOSHER
TORAH BASED "MEANS OF GRACE"
FOR FURTHER READING AND EXPLORATION

Eby, Aaron. *Biblically Kosher: A Messianic Jewish Perspective on Kashrut* (Marshfield, MO: First Fruits of Zion, 2012).

Egan, Hope. *Holy Cow! Does God Care About What We Eat?* (Littleton, CO; First Fruits of Zion, 2005).

Eisenberg, Ronald L. *The JPS Guide to Jewish Traditions* (Philadelphia: Jewish Publication Society, 2004).

Huey, Margaret McKee, ed. *Messianic Kosher Helper* (Richardson, TX: Messianic Apologetics, 2014).

McKee, J.K. *Torah In the Balance, Volume II* (Richardson, TX: Messianic Apologetics, 2015).

Kasdan, Barney. *God's Appointed Customs: A Messianic Jewish Guide to the Biblical Lifecycle and Lifestyle* (Baltimore: Lederer: 1996).

Tessler, Gordon. *The Genesis Diet* (Raleigh: Be Well Publications, 1996).

JEWISH OUTREACH AND EVANGELISM

UNIT FOUR

The Contours of Jewish Evangelism

The original mission and purpose of the Messianic movement has always been to provide a venue for Jewish outreach, evangelism, and Israel solidarity. While reaching diverse groups of people with the good news or gospel message of salvation is not easy, no matter what one's intended audience, the Apostolic Writings (New Testament) give ample testimony of how many Jewish people *in the First Century* were resistant to the news that the Messiah of Israel had arrived. So great was the agony of a figure like the Apostle Paul, that he actually wished himself accursed, to see his own flesh and blood redeemed:

"I tell the truth in Messiah—I do not lie, my conscience assuring me in the Ruach ha-Kodesh—that my sorrow is great and the anguish in my heart unending. For I would pray that I myself were cursed, banished from Messiah for the sake of my people—my own flesh and blood" (Romans 9:1-3, TLV).

While corporately in the First Century, and even until today, the Jewish people have largely dismissed Yeshua of Nazareth as the anticipated Messiah—it is not as though this has not been without a purpose. Paul noted that there has always been a remnant of Jewish Believers, himself being among them (Romans 11:5). He also detailed how "If their trespass means riches for the world, and their impoverishment means riches for the nations, how much more will their fullness mean!" (Romans 11:12, Kingdom New Testament). If a widescale Jewish dismissal of Israel's Messiah means a massive salvation of those from the world at large—**how great will it be when a concentrated salvation of the Jewish people is witnessed?** There are complications to this taking place, however, notably as it involves the behavior of the wild olive branches, non-Jewish Believers in Israel's Messiah, grafted-in to Israel's olive tree (Romans 11:17-21). History is replete that rather than being moved with mercy and compassion and understanding for Jewish people, who need the salvation of Yeshua (Romans 11:31), arrogance, disdain, discrimination, persecution, and even terrible atrocities have been committed by

The Messianic Walk

far too many of those "claiming Christ."

Every Messianic congregation or assembly, whether it is in Israel, North America, or elsewhere, is going to have some vehicle for Jewish outreach and involvement in the local Jewish community. Obviously each Jewish community is different. Here in the United States, the Jewish community in the Northeast, South Florida, Southern California, or other urban centers, is going to be a little different than the Jewish community in North Dallas, where my local congregation of Eitz Chaim is located. But regardless of how large, how small, how established, or how conservative or liberal one's local Jewish community is—there are significant contours and facets which those who are a part of a Messianic congregation need to be aware of, when involving themselves in Jewish outreach. Jewish Believers for certain need to be involved in Jewish evangelism, as they testify not only to the salvation they possess in Yeshua—but most especially how believing in Yeshua does not mean an abandonment of one's Jewish heritage or traditions. Likewise, non-Jewish Believers should also be involved in Jewish evangelism, as non-Jews in today's Messianic community can not only be used by the Lord to provoke Jewish people to faith in Messiah Yeshua (Romans 11:11), but as those who have joined in common cause and unity with Jewish Believers, as a tangible sign that past centuries of Christian anti-Semitism and discrimination are indeed something in the past.

How do any of us "evangelize"?

In contemporary evangelical Protestantism over the past half century or so, there have been scores of different methods which Believers have employed, to genuinely reach out to others with the good news. Many of us have been involved in some form of local outreach, where we have handed out tracts, or have knocked on doors, asking people about where they stand in their relationship with God. Some of these evangelistic tools and methods have taken labels such as "the Romans road," "the Four Spiritual Laws," "Evangelism Explosion," or quite possibly even "The Purpose Driven Life." But as we are probably all aware, not all of these methods work indefinitely, and some of them do not have a lasting impact—as a number of people who make a profession of faith, may not necessarily get plugged into a local assembly and network of Believers.

While we have probably all seen some of the successes and failures of customary Protestant methods of evangelism over the past three or four decades—Jewish outreach and evangelism tends to be something completely different from passing out tracts on a street corner. **Jewish evangelism is innately tied in with long-term relationship building.** History has borne out far too many examples of where Jewish populations were forced to convert to Roman Catholicism, likely involving confiscation of property, expulsion from one's home, and perhaps even the threat of death. Even Protestantism, which on the whole has been far more

The Contours of Jewish Evangelism

tolerant and respectful for Judaism, has widely expected that Jewish people who come to faith in Jesus the Messiah cease being Jewish, start being Christian, and should find themselves fully assimilated into Western Christian culture.

Consequently, with a great deal of anti-Semitic, anti-Jewish, or at least apathy toward Judaism present—when the issue of Yeshua of Nazareth is raised—seeing Jewish people truly receive the Messiah into their lives, tends to hardly be an instantaneous process. While we all might want to see the same kind of dynamic teaching and salvation present at *Shavuot*/Pentecost (Acts 2), because of too many of the forces of past history, Jewish evangelism is often a long term process. You might think that this would, of course, only be necessary if one is reaching out to Orthodox Jews who have developed opinions on the Tanach and Messianic expectation—but it even involves liberal Jews, who are nominally to non-religious, but whose Jewish identity and values are very strong. *Does receiving Yeshua mean an abandonment of one's Jewish heritage, and a betrayal of one's ancestors?*

When you get involved in Jewish evangelism, you should expect to have many meetings with an individual or family. Many of these meetings are not going to involve discussions of one's religious faith, but instead establishing trust, as you get to know a Jewish person, learn about their family history and story, how they see the world, how they see Israel, how they respond to anti-Semitism and discrimination against them, and eventually what they think of Yeshua of Nazareth at least as an historical figure. Sometimes, per the adage "so they may see your good works and glorify your Father in heaven" (Matthew 5:16, TLV), the greatest testimony of a Messianic Believer to a Jewish person is going to be in tangible actions of being their friend, helping them out, standing in solidarity with them and with the Jewish community, and being a beacon of support and stability in their life. *It might take a very long time to see your Jewish friend or Jewish neighbor be open to the good news of Messiah.*

The Terms We Use, and Communicating Well to Jewish People

All of us at some point in our lives have been told that **words mean things**. How we communicate in an ever-changing and interconnected world, is vitally important. A term or phrase can mean something positive to one group of people, and can be taken as a striking insult by another group of people. In ministry today, if a speaker tells an audience "God is raising up men in this hour to serve Him," half of your audience has been immediately lost. If a speaker tells an audience, "God is raising up men and women" or "God is raising up people," then the real message about how this is taking place can then be communicated to everyone present.

Have you ever wondered what Paul meant by saying, "To the Jews I became as a Jew, so that I might win Jews" (1 Corinthians 9:20, NASU)? Frequently, 1

The Messianic Walk

Corinthians 9:19-21 has been interpreted from the perspective that in declaring the good news, Paul would frequently change his behavior and actions, in order to do what was necessary in order to have a hearing. Was Paul a chameleon, flip-flopping around different First Century audiences in the Mediterranean? Not only this, but did Paul really not think his Jewishness was that important? While it is absolutely true that one's identity in Yeshua the Messiah and His work on the tree overrides all human achievements (Philippians 3:4-10), Paul did see value in Judaism and in his Jewish heritage (Romans 3:1-2).

So what did Paul mean when he said "To the Jews I became as a Jew"? The categories of 1 Corinthians 9:19-21 are hardly exhaustive, as there were many more groups of people Paul and company encountered in the diverse Roman Empire. It can be validly concluded that "I became as," means that Paul rhetorically identified with an audience he was tasked with declaring the good news to. *How do you best communicate the gospel to a particular group of people?* In the First Century C.E., identifying with the Jewish people involved far more than just understanding the story of Ancient Israel in the Torah and Tanach; it involved understanding the difficulties of the return of the Jewish people from Babylon exile, the fallout of the Maccabean crisis of the Second Century B.C.E., Judea as a province of the Roman Empire, and the struggles of a massive Diaspora Jewish community in the Roman Empire that faced discrimination and threats from polytheism.

In the Twentieth and Twenty-First Centuries, we should be able to easily deduce that "To the Jews I became as a Jew" would mean more than having a good understanding of Ancient Israel from the Tanach and Second Temple Judaism; it is something that involves complicated histories and diverse Jewish communities. What happened after the fall of the Second Temple? How has Roman Catholicism historically treated the Jewish people? How has Protestantism historically approached the Jewish theological tradition? What were some of the terrors perpetuated upon Jews during the Middle Ages? What were the pogroms of the Russian Empire? How and why did the Holocaust happen? What are present Christian attitudes to the existence of the State of Israel? These questions, and many more, are involved in what it means to place oneself in the position of a modern Jewish person, who needs the good news of Israel's Messiah.

Ever since the early beginnings of the modern Messianic Jewish movement, in late 1960s and early 1970s, there have been various lists composed of words common to today's evangelical Protestantism—which while meaning many positive things to most of today's non-Jewish Believers, can be quite offensive to Jewish people you are trying to develop a relationship with. Biblical Hebrew has approximately 3,500 words; Biblical Greek has approximately 5,500 words; modern English has approximately 150,000 words. There are legitimate alternatives that can be employed by today's Messianic people, instead of the more standard words or terms employed in "Christianese." While it is a process, particularly for non-

The Contours of Jewish Evangelism

Jewish Believers called by God into the Messianic movement, there are a number of terms which you need to be aware of, that do not facilitate Jewish evangelism too well. If you are ever called to speak in front of a Messianic congregation to give a testimony or issue a prayer, the following are some terms you need to really not be using:

Jesus is not the original name of the Messiah of Israel, but is instead an English transliteration of the Greek *Iēsous*, itself a Greek transliteration of the Hebrew *Yeshua*, meaning "He is salvation" (Matthew 1:21). The name "Jesus" is hardly pagan, and there were many Jews in the Diaspora who actually bore the name *Iēsous* (Colossians 4:11). While it was perfectly acceptable in the First Century C.E. for Jewish Believers in Yeshua to call the Messiah *Iēsous* in a Greek-speaking context, with *Iēsous* as the Septuagint title of the Book of Joshua—calling the Messiah Jesus in Jewish settings in the Twenty-First Century is quite complicated. Throughout history, persecution has been inflicted upon the Jewish people using the name Jesus (or its derivative forms). When many of today's Jews hear the name Jesus, they hardly think of a First Century Jewish Messiah, but instead as a figure who has been frequently responsible for enacting great tragedies upon the Jews. Today's Messianic Jewish movement uses the name **Yeshua** (also frequently spelled Y'shua) for the Messiah.

Christ is a title derived from the Greek *Christos* meaning "Anointed One," the equivalent of the Hebrew *Mashiach* or Messiah. While *Christos* does appear in the Greek Apostolic Writings, its post-First Century usage as a title has been more widely employed than Jesus, in fact, in the discrimination and persecution of Jewish people by religious authorities. Today's Messianic Jewish movement uses the title **Messiah**.

Christian, derived from *Christianos* was originally a term of ridicule, or a slur, issued against the Believers in Antioch (Acts 11:26; see NRSV which has "Christians" in quotation marks). Today there are so many denominations, sects, sub-sects, and groups which use and employ the terminology "Christian," that it is inappropriate to assume that the title "Christian" automatically means that one is a born again Believer. There are actually some today who have stopped using the terminology "Christian," and instead will call themselves a "Christ follower" or "disciple of Christ." Today's Messianic people should similarly see no problem when calling themselves a **Messiah follower** or **disciple of Messiah**. When using terminology such as "Christian" or "Christianity," it should be in reference to religious systems and institutions; **Messiah faith** or **Biblical**

The Messianic Walk

faith should not be referred to as Christianity. It is also most appropriate, given how many Jews associate the term "Christian" with Roman Catholicism and its non-Biblical to pagan traditions, to today not readily employ the terminology "Judeo-Christian," but instead "Judeo-Protestant."

The **cross** (and similarly the verb **crucify**) was the means by which Yeshua the Messiah was sacrificed for the sins of humanity by the Romans. But the cross has also been used as a symbol and banner of significant persecution by religious authorities, toward the Jewish people, for centuries. A frequent alternative employed for the term cross in today's Messianic movement is **execution-stake**, as seen in David H. Stern's Complete Jewish Bible. Messianic people will also frequently speak in terms of Yeshua being "nailed to **the tree**" (cf. Acts 5:30). A new alternative that can employed for cross would be **wooden scaffold**, as the very purpose of this form of ancient execution was to openly display the condemned, humiliating one before the public.

A **church** in the minds of many Jewish people, and for that matter many contemporary evangelicals, is a building with a steeple and stained glass windows. For others, the term church is not associated with the people of God, but instead religious institutions (or even principalities). The Greek term *ekklēsia* frequently translated the Hebrew *qahal* throughout the Septuagint, *qahal* itself often referring to the community of Ancient Israel (i.e., Deuteronomy 31:30). Many theologians today have recognized some of the complications of speaking of the people of God in terms of it being the "church," and so there are specialty English versions today which more properly translate *ekklēsia* as **assembly**, such as Young's Literal Translation or The Interlinear Bible by Jay P. Green. Today's Messianic movement very much dislikes it when its local faith community is referred to as a "church," and so one's local body should instead be called a congregation, assembly, or fellowship. (Many will employ the Yiddish *shul*, meaning school.)

Throughout a diverse array of Protestant traditions, to be sure, **baptism** for the people of God, has been approached from any number of different vantage points. The English verb baptize is derived from the Greek verb *baptizō*, but the term baptism, even from just an evangelical Protestant perspective, has a great deal of socio-religious baggage associated with it. Very early on, today's Messianic Jewish movement began employing more theologically neutral terminology such as **water immersion** or **immerse**

The Contours of Jewish Evangelism

(as would be seen in Bibles such as the Complete Jewish Bible or Tree of Life Version). Many Jewish people, when hearing the terminology "baptize," do not think of ritual immersions in water taking place, with their origins found in the purification rituals of the Tanach. When many Jewish people may hear the terminology "baptize," they think of forced baptisms of Jewish people by Roman Catholic authorities throughout history, with the intention of them abandoning their Jewish heritage and traditions.

Many people do not see a problem with using the terms **convert** or **conversion**, describing the turning of people to Messiah faith. To many Jewish people who need to hear the good news, however, describing it in terms of "conversion" would mean that they would have to abandon their Jewish heritage and the great virtues of Jewish religion, to embrace another faith. *The Messianic Scriptures are clear that the First Century Jewish Believers did not abandon Judaism.* While one may be tempted to use convert as a neutral term—certainly as it is in many non-religious contexts—it is much better to employ terminology such as **turn** or **turning**, as in "the turning of the nations" (Acts 15:3, author's rendering).

The proper name of God in the Tanach is composed of the Hebrew consonants *yud, hey, vav, hey,* often represented in English as either **YHWH** or **YHVH**. Today's Bible scholars often think that it was originally pronounced as something close to either Yahweh or Yahveh. In most English Bibles, the Divine Name is rendered as "the LORD" in SMALL CAPITAL LETTERS, going back to the Second Temple convention of not speaking the Divine Name aloud. In the time of Yeshua, the Divine Name was only spoken aloud by the high priest on *Yom Kippur* (m.*Yoma* 6:2). Yeshua and the Apostles observed the standing Jewish practice of their day, by frequently using Hebrew titles such as *Adonai* or *Elohim* for the Supreme Being, their Greek equivalents being *Kurios* and *Theos*—the equivalents of our English titles Lord and God. Many Orthodox Jews today use the title *HaShem*, meaning "the Name," to refer to God. Unfortunately, the Sacred Name Only movement has infiltrated the Messianic movement via its literature and Bible versions, as it insists that one must affluently speak the Divine Name YHWH/YHVH in order to be truly saved. Speaking the Divine Name, at a main function of one's Messianic Jewish congregation, is going to create great challenges in presenting Jewish people with the good news—as they will most probably be offended and feel insulted, given the great sanctity with which Judaism has approached it. **When in doubt, speaking of God as "God," is entirely appropriate.**

The Messianic Walk

Approaching Messianic Prophecy

Integral to being involved with Jewish outreach and evangelism, is having some knowledge of the prophecies which foretell of the arrival of Yeshua the Messiah. Most Messianic congregations have regular teachings or classes on the Messiahship of Yeshua of Nazareth, which relate to prophecies from the Tanach (Old Testament). There have also been lengthy analyses produced, ranging from Michael Brown's five-volume *Jewish Objections to Jesus* series to *Isaiah 53 Explained* by Mitch Glaser. It is critical that each of us has a cursory understanding of how many Messianic prophecies have been approached across time: from Second Temple Judaism to later Rabbinical Judaism, as well as to evangelical Protestantism and the modern Messianic Jewish movement. Eventually as you develop relationships with Jewish people—even if many of them are non-religious—the question of whether Yeshua of Nazareth is indeed the anticipated Redeemer from the Tanach Scriptures, will arise.

How should any of us approach prophecies which speak of Yeshua of Nazareth? 1 Corinthians 15:3-4 direct, "For I also passed on to you first of all what I also received—that Messiah died for our sins according to the Scriptures, that He was buried, that He was raised on the third day according to the Scriptures" (TLV). I once encountered a teacher who, in fact, denied Yeshua as the Messiah because he could not find a direct prophecy which spoke of the Messiah being raised on the third day. Too many of us, as Western people, are inclined to think that all prophecies of the Messiah to come are predictive in nature. Too often having binary minds that think in 0s and 1s, we are conditioned to approach Messianic prophecy as one predictive prophecy *equaling* one fulfillment, and so forth. Of course, it should be understood that there are indeed many predictive prophecies which foretell of the arrival of the Messiah Yeshua and His death for us (i.e., Micah 5:2; Daniel 9:23-25; Isaiah 7:14; 9:6-7; Psalm 22; Isaiah 53:5-7), but there are other factors involving Yeshua's Messiahship which must be approached more thematically or typologically (i.e., Hosea 6:2; 11:1). These often involve the identification of Yeshua the Messiah with the nation of Israel, embodying the hopes and aspirations of Israel and its kingdom. What has happened to Israel, or what has happened to significant figures in Israel's history (i.e., Moses, David), have been to some degree repeated in the life and ministry of Yeshua of Nazareth.

The Contours of Jewish Evangelism

An ongoing feature of continued study and research in Messianic theology definitely involves a refinement of our understanding and approach to Yeshua's Messiahship. As the Messianic Jewish movement grew throughout the 1970s and into the 1990s, the Jewish anti-missionary movement also grew. Mainly made up of Orthodox Jews, the anti-missionary movement specifically targets Messianic Jewish Believers, in order to see them deny Yeshua as the Messiah. Frequently Jewish anti-missionaries will appear at Messianic Jewish conference events, or perhaps will even visit your own local congregation. Prominent Messianic Jewish evangelistic organizations tend to be those best equipped to handle some of the customary arguments of the anti-missionaries. Yet it also needs to be recognized that since the 1990s, as many more non-Jewish Believers have been directed into the Messianic movement, that the anti-missionary movement has been targeting many of these people as potential proselytes to the Synagogue. The Jewish anti-missionary movement affects everyone who is involved with declaring the good news that Yeshua is the Messiah of Israel.

Theological and Historical Complications

Having some handle on the Messianic prophecies of the Tanach is not going to be enough, in order to reach out with the good news to your Jewish friends and neighbors, as there are theological and historical complications you need to be conscious of. Some significant theological impediments toward reaching Jewish people, with the good news, include the errant Christian theologies of supersessionism and dispensationalism. Supersessionism is more commonly known as **replacement theology**, the idea that since the Jewish people have corporately rejected the Messiah, that God has rejected His people Israel, and has transferred the promises He gave to Israel to a new, independent "Church" entity. Prophecies in the Tanach which speak to the restoration of Israel in the end-times are not to be taken literally, but are instead to be allegorized as signs of spiritual bounty for the faith community. **Dispensationalism**, while rightly affirming God's continued fidelity to His promises with Israel and the Patriarchs, wrongly tends to divide up God's Word, believing that in the present with the widescale Jewish rejection of Yeshua, that God has presently put Israel aside and is working through the non-Jewish Christian Church. This will only change until the pre-tribulation rapture has taken place, and then God once again resumes His program with Israel. For non-Jewish Believers involved in Jewish outreach, these two extremes are to be avoided by stressing oneself as a fellow member of Israel's Commonwealth (Ephesians 2:11-13), who is actively interested and involved in the restoration of Israel's Kingdom (Acts 1:6).

The Messianic Walk

More historically, significant impediments are present when non-Jewish Believers mainly, but also some Jewish Believers raised in minimally religious families, assume things about Judaism, Jewish tradition, and Jewish culture *without doing any research*. Time and time again, people in today's Messianic movement have been caught saying inappropriate things about "the Rabbis" or "the Talmud," without ever having read or consulted what such Rabbis or what the Talmud has actually said. Perhaps in the diverse array of ancient Jewish literature there are incorrect statements made, and incorrect conclusions drawn, about a whole host of issues (among the many things which are correct), but misunderstanding and miscommunication occur when people are unwilling to give others a hearing. It is unfair and inappropriate to make conclusions about Judaism and Jewish history, without having done some homework first!

Yeshua the Messiah issued the ever-imperative word, "salvation is from the Jews" (John 4:22, TLV). Each of us in today's Messianic movement needs to recognize how unique and distinct the Jewish people are, as the bearers of the Messiah (Romans 9:5) to the entire world. Jewish outreach and evangelism is not something easy—and your Messianic congregation and venue is different than someone else's—**but it is absolutely vital for each Messianic person to be contributing to this cause in some way!**

How Do We Know that Yeshua of Nazareth is the Messiah?

Why do any of us believe that Yeshua (Jesus) of Nazareth, is the prophesied Messiah of Israel? As I have asked this question among many people in today's Messianic movement over the years—while I have found many people who have sincerely done their homework, and have investigated various Tanach prophecies and Second Temple Jewish expectations—I have found far many more who will give subjective answers based on their supernatural experiences. While it is commendable for us to know that on a particular date we were cleansed of our sins and redeemed by the atoning work of Yeshua, our supernatural experiences can never be used as a substitute for theologically processing *why* we believe that Yeshua is the Messiah. When visiting the synagogue in Berea, it is said that the people "received the message with goodwill, searching the Scriptures each day to see whether these things were true" (Acts 17:11, TLV). They heard the message that the Messiah of Israel had arrived, and they checked it against the Tanach. Unfortunately for far too many of today's Believers, we have simply been given Yeshua as the Messiah, and have not been forced into thinking through why we should even place our trust in Him.

Today's Messianic community is a venue for Jewish outreach and evangelism. Unlike more customary Protestant evangelism, where the main purpose is to reach out with the love of the Lord to a hurting world beset by sin—the Messianic community has to go further, in invoking the First Century dynamics of "God

The Messianic Walk

brought to Israel a Savior—Yeshua" (Acts 13:23, TLV), in actualy proving to some significant degree that Yeshua is the anticipated Messiah. For most of today's Messianic people, when presenting and/or defending the Messiahship of Yeshua of Nazareth, they will find themselves mainly resorting to various "proof texts" of Messianic prophecy. While not at all improper, many of us have little or no understanding as to why, and most especially how, the concept of a Messiah had developed by the period of Second Temple Judaism. We do not often consider how at various points, particularly crisis moments, in Biblical history, the concept of a Messiah who would resolve the problems of Israel and humanity, would substantially advance.

Many of today's Messianic people are involved in Jewish outreach and evangelism via their local congregation, and/or one of the many opportunities available through a major ministry operating in Israel or in a large Diaspora Jewish sector. These people do tend to be prepared, somewhat, for having to explain why they believe that Yeshua is the Messiah of Israel. Others, however, who are interested in Jewish outreach, may not be as adequately prepared. More disturbing, to be sure, would be those in positions of Messianic congregational leadership and teaching, who are not as well equipped as they ought to be, regarding the Messiahship of Yeshua of Nazareth. Fortunately, regardless of where we have been in our individual studies, the Lord will use circumstances to focus our attention on the necessary investigations that we need to undertake, in order to be ready to best declare the good news of Israel's Messiah to His Jewish people.

At one point in your Messianic experience, it is likely that you have encountered different materials or books or social media circulate in your local assembly, which at least questions whether or not Yeshua of Nazareth is the prophesied Messiah. *It is no more inappropriate to ask whether Yeshua is the Messiah, than it is inappropriate to ask whether or not there is a God.* **All of us, in trying to figure out who we are as spiritual human beings, need to ask the question of whether Yeshua is the Messiah.** Not infrequently, in thinking themselves to be prepared to speak of the good news of Yeshua to various Orthodox Jews, for example, one can encounter various Messianic people begin to seriously question whether He is truly the Messiah of Israel. When you see Messianics being influenced more by the people they are hoping to influence, it is a serious cause for concern. Every person, Jewish or non-Jewish, who is a part of today's Messianic movement, is a target for being influenced by the Jewish anti-missionary movement: Jewish groups whose mission it is to specifically speak out against the Messiahship of Yeshua of Nazareth.

What do we do when any of us hear some seemingly convincing arguments against Yeshua being the Messiah? Whether we realize it or not, the Lord does not intend us to cover our ears, hide under our beds, and hum very loudly as though we did not hear anything. Instead, this is a time for us to learn, to truly

How Do We Know That Yeshua of Nazareth is the Messiah?

consider why we believe that Yeshua is the Messiah, and to have theological confirmation in our minds of what we know in our hearts. Believe it or not, this is not something limited to an individual here or there; this is a group effort. The belief that Yeshua is the Messiah of Israel is something that Messianic congregations are to boldly declare to the Jewish community and to the world. But what does your congregation, fellowship, or study group do about this?

Does your assembly regularly have *Shabbat* messages, during the main service, on the Messiahship of Yeshua? Some Messianic congregations certainly do, but some Messianic congregations do not. What is the location of your assembly and its demographic profile? Some Messianic congregations' leadership are able to fairly balance the main Messianic mission of Jewish outreach and evangelism, while at the same time welcoming in non-Jewish Believers wanting to take hold of their faith heritage in Israel's Scriptures. Yet, some Messianic congregations can be so utterly overwhelmed with non-Jewish people, that the assembly becomes more about Hebrew Roots or Jewish Roots or Torah study, than it does about Jewish evangelism. A congregation focused on Jewish evangelism, will by necessity be teaching its people about the Messiahship of Yeshua. None of us wants to be open season for a personal visit from a Jewish anti-missionary, and see our faith shaken, when hearing claims against Yeshua—because little or no study on the Messiahship of Yeshua of Nazareth has been conducted.

The Concept of a Messiah in Second Temple Judaism

Ranging across the spectrum of Jewish history and theology, it is easily witnessed that there is a diverse array of options and opinions available at one's disposal, regarding the concept of "the Messiah." Those who place some importance on the life and ministry of Yeshua of Nazareth, must by necessity consider the ideas of a Messiah figure circulating within contemporary Second Temple Judaism. It is safe to say that there is no single school of thought regarding a Messiah in Second Temple Judaism, although it is widely agreed that the ideas of a Messiah figure had been piqued and honed as a consequence of the fall of Israel's Kingdom and the consequences of the exile. *That someone was to arise within the community of Israel, and fix the problems of the exile, was the major impetus behind Messianism.* Various groups within Second Temple Judaism—especially including the Pharisees and the Qumran community—had opinions about a kingly or anointed figure who would come and return Israel to its fullness. These opinions, however, were not unified.

While today's evangelical Protestants are likely to think in terms of the Messiah being a figure who would resolve the human sin problem, Ancient Jews were primarily looking for a Messiah to resolve the political disposition of Israel. Following the return of the Jewish exiles from Babylon and the reconstruction of Jerusalem and the Temple, there was still no political autonomy for Israel, and the

The Messianic Walk

Davidic throne was vacant. What did this mean? How could God allow this? This understandably focused the attention of many Jews on prophetic declarations and oracles speaking to the reconstitution of Israel's Kingdom and the Davidic monarchy. The Maccabean crisis of the Second Century B.C.E., though, saw a shift in some of the ideas of Messianism toward an eschatological state of being, with discussions and speculations associated with the Kingdom of Heaven, the resurrection of the dead, and the last judgment. Ideas of an entirely political Messiah figure were steadily meshed with ideas of a spiritual or priestly and/or prophetic Messiah figure—in no small part due to the religious corruption present in the First Century B.C.E. As noted by C.A. Evans in *Dictionary of New Testament Background*,

"In reaction to the oppression of Greek and Roman rule, and in response to what was perceived as usurpation of the high priesthood on the part of the Hasmoneans and their successors, hopes for the appearance of a righteous king and/or priest began to be expressed. The later usurpation of Israel's throne by Herod and his successors only fueled these hopes."[1]

Some of the major Tanach concepts of Second Temple Judaism, would have included the raising of David (Ezekiel 34:23-24; 37:24; Hosea 3:5), and the anticipation of some sort of new age for Israel (Isaiah 63:4; 65:25; Jeremiah 31:31-34; 34:16; Ezekiel 48:35). Intertwined within this are not just emphases on political independence and the restoration of the Davidic monarchy, but also the return of all of the exiles of Israel to the Promised Land, the restoration of proper Temple worship and a just priesthood, and most especially a commitment on the part of Israel to obey God's Torah.

While one's review of the Messianic claims of Yeshua of Nazareth, necessarily require an examination of the Tanach Scriptures and Apostolic Writings—various strata of extra-Biblical literature play some role in us considering various expectations present among Second Temple Jews. Pulling a number of themes from Isaiah 11; Ezekiel 34; and Psalm 2; and communicating in a style not unlike Psalm 89, the First Century B.C.E. *Psalms of Solomon* 17:21-25 witnesses the Son of David purging Jerusalem and destroying the God-less:

"See, Lord, and raise up for them their king, the son of David, to rule over your servant Israel in the time known to you, O God. Undergird him with the strength to destroy the unrighteous rulers, to purge Jerusalem from gentiles who trample her to destruction; in wisdom and in righteousness to drive out the sinners from the inheritance; to smash the arrogance of sinners like a potter's jar; to shatter all their substance with an iron rod; to destroy the unlawful nations with the word of

---

[1] C.A. Evans, "Messianism," in Craig A. Evans and Stanley E. Porter, eds., *Dictionary of New Testament Background* (Downers Grove, IL: InterVarsity, 2000), 699.

How Do We Know That Yeshua of Nazareth is the Messiah?

his mouth; at his warning the nations will flee from his presence; and he will condemn sinners by the thoughts of their hearts" (*Psalms of Solomon* 17:21-25).[2]

Likely appropriating themes from Zechariah 3, it is witnessed in the Dead Sea Scrolls that the Qumran community believed itself to be an established enclave "until there come the Prophet and the Messiahs of Aaron and Israel" (1QS 9.11).[3] The Messiah of Israel is approached as being a priestly type of figure, as seen in the expectation, "The procedure for the [mee]ting of the men of reputation [when they are called] to the banquet held by the society of the *Yahad*, when [God] has fa[th]ered (?) the Messiah (or when the Messiah has been revealed) among them: [the Priest,] as head of the entire congregation of Israel, shall enter first" (1QSa 2.11-12).[4] That the Messiah would be a priestly king is witnessed in additional remarks witnessed in the DSS:

> "This is the rule for those who live in camps, who live by these rules in the era of wickedness, until the appearance of the Messiah of Aaron" (CD 12.23).[5]

> "And this is the exposition of the regulations by which [they shall be governed in the age of wickedness until the appearance of the Messi]ah of Aaron and of Israel" (CD 14.19).[6]

> "they will escape in the time of punishment, but all the rest will be handed over to the sword when the Messiah of Aaron and of Israel comes" (CD 19.10).[7]

> "the Beloved Teacher dies until the Messiah from Aaron and from Israel appears" (CD 20.1).[8]

That the Messiah was anticipated to be some kind of a priestly king, a merging of the vocations of Levi and Judah, is also seen in statements made throughout the Pseudepigrapha:

> "When vengeance will have come upon them from the Lord, the priesthood will lapse. And then the Lord will raise up a new priest to whom all the words of the Lord will be revealed. He shall effect the judgment of truth over the earth for many days. And his star shall rise in heaven like a king; kindling the light of

---

[2] R.B. Wright, trans., "Psalms of Solomon," in James H. Charlesworth ed., *The Old Testament Pseudepigrapha*, Vol 2 (New York: Doubleday, 1985), 667.

[3] Michael Wise, Martin Abegg, Jr., and Edward Cook, trans., *The Dead Sea Scrolls: A New Translation* (San Francisco: HarperCollins, 1996), 139.

[4] Ibid., 147.

[5] Ibid., 70.

[6] Ibid., 72.

[7] Ibid., 58.

[8] Ibid., 59.

The Messianic Walk

knowledge as day is illumined by the sun. And he shall be extolled by the whole inhabited world. This one will shine forth like the sun in the earth; he shall take away all darkness from under heaven, and there shall be peace in all the earth. The heavens shall greatly rejoice in his days and the earth shall be glad; the clouds will be filled with joy and the knowledge of the Lord will be poured out on the earth like the water of the seas. And the angels of glory of the Lord's presence will be made glad by him. The heavens will be opened, and from the temple of glory sanctification will come upon him, with a fatherly voice, as from Abraham to Isaac. And the glory of the Most High shall burst forth upon him. And the spirit of understanding and sanctification shall rest upon him [in the water]. For he shall give the majesty of the Lord to those who are his sons in truth forever. And there shall be no successor for him from generation to generation forever. And in his priesthood the nations shall be multiplied in knowledge on the earth, and they shall be illumined by the grace of the Lord, but Israel shall be diminished by her ignorance and darkened by her grief. In his priesthood sin shall cease and lawless men shall find rest in him. And he shall open the gates of paradise; he shall remove the sword that has threatened since Adam, and he will grant to the saints to eat of the tree of life. The spirit of holiness shall be upon them. And Beliar shall be bound by him. And he shall grant to his children the authority to trample on wicked spirits. And the Lord will rejoice in his children; he will be well pleased by his beloved ones forever. Then Abraham, Isaac, and Jacob will rejoice, and I shall be glad, and all the saints shall be clothed in righteousness" (*Testament of Levi* 18).[9]

"To me God has given the kingship and to him, the priesthood; and he has subjected the kingship to the priesthood. To me he gave earthly matters and to Levi, heavenly matters. As heaven is superior to the earth, so is God's priesthood superior to the kingdom on earth, unless through sin it falls away from the Lord and is dominated by the earthly kingdom. For the Lord chose him over you to draw near to him, to eat at his table to present as offerings the costly things of the sons of Israel....And after this there shall arise for you a Star from Jacob in peace: And a man shall arise from my posterity like the Sun of righteousness, walking with the sons of men in gentleness and righteousness, and in him will be found no sin. And the heavens will be opened upon him to pour out the spirit as a blessing of the Holy Father. And he will pour the spirit of grace on you. And you shall be as sons in truth, and you will walk in his first and final decrees. This is the Shoot of God Most High; this is the foundation for the life of all humanity. Then he will illumine the scepter of my kingdom, and from your root will arise the Shoot, and through it will arise the rod of righteousness for the nations, to judge and to save all that call on the Lord" (*Testament of Judah* 21:2-5; 24).[10]

---

[9] H.C. Kee, trans., "Testaments of the Twelve Patriarchs," in James H. Charlesworth, ed., *The Old Testament Pseudepigrapha*, Vol 1 (New York: Doubleday, 1983), pp 794-795.
[10] Ibid., pp 800, 801.

How Do We Know That Yeshua of Nazareth is the Messiah?

"And a spirit of prophecy came down upon his mouth. And he took Levi in his right hand and Judah in his left hand. And he turned to Levi first and he began to bless him first, and he said to him, 'May the God of all, i.e. the LORD of all ages, bless you and your sons in all ages. May the LORD give you and your seed very great honor. May he draw you and your seed near to him from all flesh to serve in his sanctuary as the angels of the presence and the holy ones. May your sons' seed be like them with respect to honor and greatness and sanctification. And may he make them great in every age. And they will become judges and rulers and leaders for all of the seed of the sons of Jacob. The word of the LORD they will speak righteously, and all of his judgments they will execute righteously. And they will tell my ways to Jacob, and my paths to Israel. The blessing of the LORD shall be placed in their mouth, so that they might bless all of the seed of the beloved. (As for) you, your mother has named you 'Levi,' and truly she has named you. You will be joined to the LORD and be the companion of all the sons of Jacob. His table will belong to you, and you and your sons will eat (from) it, and in all generations your table will be full, and your food will not be lacking in any age. And all who hate you will fall before you, and all your enemies will be uprooted and perish, and whoever blesses you will be blessed, and any nation which curses you will be cursed.' And to Judah he said: 'May the LORD give you might and strength to tread upon all who hate you. Be a prince, you and one of your sons for the sons of Jacob; may your name and the name of your son be one which travels and goes about in all the lands and cities. Then may the nations fear before your face, and all of the nations tremble, [and every nation trembles]. And with you will be the help of Jacob and with you will be found the salvation of Israel. And on the day when you sit on your righteous throne of honor, there will be great peace for all the seed of the beloved's sons. Whoever blesses you will be blessed, and all who hate you and afflict you and curse you will be uprooted and destroyed from the earth and they shall be cursed'" (*Jubilees* 31:12-20).[11]

Noting a number of Tanach passages (Deuteronomy 5:28-29; 18:18-19; Numbers 24:15-17; Deuteronomy 33:8-11; Joshua 6:26), the DSS also catalogue some of the priestly expectations of the Messiah (4Q175).[12]

While a controversial text to be certain, that some Messianic ideas are present in the Book of *1 Enoch* is unavoidable. Perhaps with some allusions intended to Psalm 2; the Son of Man in Daniel 7:13; and even the Servant of Isaiah 49; 52:13-53:12, the Messiah is depicted as a transcendent Heavenly figure:

"In those days, the kings of the earth and the mighty landowners shall be humiliated on account of the deeds of their hands. Therefore, on the day of their misery and weariness, they will not be able to save themselves. I shall deliver them

---

[11] O.S. Wintermute, "Jubilees," in James H. Charlesworth ed., *The Old Testament Pseudepigrapha*, Vol 2 (New York: Doubleday, 1985), pp 115-116.

[12] Wise, Abegg, and Cook, pp 230-231.

into the hands of the my elect ones like grass in the fire and like lead in the water, so they shall burn before the face of the holy ones and sink before their sight, and no place will be found for them. On the day of their weariness, there shall be an obstacle on the earth and they shall fall on their faces; and they shall not rise up (again), nor anyone (be found) who will take them with his hands and raise them up. For they have denied the Lord of the Spirits and his Messiah. Blessed be the name of the Lord of the Spirits....For his might is in all the mysteries of righteousness, and oppression will vanish like a shadow having no foundations. The Elect One stands before the Lord of the Spirits; his glory is forever and ever and his power is unto all generations. In him dwells the spirit of wisdom, the spirit which gives thoughtfulness, the spirit of knowledge and strength, and the spirit of those who have fallen asleep in righteousness....And he said to me, 'All these things which you have seen happen by the authority of his Messiah so that he may give orders and be praised upon the earth'" (*1 Enoch* 48:8-10; 49:2-3; 52:4).[13]

Ideas of a Messianic figure functioning in roles of king, priest, prophet, and being exalted in Heaven, are witnessed across a broad selection of excerpts from Second Temple Jewish literature. And, there are doubtlessly other avenues or contours of Messianic expectation, to be considered and explored, as well. When Yeshua of Nazareth entered in on the scene in the First Century, in the world of Second Temple Judaism, there were various expectations—some more refined than others—of what the Messiah was likely going to do. While Jewish anti-missionaries will be seen to frequently dismiss the Messianic claims of Yeshua of Nazareth, they are also likely to be seen doing so without any engagement with some of the expectations of the broad time period in which He actually lived—and instead are more concerned with post-First Century C.E. diatribes and debates between the Jewish Synagogue and institutional Christian Church.

The Messianic Expectation from the Tanach

When considering the Messiahship of Yeshua of Nazareth, many people automatically assume that there are simply lists and collections of predictive prophecies in the Tanach (Old Testament) which were then fulfilled in His life and activities. It is to be properly recognized how there are various predictive prophecies in the Tanach, which are afforded fulfillment in the Apostolic Writings. Yet it is also clear that there are some passages in the Tanach, specifically ascribed to Yeshua of Nazareth, where a singular figure was not the original subject. And, there are also various Tanach passages applied to Yeshua, which raise some questions about authorial intent, among other things. While many laypersons do find themselves caught off guard by Tanach ascriptions to Yeshua of Nazareth,

---

[13] E. Isaac, trans., "1 (Ethiopic Apocalypse) of Enoch," in *The Old Testament Pseudepigrapha*, Vol 1, pp 35-36, 37.

How Do We Know That Yeshua of Nazareth is the Messiah?

theologians and commentators have certainly proposed various solutions to the challenges and difficulties presented. In his 1995 resource *The Messiah in the Old Testament*, Walter C. Kaiser offers three significant categories for readers approaching Tanach prophecy:

1. "***Direct prophecies*** are those in which the OT author looked directly at the messianic age, and his readers understood it as a prophecy about the Messiah."[14] Referenced as direct prophecies of the coming Messiah are Micah 5:1: "And you, O Bethlehem of Ephrath, last among the clans of Judah, from you one shall come forth to rule Israel for Me – one whose origin is from of old, from ancient times" (NJPS; cf. Matthew 2:6). Malachi 3:1: "Behold, I am sending My messenger to clear the way before Me..." (NJPS; cf. Mark 1:2; Matthew 11:10; Luke 7:27). Zechariah 9:9: "Rejoice greatly, fair Zion; raise a shout, fair Jerusalem! Lo, your king is coming to you. He is victorious, triumphant, yet humble, riding on an ass, on a donkey foaled by a she-ass" (NJPS; cf. Matthew 21:5; John 12:15).

2. "***Typical prophecies*** are different from direct prophecies in that their immediately referent in their own day was separated from that to which their ultimate referent pointed, though they were joined as one single meaning in that they shared at least one thing in common, which was at the heart of the prediction. In this category we have persons, institutions, or events that were *divinely designated* in the OT text to be models, previews, or pictures of something that was to come in the days of Messiah."[15] The Torah direction regarding the construction of the Tabernacle is noted: "And let them make Me a sanctuary that I may dwell among them. Exactly as I show you – the pattern of the Tabernacle and the pattern of all its furnishings – so shall you make it...Note well, and follow the patterns for them that are being shown you on the mountain" (Exodus 25:8-9, 40, NJPS). Since there was a Heavenly original for the Earthly implements, in dealing with various Messianic prophecies, so was there some kind of precedent in the Biblical record which found its ultimate fulfillment in the activities of Yeshua of Nazareth.

3. "The third type of prophecies quoted in the NT are ***applications***. Here the language of the OT text is used or appropriated, but no specific prediction was intended by the OT or claimed by the NT writer."[16] Matthew 2:23 is offered as an example of this: "and came and dwelt in

---

[14] Walter C. Kaiser, *The Messiah in the Old Testament* (Grand Rapids: Zondervan, 1995), 33.
[15] Ibid., 34.
[16] Ibid., 35.

a city called Nazareth, that what was spoken through the prophets might be fulfilled, 'He shall be called a Nazarene'" (author's rendering). Noted is the word of Isaiah 11:1 and the Hebrew *netzer* for "branch" (RSV/NRSV/ESV, NASU, NIV) or "twig" (NJPS): "A staff will emerge from the stump of Jesse and a shoot [*netzer*] will sprout from his roots" (ATS). Literary devices of some sort have been employed to posit Messianic fulfillment in the life of Yeshua.

Most of today's evangelical theologians and pastors—and by extension a wide number of Messianic congregational leaders and teachers—have been trained to read and interpret the Scriptures using the common historical-grammatical approach. Such a method follows the major premise of reading a Bible passage for what it meant to its original audience first, before deducing modern principles. Our ultimate appeal cannot be to English translations, but instead to the Hebrew and Greek source text. Investigation and consideration for some historical or cultural background, perhaps from some bodies of extra-Biblical literature or material, may be conducted. For many Tanach passages that are Messianic in nature, employing common historical-grammatical approaches, is entirely sufficient. However, it is clear enough that the fulfillment of various Tanach expectations can require some multi-dimensional thinking, particularly in terms if whether a previous figure or event in Ancient Israel represented something which would be witnessed later in the activities of Yeshua of Nazareth. This is where trying to not only enter into the reasoning processes of various Biblical authors is necessary, but also some consultation with Second Temple Jewish hermeneutics.

In a great deal of the anti-missionary materials that one will encounter, it will be frequently witnessed that the Messiahship of Yeshua of Nazareth is dismissed almost entirely on the basis of Him not accomplishing direct prophecies. Almost all appeals to the Tanach of Him embodying in His actions, things once witnessed in the lives of important figures such as Moses or David, or the corporate experience of the people of Israel, do not tend to be too widely considered. Still, it is to be appreciated that an author like David Klinghoffer has to admit, "it might be objected that while the Gospels' interpretations of these verses may be highly imaginative—or, to put it another way, highly strained—rabbinic exegesis is no less so...[W]hy would first-century believers in rabbinic Judaism reject Matthew's or John's understanding of the prophecies in question, subjecting them to a higher level of scrutiny than was applied to the teachings of the rabbis?"[17] Klinghoffer hardly agrees with the conclusions of the Apostolic Writings, but he at least acknowledges that some of its methodology is not at all irregular to Second Temple Judaism and the time thereafter.

---

[17] David Klinghoffer, *Why the Jews Rejected Jesus* (New York: Three Leaves Press, 2005), 85.

How Do We Know That Yeshua of Nazareth is the Messiah?

While predictive prophecies from the Tanach, and various other typologies, may tend to garner a sufficient amount of our attention in reviewing the Messiahship of Yeshua—having a wider view of the history and narratives of the Tanach is also most imperative. In his 1992 book, *Knowing Jesus Through the Old Testament*, Christopher J.H. Wright indicates the significance of "working back from actual events which happened in the...life of Jesus to certain Hebrew scriptures in which [one] now sees a deeper significance than they could have had before."[18] Sometimes today's Messianic community is not as adequately prepared as it thinks it is, in terms of understanding the Tanach Scriptures—as our studies tend to be focused more on the weekly Torah portions than anything else. Wright properly responds to the common evangelical dilemma of only looking at the Tanach as a collection of prophecy predictions about the Messiah. He observes, "the Old Testament is much more than a promise box full of blessed predictions about Jesus. It is primarily a story—*the* story of the acts of God in human history out of which those promises arose and in relation to which only they make sense."[19]

All of us, in our wanting to see the Messiahship of Yeshua properly defended, need to do more than love Him; we also need to be able to love the Scriptures which speak of Him and to His work, and inform us as to His worldview and values. For some who have either dismissed the possibility of Yeshua as Messiah, or worse, once expressed belief in Him—their denial may have taken place because Believers have not engaged sufficiently with the Tanach Scriptures on a whole panoply of issues directly and indirectly related to His Messiahship.

Tanach Prophecies Fulfilled by, or Involving, Yeshua of Nazareth

The First Century followers of Yeshua of Nazareth, whether it be those who encountered Him in person firsthand, encountered those who encountered Him firsthand, or simply heard enough about Him and saw supernatural actions performed in His name or authority—knew that they had to turn to the Tanach, the Scriptures of Israel, for confirmation regarding who He was. *Was Yeshua the Messiah of Israel?* While one's investigation of the Scriptures, for confirmation that Yeshua of Nazareth is the anticipated Messiah of Israel, can seemingly be endless—there is, nevertheless, a significant category of references to be recognized as significant, in order for a Bible reader to begin his or her investigation into the Messiahship of Yeshua.[20]

---

[18] Christopher J.H. Wright, *Knowing Jesus Through the Old Testament* (Downers Grove, IL: IVP Academic, 1992), 27.

[19] Ibid.

[20] The list followed in this article has been provided generously by Barry Rubin, gen. ed., *The Complete Jewish Study Bible* (Peabody, MA: Hendrickson, 2016), pp li-liv.

The Messianic Walk

Genesis 3:15: The seed of the woman would crush the head of the serpent

After Adam and Eve eat the forbidden fruit, it is decreed that the seed, a descendant, of the woman, would crush the head of the serpent, Satan (Genesis 3:15). Yeshua was born of a woman (Galatians 4:4), and was sent to destroy Satan's works (1 John 3:4).

Genesis 12:3: The seed of Abraham

The seed or posterity of Abraham was to bless all families of Planet Earth (Genesis 12:3). Yeshua the Messiah, and the redemption He provides, is to be recognized as the major fulfillment of this promise (Matthew 1:1; Acts 3:25; Galatians 3:16).

Genesis 17:19; 21:12: The seed of Isaac

Abraham was explicitly told by God that his son Isaac would be the child of promise (Genesis 17:19; 21:12; cf. Hebrews 11:17-19). Yeshua of Nazareth is a descendant of Isaac (Matthew 1:2; Luke 3:34).

Genesis 38:14; Numbers 24:17, 19: The seed of Jacob who will have dominion

Jacob was told by God that by his seed the families of Planet Earth would be blessed (Genesis 38:14). Balaam decreed that a star would come forth from Jacob (Numbers 24:17) who would have dominion (Numbers 24:19). Yeshua of Nazareth is a descendant of Jacob (Matthew 1:2; Luke 3:34), and is "the bright morning star" (Revelation 22:16).

2 Samuel 7:12-13; Isaiah 9:7; 11:1-5; Jeremiah 23:5: A descendant of Judah

The Prophet Nathan told David that a great descendant would come forth from him, whose throne would be established forever (2 Samuel 7:12-13). The Prophet Isaiah foretold of a righteous King who would have an everlasting government of peace (Isaiah 9:7), this King would come from Jesse and would judge the world in righteousness (Isaiah 11:1-5). The Prophet Jeremiah also decreed of a righteous Branch which would come from David, acting wisely and justly (Jeremiah 23:5).

Micah 5:2: Have Eternal Origins

The Prophet Micah decreed that the Messiah would have origins "from the days of eternity" (Micah 5:2, TLV). The Apostolic Writings all affirm that Yeshua had origins from outside this universe, at least implying some unique supernatural nature (John 1:1, 14; 8:58; Ephesians 1:3-4; Colossians 1:15-19; Revelation 1:8).

How Do We Know That Yeshua of Nazareth is the Messiah?

Psalm 2:7; Proverbs 30:4: The Son of God
Psalm 2:7 speaks of God's anointed, "You are My Son, today I have begotten You" (NASU), with Proverbs 30:4 raising the question, "Who has ascended into heaven and descended? Who has gathered the wind in His fists? Who has wrapped the waters in His garment? Who has established all the ends of the earth? What is His name or His son's name? Surely you know!" (NASU). Yeshua of Nazareth is regarded as God's beloved Son (Matthew 3:17), the Son of the Most High (Luke 1:32).

Isaiah 9:6-7; Jeremiah 23:5-6: Bear the Name of God
The Prophet Isaiah decreed of the Messiah, that "His Name will be called Wonderful Counselor, Mighty God My Father of Eternity, Prince of Peace" (Isaiah 9:6, TLV). The Prophet Jeremiah foretold that the Messiah's name would be "The LORD our righteousness" (Jeremiah 23:6, NASU). And the exclamation of Philippians 2:9-11 is that at the name of Yeshua every knee will bow and confess that He is Lord (YHWH).

Daniel 9:24-26: Come 483 years after the rebuilding of Jerusalem's wall
The Prophet Daniel foretold that "from the issuing of a decree to restore and rebuild Jerusalem until Messiah the Prince *there will be* seven weeks and sixty-two weeks" (Daniel 9:25, NASU). 483 years after the rebuilding of the wall of Jerusalem, the Messiah arrived on the scene (Matthew 2:1, 16, 19; Luke 3:1, 23).

Isaiah 7:14: Born of a virgin
The Prophet Isaiah foretold of how "*ADONAI* Himself will give you a sign: Behold, the virgin will conceive" (Isaiah 7:14, TLV). The Hebrew *almah* was rendered in the Greek Septuagint as *parthenos* or "virgin." This word is applied to the miraculous birth of Yeshua (Matthew 1:18-2:1; Luke 1:26-35).

Micah 5:2: Born in Bethlehem
The Prophet Micah spoke, "But you, Bethlehem Ephrathah—least among the clans of Judah—from you will come out to Me One to be ruler in Israel" (Micah 5:2, TLV). Yeshua was born in Bethlehem (Matthew 1:18-2:1; Luke 1:26-35).

Psalm 72:10-11: Adored by the great
The Messiah is to be honored by both kings and nations (Psalm 72:10-11). Magi from the East came to worship the child Yeshua (Matthew 2:1-11).

The Messianic Walk

Isaiah 40:3-5; Malachi 3:1: Preceded by a voice crying in the wilderness

Isaiah foretells of a voice crying in the wilderness, preceding the Messiah (Isaiah 40:3-5), and Malachi spoke of a messenger coming before the Lord (Malachi 3:1). These prophecies are applied to the unique figure of John the Immerser/Baptist (Matthew 3:1-3; Luke 1:17; 3:2-6), who announced the arrival of Yeshua.

Isaiah 11:2; 61:1; Psalm 45:7: Anointed with the Spirit of God

The Messiah was to be anointed and empowered with the Spirit of God in a very unique and significant way (Isaiah 11:2; 61:1; Psalm 45:7). Yeshua is noted as having the Spirit rest on Him at His immersion by John (Matthew 3:16); Yeshua is One who speaks the words of God because of the Spirit (John 3:34); Yeshua performed good works precisely because of the Spirit (Acts 10:38).

Deuteronomy 18:15, 18: A prophet like Moses

Moses told the Ancient Israelites that a prophet like him could arise in the future, and that the people were to heed anything that such a prophet would tell them, or face disastrous consequences (Deuteronomy 18:15, 18). The ultimate example of such a prophet is considered to be Yeshua the Messiah (Acts 3:20-22), as heeding or not heeding His words have eternal repercussions.

Isaiah 61:1-2: Possess a ministry promoting human wholeness

The Messiah's ministry will involve a significant proclamation of human wholeness to those who are oppressed: "To bring good news to the afflicted; He has sent me to bind up the brokenhearted, to proclaim liberty to captives and freedom to prisoners" (Isaiah 61:1, NASU). Yeshua specifically applied this word to Himself, at His home synagogue in Nazareth (Luke 4:18-19).

Isaiah 35:5-6; 42:18: Possess a healing ministry

Isaiah spoke of how the restoration of Zion would involve various physical acts of healing (Isaiah 35:5-6; 42:18). Certainly, healing is a significant feature of the actions of Yeshua (i.e., Matthew 11:5).

Isaiah 9:1-2: Minister in the Galilee

The Prophet Isaiah spoke of how "He will bring glory—by the way of the sea, beyond the Jordan—Galilee of the Gentiles" (Isaiah 9:1, TLV). The Messiah's ministry would involve how "The people walking in darkness will see a great light. Upon those dwelling in the land of the shadow of death, light will shine" (Isaiah 9:2, TLV). This prophetic word is specifically applied to Yeshua (Matthew 4:12-16).

How Do We Know That Yeshua of Nazareth is the Messiah?

Isaiah 40:11; 42:3: Tender and Compassionate
The Prophet Isaiah said, "Like a shepherd, He tends His flock. He gathers the lambs in His arms carries them in his bosom, and gently guides nursing ewes" (Isaiah 40:11, TLV). Justice will be fairly implemented (Isaiah 42:3). Yeshua was tactful in His ministry (Matthew 12:15, 20), and He participated in the human experience, being able to identify with the struggles of men and women (Hebrews 4:15).

Isaiah 42:2: Meekness
The Prophet Isaiah decreed of the Servant, "He will not cry out or raise *His voice*, nor make His voice heard in the street" (Isaiah 42:2, NASU). Yeshua issued instructions for His presence to not be widely known, even after performing miracles (Matthew 12:15-16, 19).

Isaiah 53:9: Sinless and Guileless
The Prophet Isaiah said, "His grave was assigned with wicked men, yet He was with a rich man in His death, because He had done no violence, nor was there any deceit in His mouth" (Isaiah 53:9, NASU). 1 Peter 2:22 applies this word to the activity of Yeshua.

Isaiah 53:11-12; Psalm 69:9: Bear what is due to others
The Prophet Isaiah foretold that the Servant will bear the transgressions and sin of many (Isaiah 53:11-12), echoed by Psalm 69:9. In Romans 15:3 Paul attests to how Yeshua was not concerned with pleasing Himself, but instead how the reproaches of others fell on Him.

Psalm 110:4: Serve in a priestly capacity
Psalm 110:4 speaks of God's anointed serving in a priestly capacity like Melchizedek. Throughout the Epistle to the Hebrews, Yeshua being the ultimate high priest, like the example of Melchizedek, is emphasized (Hebrews 5:5-6; 6:20; 7:15-17).

Zechariah 9:9: Enter into Jerusalem on a donkey
The Prophet Zechariah foretold, "Rejoice greatly, O daughter of Zion! Shout *in triumph*, O daughter of Jerusalem! Behold, your king is coming to you; He is just and endowed with salvation, humble, and mounted on a donkey, even on a colt, the foal of a donkey" (Zechariah 9:9, NASU). This word is applied to how Yeshua entered into Jerusalem, in the days before His execution (Matthew 21:1-11; Mark 11:1-11).

Malachi 3:1: Enter into the Temple with authority
Malachi 3:1 says that God's messenger "will suddenly come to His temple" (NASU). It can certainly be said that when Yeshua entered into the Temple complex, He disrupted the normal flow of activities (Matthew 21:12-24:1; Luke 2:27-38, 45-50; John 2:13-22).

Isaiah 49:7; Psalm 69:4: Be hated without a cause
Isaiah 49:7 speaks of "the One the nation abhors" (TLV). The prayer of David in Psalm 69:4 is, "Those who hate me without a cause outnumber the hairs of my head. Powerful are my enemies who would destroy me with lies" (TLV). Yeshua was unjustly hated (John 15:24-25).

Isaiah 53:2-3; 63:3, 5; Psalm 69:9(8): Rejected by His Own People
The Messiah was to be a figure largely rejected. "He was despised and rejected by others; a man of suffering and acquainted with infirmity; and as one from whom others hide their faces he was despised, and we held him of no account" (Isaiah 53:3, NRSV). Isaiah also decreed, "I have trodden the wine trough alone, and from the peoples there was no man with Me. I also trod them in My anger and trampled them in My wrath" (Isaiah 63:3, NASU). Frequently in the Gospels, Yeshua of Nazareth is dismissed as a nobody (Mark 6:3; John 7:3-5), and He has to find His own way (Luke 9:58). It is explicitly reported that His own Jewish people largely did not receive Him (John 1:11).

Psalm 118:22: Rejected by the Jewish Leadership
It was anticipated in Psalm 118:22, "The stone the builders rejected has become the capstone" (TLV). Yeshua applies this word to Himself, in how He is rejected by various Jewish religious leaders (Matthew 21:42; cf. John 7:48).

Psalm 2:1-2: Plotted Against by Jews and Pagans
Psalm 2:1-2 speaks of a conspiracy against the Lord and His Anointed from the nations of Planet Earth: "Why do nations assemble, and peoples plot vain things; kings of the earth take their stand, and regents intrigue together against the LORD and against His anointed?" (NJPS). This word is specifically applied to the death of Yeshua, enacted by a conspiracy of both the Romans and Jewish religious leaders.

Psalm 41:10(9); 55:13-15(12-14): Betrayed by a Friend
King David cried to the Lord, "Even my close friend in whom I trusted, who ate my bread, has lifted up his heel against me" (Psalm 41:9, NASU). Yeshua was betrayed to the Romans by Judas Iscariot (Matthew 26:21-25, 47-50; Acts 1:16-18), with the tenor of David's word invoked (John 13:18-21).

How Do We Know That Yeshua of Nazareth is the Messiah?

Zechariah 11:12: Be Sold for Thirty Pieces of Silver
Zechariah 11:12 says, "Then I said to them, 'If it seems good to you, pay me my wages, but if not, don't bother!' So they weighed out my wages—30 pieces of silver" (TLV). Judas Iscariot betrayed Yeshua for thirty pieces of silver (Matthew 26:15).

Zechariah 11:13: Betrayal Price Thrown into Temple Treasury
The price paid in Zechariah 11:12 is thrown into the Temple treasury: "Then ADONAI said to me, 'Throw it to the potter—that exorbitant price at which they valued Me!' So I took the 30 pieces of silver and threw them into the House of ADONAI, to the potter" (Zechariah 11:13, TLV). This is applied to what Judas did with the betrayal price that he received (Matthew 27:6-7).

Zechariah 13:7: Be Forsaken by His Own Disciples
Zechariah 13:7 declares, "'Awake, O sword, against My Shepherd, and against the man, My Associate,' declares the LORD of hosts. 'Strike the Shepherd that the sheep may be scattered; and I will turn My hand against the little ones'" (NASU). This word is applied to how subsequent to the arrest of Yeshua by the Romans, His Disciples scattered themselves (Matthew 26:31, 56).

Micah 4:14(5:1): Be Struck on the Cheek
Micah 5:1 says, "Now gather yourself in troops, O Daughter of Troops. He has laid siege against us. With a staff they have struck the Judge of Israel on the cheek" (TLV). Yeshua was unjustly beaten by the Romans, and mocked, as though He were a humiliated leader of Israel (Matthew 27:30).

Isaiah 50:6: Be Spat On
The Prophet Isaiah declared of the Servant, "I gave My back to those who strike Me, and My cheeks to those who pluck out the beard; I did not cover My face from humiliation and spitting" (NASU). Yeshua was beaten and spat on by both the Jewish religious leaders (Matthew 26:67) and Roman soldiers (Matthew 27:30).

Psalm 22:8-9(7-8): Be Mocked
King David exclaimed, "'Commit *yourself* to the LORD; let Him deliver him; let Him rescue him, because He delights in him'" (Psalm 22:8, NASU). While Yeshua is surely mocked before His execution (Matthew 26:67-68; 27:31), this word is specifically echoed by the religious leaders as He is dying (Matthew 27:39-44).

Isaiah 50:6: Be Beaten
The Prophet Isaiah foretold of the Servant, "I gave My back to those who strike, and My cheeks to those pulling out My beard; I did not hide My face from humiliation and spitting" (Isaiah 50:6, TLV). Yeshua was thoroughly beaten before His execution (Matthew 26:67; 27:26, 30).

The Messianic Walk

Psalm 22:16(15); Zechariah 12:10: Hands and Feet Pierced
Taking into consideration the textual witnesses of the Septuagint and other Hebrew manuscripts, Psalm 22:15 decrees, "For dogs have surrounded me. A band of evildoers has closed in on me. They pierced my hands and my feet" (Psalm 22:16, TLV). Zechariah 12:10 further states, "Then I will pour out on the house of David and the inhabitants of Jerusalem a spirit of grace and supplication, when they will look toward Me whom they pierced. They will mourn for him as one mourns for an only son and grieve bitterly for him, as one grieves for a firstborn" (TLV). These words are applied to the execution of Yeshua, being crucified by the Romans (Matthew 27:35; Luke 24:39; John 19:18, 34-37; 20:20-28; cf. Revelation 1:7).

Psalm 22:16(15): Thirsty During His Execution
King David said, "my vigor dries up like a shard; my tongue cleaves to my palate; You commit me to the dust of death" (Psalm 22:16, NJPS). During the execution of Yeshua, He experienced great thirst (John 19:28).

Psalm 69:22(21): Given Vinegar to Quench Thirst
King David said, "They give me gall for food, vinegar to quench my thirst" (Psalm 69:22, NJPS). During the execution of Yeshua, He was given vinegar to quench His thirst (Matthew 27:34).

Exodus 12:46; Psalm 34:21(20): Be Executed Without a Broken Bone
The Passover lamb was to be eaten without any broken bones (Exodus 12:46), and it is said of the righteous, "He {the Lord} keeps all his bones, not one of them is broken" (Psalm 34:20, NASU). When Yeshua was executed, not a single bone of His body was broken (John 19:33-36).

Isaiah 53:12: Be Considered a Transgressor
Isaiah 53:12 says of the Servant that He will be regarded as a transgressor: "I will allot Him a portion with the great, and He will divide the booty with the strong; because He poured out Himself to death, and was numbered with the transgressors; yet He Himself bore the sin of many, and interceded for the transgressors" (NASU). Yeshua was executed right alongside of known criminals (Luke 23:32).

Daniel 9:24-26: Be "cut off and have nothing. . ."
Speaking of the rebuilding of Jerusalem, Daniel prophesied, "it will be built again, with plaza and moat, even in times of distress. Then after the sixty-two weeks the Messiah will be cut off and have nothing" (Daniel 9:24b-25a, NASU). Yeshua of Nazareth was cut off after sixty-nine weeks (Daniel 9:24a) via His death (Romans 5:6; 1 Peter 3:18).

How Do We Know That Yeshua of Nazareth is the Messiah?

Isaiah 53:5-7, 12: Death Would Atone for Sins of Humanity
Isaiah spoke of how the iniquities of all would fall upon the Servant (Isaiah 53:5-7, 12). The death of Yeshua is portrayed in the Apostolic Writings as affecting the entire human race (Mark 10:45; John 1:29; 3:16; Acts 8:30-35).

Isaiah 53:9: Be Buried With the Rich
Isaiah 53:9 speaks of how "His grave was assigned with wicked men, yet He was with a rich man in His death, because He had done no violence, nor was there any deceit in His mouth" (NASU). Yeshua was interred in the tomb intended for Joseph of Arimathea (Matthew 27:57-60).

Isaiah 53:9-10; Psalm 2:7-8; 16:10: Be Raised From the Dead
Isaiah 53:10 foretold, "He will see *His* offspring, He will prolong *His* days, and the good pleasure of the LORD will prosper in His hand" (NASU). Psalm 2:8 states, "I will surely give the nations as Your inheritance, and the *very* ends of the earth as Your possession" (NASU). Psalm 16:10 explicitly remarks, though, "For You will not abandon my soul to Sheol; nor will You allow Your Holy One to undergo decay" (NASU). These words have all been applied to the resurrection of Yeshua from the dead (Matthew 28:1-20; Acts 2:23-36; 13:33-37; 1 Corinthians 15:4-6).

Psalm 16:11; 68:19(18); 110:1: Ascend to Right Hand of God
The right hand of God is a place of blessing and honor (Psalm 16:11), as is ascending into God's presence (Psalm 68:19). Psalm 110:1 explicitly states, "The LORD says to my Lord: 'Sit at My right hand Until I make Your enemies a footstool for Your feet'" (NASU). Yeshua ascended into Heaven (Luke 24:51; Acts 1:9-11), at the right hand of God (Acts 7:55; Hebrews 1:3).

Zechariah 6:13: Exercise Priestly Office in Heaven
Zechariah 6:13 explains, "He will build the Temple of *ADONAI*. He will bear splendor and sit and rule on His throne. Thus He will be a kohen [priest] on His throne. So a counsel of shalom will be between them both" (TLV). Romans 8:34 speaks of how "the Messiah Yeshua, who died and—more than that—has been raised, is at the right hand of God and is actually pleading on our behalf!" (CJB). Hebrews 7:25-8:2 explicitly goes into detail regarding the priestly ministry of Yeshua in the Heavenly Temple.

Isaiah 28:16; Psalm 118:22-23: Be the Cornerstone
Isaiah 28:16 declares, "Therefore thus says the Lord GOD, 'Behold, I am laying in Zion a stone, a tested stone, a costly cornerstone *for* the foundation, firmly placed. He who believes *in it* will not be disturbed'" (NASU). Psalm 118:22-23 further states, "The stone which the builders rejected has become the chief corner *stone*. This is the LORD's doing; it is marvelous in our eyes" (NASU). Yeshua is explicitly noted to be the Cornerstone (Ephesians 2:20), widely rejected by the

The Messianic Walk

Jewish religious leaders (Matthew 21:42; 1 Peter 2:5-7).

Isaiah 11:10; 42:1:
Be Sought After by the Jewish People and the Nations
Isaiah 11:10 decrees, "Then in that day the nations will resort to the root of Jesse, who will stand as a signal for the peoples; and His resting place will be glorious" (NASU). Isaiah 42:1 also states, "Behold, My Servant, whom I uphold; My chosen one *in whom* My soul delights. I have put My Spirit upon Him; He will bring forth justice to the nations" (NASU). The arrival of the Messiah will have an affect not only on Israel, but also the world at large (Acts 10:45-46; 13:46-48).

Isaiah 11:10; 42:1-4; 49:1-6: Be Accepted by the Nations
Isaiah 11:10 and 42:1-4 indicate that the Servant will be accepted by the peoples of Planet Earth. Isaiah 49:6 further states how the restoration of Israel's Kingdom and the salvation of the Earth are tied together: "It is too small a thing that You should be My Servant to raise up the tribes of Jacob and to restore the preserved ones of Israel; I will also make You a light of the nations so that My salvation may reach to the end of the earth" (NASU). Yeshua is represented as having a ministry that affected more than just His fellow Jews (Matthew 12:18-21; cf. Romans 9:30; 20:20; 11:11; 15:10).

Psalm 2:6: Be the King
Psalm 2:6 exclaims, "But as for Me, I have installed My King upon Zion, My holy mountain" (NASU). Yeshua, however, attested before Pontius Pilate that His Kingdom was not a worldly realm (John 18:33-37).

Zechariah 12:10; Psalm 22:17(16): Be Seen by Israel as Pierced
Factoring in the different witnesses of the Septuagint and other Hebrew fragments, the Messiah's being pierced at His execution would have a reverberating effect to His own Jewish people (Luke 24:39; John 19:34-37; Revelation 1:7).

Patiently Waiting for the Restoration of Israel

Having a good handle on an entire series of Bible passages from the Tanach (OT), which in some form or fashion have been applied to Yeshua of Nazareth, is very important when involving oneself in Jewish outreach and evangelism. Many who prepare to go out into the Jewish community, or even just talk to a Jewish friend or neighbor about Yeshua—will for the first time ever, as a result of such preparations, receive some significant level of confirmation that Yeshua truly is the anticipated Messiah of Israel. Indeed, the Bible passages that we have just summarized in this analysis, represent many of the key concepts and ideas that surround the work and activities of Yeshua of Nazareth. Each one of us has a responsibility to ourselves, and to our fellow brothers and sisters, to see that at

How Do We Know That Yeshua of Nazareth is the Messiah?

some time in our faith experience, **we know why we truly believe that Yeshua is the Messiah.** And from that probing of God's Word, we should then be able to hopefully better communicate such truths as we reach out with the Messianic movement's definite mission of impacting the Jewish community with the good news!

One of the certain expectations of Yeshua as Messiah, was His widescale rejection by the Jewish religious leaders. Indeed, Isaiah 50:6 declared, "I gave My back to those who strike, and My cheeks to those pulling out My beard; I did not hide My face from humiliation and spitting" (TLV). When involving oneself in Jewish outreach and evangelism—in no small part due to Christian anti-Semitism from past centuries, but also today due in large part due to liberal, progressive Judaism—those who reach out with the good news of Israel's Messiah to His Jewish people, are more likely going to be rejected than welcomed. While today's Messianics, and especially Messianic Jewish congregational leaders, can all give testimonies to how debating various Tanach passages with Orthodox Jews did not turn out too successfully—more often than not your experience in reaching out with the good news is going to involve liberal Jews whose spiritual experiences with God are quite nominal. Today's Messianic Believers, Jewish *or* non-Jewish, know more about the Holy Scriptures than most of today's Jewish people in North America. To them, the Bible is a collection of interesting stories. So, should you be rejected, or dismissed, or just ignored by such people—know that a great deal of the dismissal of Yeshua you may witness, **is more of a rejection of God.**

It is vital that each one of us, in our investigations involving the Messiahship of Yeshua, not forget the very heart of Yeshua for the redemption of His Jewish people and the City of Jerusalem. As our Lord prayed fervently in Matthew 23:37-39, "Yerushalayim! Yerushalayim! You kill the prophets! You stone those who are sent to you! How often I wanted to gather your children, just as a hen gathers her chickens under her wings, but you refused! Look! God is abandoning your house to you, leaving it desolate. For I tell you, from now on, you will not see me again until you say, 'Blessed is he who comes in the name of *Adonai*'" (CJB). Circumstances within modern Israel and the Jewish community have to change so that people naturally are inclined to wish upon others, good tidings from the God of Israel. The only real way that this will happen, is for those who already know the God of Israel and His Son, Yeshua, to love those in the Jewish community who need Him. And, for those who should know the God of Israel to realize that they truly need Him.

Knowing that Yeshua of Nazareth is the Messiah of Israel certainly involves the necessary study of Holy Scripture, to confirm that He is the One anticipated to bring redemption to Israel and the world. Knowing that Yeshua of Nazareth is the Messiah of Israel also involves each of us diligently following Him, as those who have placed our trust in His work, and who have the confidence that He will return again. We each need to be patient as we experientially know Him, and represent

The Messianic Walk

Him not just to a world which needs His salvation and to heed His teachings and example—but most especially those of His very Jewish people!

The Wild and Wonderful World of the Broad Messianic Movement

Any one of us, who has read the Gospels and Acts, is undeniably struck by the fact that the message of the arrival of Israel's Messiah, was first proclaimed to the Jewish people—**and the necessity of proclaiming the good news to today's Jewish people is hardly on the spiritual radar of contemporary evangelicalism.** With a handful of exceptions (i.e., Matthew 8:9; Luke 7:8), the quantitative declaration of the good news, to those of the nations, did not take place until after Peter's vision in Acts ch. 10. Of course, as a Tanach prophecy like Isaiah 49:6 would declare, "It is too trifling a thing that You should be My servant to raise up the tribes of Jacob and restore the preserved ones of Israel. So I will give You as a light for the nations, that You should be My salvation to the end of the earth" (TLV). However, given some of the controversies regarding the inclusion of Greek and Roman Believers in the First Century Body of Messiah—particularly as seen in parts of Galatians and Romans—many of the Jewish Believers did not consider the anticipated restoration of Israel's Kingdom (Acts 1:6) to be intertwined with the salvation of people from the masses of humanity.

History has borne out that by the mid-First Century, more people from the nations at large were receiving Israel's Messiah, than the Messiah's own Jewish people. In Romans chs. 9-11, the Apostle Paul was distraught over the widescale dismissal of Yeshua by his fellow Jews, but did recognize that it had to be a part of God's plan. Non-Jewish Believers would have a responsibility, though, of provoking

The Messianic Walk

Jewish people to jealousy for faith in Yeshua (Romans 11:11), not be arrogant against the natural branches (Romans 11:18), and be vessels of grace and mercy to the Jewish people (Romans 11:30-31). Unfortunately, Paul's direction has not been implemented over the centuries—and rather than seeing non-Jewish Believers in Israel's Messiah demonstrate His love to the Jewish people, instead discrimination, persecution, and atrocities have taken place. Only in our generation, perhaps, have some of the directions of Romans chs. 9-11 been taken more seriously by non-Jewish Messiah followers.

The Messianic Jewish Movement

The development of today's modern Messianic Jewish movement goes back to the late 1960s and early 1970s, as Jewish Believers in Israel's Messiah established congregations, synagogues, and assemblies with the mission of facilitating **Jewish outreach, Jewish evangelism, and solidarity with the State of Israel.** This is a mission which continues to our present day, and should ever be on the hearts and minds of those involved with today's Messianic congregations. A major reason, for the establishment of Messianic Jewish congregations, was to combat the errant idea that Jewish people, who come to faith in Israel's Messiah, stop being Jewish, start being "Christian," and should readily assimilate into a non-Jewish Christian Church system and culture. In stark contrast to this, Jewish people coming to faith in Israel's Messiah, hardly stop being Jewish; some would say that being a Believer in Israel's Messiah is one of the most Jewish things that one can do. The Messianic Jewish movement is present, to particularly communicate to the wider non-believing Jewish community, that expressing faith in Yeshua of Nazareth does not mean an abandonment of one's Jewish heritage and traditions. For much of Messianic Judaism's modern history, these convictions have put it at odds with a great deal of traditional Christianity.

Throughout much of the 1980s and into the 1990s, Messianic Judaism grew, primarily in North America, with the establishment of congregations to reach out to the local Jewish community in their immediate vicinity. This mission continues to our present day. However, while the original vision and purpose of the Messianic Jewish movement innately involved Jewish outreach, evangelism, and Israel solidarity—Messianic Jewish rabbis and congregational leaders frequently do get invited to speak at evangelical churches, and in particular speak not only on the Messiah in the Biblical festivals, but frequently host Passover *seder* presentations. The late 1990s saw a wide number of non-Jewish Believers being called into the Messianic community, for a variety of reasons. Many of these reasons involved evangelical Believers wanting to partake of their Jewish Roots in tangible ways, learning about the Tanach or Old Testament on a more regular basis, and participating in things that Yeshua and His first followers did. Some Messianic Jewish congregations were very welcoming of such non-Jewish Believers as their

The Wild and Wonderful World of the Broad Messianic Movement

fellow brothers and sisters, actually concluding that as the Messiah's return was steadily approaching, that the Messianic movement would probably start looking more and more like the First Century *ekklēsia*. Others, however, did not act so positively toward the large numbers of non-Jewish Believers coming into their ranks. Were these people going to help aid Jewish outreach and evangelism, or bring an all new series of issues (and problems) into the assembly?

Following the turn of the Millennium in the early 2000s, there were varied Messianic Jewish reactions to the many non-Jewish Believers coming into the Messianic movement. Some of these reactions were positive, and others were negative. Messianic Jewish leaders have properly emphasized that non-Jewish Believers need to be supernaturally called into the Messianic movement (certainly at this phase of its development), and committed to Jewish ministry, even though it will obviously involve some significant investigation and study of their own faith heritage in Israel's Scriptures. *This would also necessarily include being sensitive to Jewish concerns and historical resistance to Yeshua the Messiah.* Many Messianic Jewish leaders have eagerly embraced non-Jewish participation in the Messianic Jewish movement, with an emphasis on congregations representing the "one new man" or "one new humanity" of Ephesians 2:15, where all can confess sins of prejudice and misunderstanding to each other, and we can pool our talents and resources for the salvation and restoration of Israel (cf. Romans 11:26). Other sectors of the Messianic Jewish movement have not been so welcoming of non-Jewish Believers in its ranks. And, because of this, a number of movements or sub-movements spun off of the Messianic Jewish movement, from the 1980s to the 2000s.

It is safe to say, that just as many of the First Century Jewish Believers did not anticipate many Greeks and Romans embracing faith in Israel's Messiah—so did a number of Messianic Judaism's early pioneers not prepare themselves sufficiently for non-Jewish Believers coming into the Messianic movement. The salvation of the nations at large was anticipated in the Tanach, and in the case of non-Jewish Believers being drawn into the Messianic movement in significant numbers, in modern times, it is also prophesied that the nations will stream to Zion to be taught God's Instruction, resulting in worldwide peace (Isaiah 2:2-4; Micah 4:1-3). These prophecies are taking place in our day, just as in our day more Jewish people have come to Messiah faith than since the times of the Messiah. Yet, a holy message of seeing all of God's people with a faith grounded in all of God's Word, has been frequently used in an inappropriate manner to promote division, rather than to better understand the ways of God, so that we can better and more genuinely understand the two critical commands of loving Him and neighbor (Deuteronomy 6:5; Leviticus 19:18).

The Messianic Walk

The One Law/One Torah Sub-Movement

In the early 2000s, a prominent movement that broke off of Messianic Judaism, is frequently known by the label of **One Law/One Torah.** To its credit, it honestly sought an answer for the place of non-Jewish Believers within the Commonwealth of Israel (Ephesians 2:11-13) as co-heirs with Jewish Believers (Ephesians 3:6). It usefully decided that non-Jewish Believers in the Messianic movement are like the sojourners or *gerim* who entered into Ancient Israel, professing belief in Israel's God, and entering into the community. Because sojourners or *gerim* could be among those easily taken advantage of, the Torah includes explicit instruction to the Israelites that they were to be shown hospitality. The sojourner in Ancient Israel was to actually be treated by the native born as though he were native born: "When a stranger resides with you in your land, you shall not do him wrong. The stranger who resides with you shall be to you as the native among you, and you shall love him as yourself, for you were aliens in the land of Egypt; I am the LORD your God" (Leviticus 19:33-34, NASU). It was hardly unreasonable or unfair to suggest that non-Jewish Believers, in today's Messianic movement, be shown the same welcome that sojourners in Ancient Israel were demonstrated.

Much of the One Law/One Torah sub-movement's ideology is focused around a number of Torah passages which stress either "one law" or "one statute" to be followed by those within the community of Ancient Israel (i.e., Exodus 12:48-49; Leviticus 24:22; Numbers 9:14; 15:15-16). A statement such as "There shall be one standard for you; it shall be for the stranger as well as the native, for I am the LORD your God" (Leviticus 24:22, NASU), would be applied by proponents of a One Torah theology as a universal statement for all in the community of Ancient Israel following the same Torah. While passages that use terminology such as "one law" or "one statute" should be able to be examined for what they mean within Torah jurisprudence—are such remarks involving "one law" or "one statute" universal statements, or principally statements regarding the legislation immediately detailed?

Leviticus 24:22, for example, is immediately preceded by how natives and sojourners, equally within Ancient Israel, were to be stoned to death for blasphemy: "Moreover, the one who blasphemes the name of the LORD shall surely be put to death; all the congregation shall certainly stone him. The alien as well as the native, when he blasphemes the Name, shall be put to death" (Leviticus 24:16, NASU). When an act of blasphemy was committed within Ancient Israel, by either a native or a sojourner, the uniform penalty of capital punishment was to be enacted. It was not as though a native born could be issued a corporal punishment such as a flogging, or have to pay a heavy fine—with the sojourner only subject to capital punishment. In high legal matters where the native born of Israel might have been shown preferential treatment or special favors, there was to be a uniform standard.

The Wild and Wonderful World of the Broad Messianic Movement

The Torah's instruction includes a number of significant areas detailing both the native born Israelite's, and well as the sojourner's, obedience and standing (Exodus 12:10; Leviticus 16:29; 17:15; 18:26; Numbers 35:15; Deuteronomy 1:16). And frequently, sojourners were to be regarded as a part of the broad community of Israel. However, it is hardly as though there were no differences of any kind between the two. Sojourners, unless being circumcised and intermarrying into one of the Twelve Tribes of Israel, did not have any sort of ancestral claim on the Promised Land. Likewise, due to their frequently low economic status, sojourners in Ancient Israel were often recipients of welfare (Leviticus 19:10; 23:22; Deuteronomy 10:18; 14:21). While sojourners and natives in the community of Ancient Israel had a great deal in common, there were also differences as well. Advocates of a One Law/One Torah theology, do not tend to be willing to discuss those differences.

While there are well-meaning and sincere advocates of a One Law/One Torah theology, who have made useful theological contributions, there is a deep ideological problem with emphasizing Bible passages that use the terminology "one law" or "one statute" as a credo. Each one of these passages involves an original setting in Ancient Israel that has been *directly affected* by the death, burial, and resurrection of Yeshua the Messiah—and the post-resurrection era in which we live. A frequent criticism of those who identify as One Law/One Torah, is that they are very legalistic and rigid in their approach to Moses' Teaching. This is hardly a surprise if "one law" originally involved settings such as uniform capital punishment for those in Ancient Israel! Yeshua the Messiah, via His sacrifice on the tree, absorbed the capital penalties of the Torah onto Himself (Colossians 2:14).

Rather than emphasize passages that employ "one law" terminology, it is far better to stress education and training in Moses' Teaching, for the Jewish and non-Jewish Believers who make up today's Messianic movement: "Assemble the people, the men and the women and children and the alien who is in your town, so that they may hear and learn and fear the LORD your God, and be careful to observe all the words of this law" (Deuteronomy 31:12, NASU). An educational model, of receiving Torah instruction, will facilitate the work of the Holy Spirit via the power of the New Covenant, which is to supernaturally transcribe God's commandments onto a redeemed heart and mind (Jeremiah 31:31-34; Ezekiel 36:25-27). A redeemed heart and mind are not rigid and inflexible when it comes to implementing God's Instruction in complicated Twenty-First Century circumstances.

The Two-House Sub-Movement

Around the turn of the Millennium, and extending into the early 2000s, another major sect that spun off of Messianic Judaism was the **Two-House** movement. Many of the people, who were initially involved in the Two-House sub-movement, had been non-Jewish Believers who had felt unwelcomed or dismissed from

The Messianic Walk

Messianic Judaism. In feeling spurned or marginalized in Messianic Jewish settings, and also concluding that they could not return to their previous Christian experience, a wide array of questions about *why* they had been drawn toward the Messianic movement and their faith heritage in Israel's Scriptures were being asked. A number of today's Messianic Jews are of the opinion that various non-Jewish Believers in the Messianic movement are indeed here because they have distant Jewish ancestry which has asserted itself in some way, as the Messiah's return draws closer. People, who identify as being Two-House, think that most of today's non-Jewish Believers, involved in today's "things Messianic," are here, in slight contrast, because they are most probably descendants of the Ten Lost Tribes.

Anyone who studies the Tanach Scriptures should very much be aware of how following the death of King Solomon, the Kingdom of Israel split into the Northern Kingdom of Israel or Ephraim, and the Southern Kingdom of Judah. The Divided Kingdom era is a part of legitimate Biblical history, recorded in the Books of Kings and Books of Chronicles, and reflected in the Prophets. As a matter of Biblical history, it also has to be recognized that when the Northern Kingdom of Israel/Ephraim fell to the expanding Assyrian Empire in 722-721 B.C.E., that a sizeable enough part of its population was deported. Many of these people, in being forcibly transversed to other parts of the Assyrian Empire, in the Middle East, were forced to intermarry with other conquered peoples. Anyone involved in Biblical Studies has to acknowledge that the exact whereabouts, of what are commonly called the Ten Lost Tribes, has been a matter of much speculation—as well as myth—throughout history.

There are Tanach prophecies, detailing the final restoration of Israel's Kingdom, which surely involve the reunion of people from both the Northern and Southern Kingdoms (i.e., Isaiah 11:12-16; Jeremiah 31:6-10; Ezekiel 37:15-28; Zechariah 10:6-10). The famed two-stick oracle of Ezekiel 37:15-28, for example, is recognized as being a futuristic, yet-to-be fulfilled prophecy, by both Jewish and Christian commentators alike—and for many of the latter, as something which will be directly involved with the Messiah's Second Coming. Certainly as a matter of Bible study and eschatology, considering prophetic passages of the Tanach which involve the Northern and Southern Kingdoms as participants, should not be a huge issue. If, for example, there are people who are descendants of the exiled Northern Kingdom, to be reunited with those of the Southern Kingdom, *before the Messiah's return*, then it is something for us to contemplate in regard to how soon, or how not so soon, Yeshua will come back.

Among both Jewish and Christian Bible scholars today, it is recognized that in spite of some of the unwarranted speculation and mythology that has been witnessed in history regarding the Ten Lost Tribes—that there are pockets of people groups on Earth today, who are separate from the Jewish community, but nevertheless have some oral traditions or customs going back to Ancient Israel.

The Wild and Wonderful World of the Broad Messianic Movement

There are pockets of people in remote corners of places like Southeast Asia, South Asia, the Middle East, the Eastern Mediterranean basin, and the environs of Central Africa, who claim to be descendants of the exiled Northern Kingdom—and have been confirmed as likely members of the Ten Lost Tribes by Jewish authorities in Israel, usually enjoined by DNA analysis. These are the areas which generally fall within the sphere of influence of the old Assyrian, Babylonian, and Persian Empires, and where the exiles of the Northern Kingdom could have been legitimately deported, scattered, and/or assimilated (cf. Jeremiah 31:10; Hosea 8:8-9; Amos 9:8-9).

The Two-House sub-movement, in originally seeking an answer for the place of many non-Jewish Believers in today's Messianic movement, drew the assumption that they are most probably descendants of the Ten Lost Tribes—even though such people had no quantitative evidence for Semitic ancestry. The Two-House sub-movement widely believes that there are hundreds of millions, or even billions, of physical descendants of Abraham, Isaac, and Jacob on Planet Earth today, in spite of the Torah word that the numbers of Israel will not be so numerous (Deuteronomy 28:62).

In spite of the non-Jews who make up the Two-House sub-movement, self-identifying as "Ephraim"—and wanting some kind of reunion with "Judah"—the Two-House sub-movement is broadly hostile to a great deal of mainline Jewish traditions and customs. This is most frequently evident by Two-House people often following a different calendar for the appointed times than the mainstream Jewish calendar, affluent use of the Divine Name YHWH/YHVH rather than acceptable titles such as God or Lord, and even a tacit acceptance of polygamy by some of its leaders. (A few of those within the Two-House sub-movement do not believe that today's Ashkenazic Jews are legitimate Semites, they think that the State of Israel is a Luciferian counterfeit, and they are even Holocaust deniers.) **Messianic Judaism has had every reason to at least be concerned, when people identifying as "Two-House" visit its assemblies.**

The place of non-Jewish Believers within Messianic congregations, definitely needs to be one where they are welcomed as equal brothers and sisters in the Lord, with gifts and talents and skills which need to be appreciated and used. One does not have to be of physical Israel in order to be accepted into the Kingdom of God—because physical ancestry *of any kind* hardly merits someone eternal salvation (cf. Romans 2:9). As a matter of our Biblical Studies, we do need to carefully and reasonably be able to discuss the Divided Kingdom era of Ancient Israel's history, and be able to sort through much of the fact and fiction involved with the deportation of exiles from the Northern Kingdom by Assyria. Various Messianic Jewish ministries of today have recognized legitimate people groups from Asia and Africa descended from the Ten Lost Tribes, and it is likely these people who will be among the participants in prophecies like Ezekiel 37:15-28.

The Messianic Walk

The Hebrew Roots Movement

There are many non-Jewish Believers, who in the 2000s felt unwelcome in various Messianic Jewish congregations, felt welcomed in the Two-House sub-movement, identified as some sort of "Israelite" for a season—but then who thankfully saw some of the extremism present in the Two-House sub-movement regarding the Lost Tribes and physical identity. By the late 2000s and into the 2010s, many who had been involved in the Two-House sub-movement, legitimately tried to shed some of the tall tales involving the Lost Tribes, and instead attempted to focus more on what it meant for non-Jewish Believers to be grafted-in to the olive tree of Israel (Romans 11:16-17ff), and more consciously associating with their faith heritage in the Tanach Scriptures. Many non-Jews had been a part of the Two-House sub-movement, for a season—not necessarily because they thought they were members of the Ten Lost Tribes—but instead because they felt more welcomed and included than they would be in various Messianic Jewish venues.

In the 1990s, when one encountered the term "Hebrew Roots" being used, it was most probably employed by various evangelical Christian teachers trying to stress how Christian people have a faith heritage in the Old Testament, the Bible of Jesus, and that it is important for people to understand the richness of the Hebrew language and how the Tanach points to the Messiah. The term "Hebrew Roots," for many, was a synonym for "Jewish Roots," or the term "Hebrew Roots" was used as a compliment to the term "Jewish Roots." The term "Hebrew Roots" was a term which could be employed to specifically emphasize the foundational importance of the Hebrew Scriptures, the importance of Hebrew language study, and getting Christian people plugged into more detailed examination of the Old Testament. The term "Jewish Roots" could be used to emphasize study of the Second Temple Judaism of Yeshua and His first disciples, the necessary examination of the broad history of this period and immediately thereafter, as well as a review of significant bodies of extra-Biblical and Rabbinical literature germane to this time. Certainly in many of my own writings, I have stressed how we all have Hebrew Roots in the Tanach Scriptures, and Jewish Roots in the Second Temple faith of Yeshua and His early disciples.

As various non-Jewish people sought to distance themselves from the label "Two-House" in the late 2000s and early 2010s, many of them instead began to use the term **Hebrew Roots**. For some of these people, this involved a sincere desire of wanting to study the Tanach Scriptures and live in a similar manner to Yeshua and His first followers. Many who have used the term "Hebrew Roots" have done so to legitimately stress a Biblical faith rooted in the Tanach Scriptures. For others, however, the term "Hebrew Roots" became a moniker to be sensationalized and abused, as in the late 2010s the term "Hebrew Roots" has become something largely associated with a non-Jewish movement, **not at all interested in Jewish outreach or evangelism,** widely dismissive of mainline Jewish traditions and customs, and at times with an even wider array of problems than those identifying as Two-House ever had. Many non-Jewish people who are involved in "Hebrew Roots" not only have a great deal of unfair disdain toward the Jewish Synagogue, but also the positive legacy of evangelical Protestantism. An entire host of sensationalistic hype is today connected to the label "Hebrew Roots," not only involving a great deal of end-time paranoia and fear, but also conspiracy theories, postulations about the Nephilim of Genesis 6, and most recently Flat Earth—among other things. **It is an understatement to say that today, when the term "Hebrew Roots" is invoked, that many of today's Messianic Jewish leaders and teachers get tense.**

Navigating Our Future

The emergence of today's Messianic movement on the scene, represents the last final spiritual move of God, *before* the final stretch of history culminating in the return of Israel's Messiah. At no time in history, since the First Century C.E., have more Jewish people come to faith in Yeshua of Nazareth. And, similar to the First Century Body of Messiah, many non-Jewish Believers are in close, regular communion with these Jewish Believers. In no uncertain terms, a number of the issues which arose in the First Century, are manifesting themselves today in various forms. But, unlike the past, we have the teacher of history to inform us about mistakes which do not have to be repeated!

A number of the early Messianic Jewish pioneers could not have foreseen how today, as the 2010s close, that there are additional sectors using the term "Messianic." Within the Tanach, it is legitimately anticipated how those from the nations will be involved in the restoration of Israel, contributing their various riches (Isaiah 45:14; 61:6; Micah 4:13). Because of the provision of the Messiah to those of the nations, non-Jewish Believers are to provide blessings to the Jewish people, and Jewish and non-Jewish followers of Israel's God are to be equal (2 Corinthians 8:13-14). All of us who have been chosen, to be a part of the Messianic movement at this time in history, are to pool our gifts, talents, and resources for the work which sits directly in front of us. **This work directly concerns the salvation of Jewish people.** As Romans 11:16 should astutely remind each of us, "For if their rejection leads to the reconciliation of the world, what will their acceptance be but life from the dead?" (TLV).

How concerned are the non-Jewish sub-movements or spin-offs, we have just reviewed, with the original Messianic Jewish vision of Jewish outreach, Jewish evangelism, and Israel solidarity? As things stand today, with the 2020s on our doorstep, it is fair to say that the non-Jewish people identifying as One Law/One Torah, Two-House, or even Hebrew Roots, are not too concerned as they should

The Messianic Walk

be, with seeing their Jewish neighbors and friends come to Messiah faith. While these people have appreciably come to a knowledge of their spiritual heritage in the Scriptures of Israel, being better educated and informed to various degrees—are they able to take such knowledge and information, and contribute to developing relationships with Jewish people who need the salvation of Yeshua? Are they helping to facilitate a more stable and effective Messianic movement, or are they fracturing it further and further? When difficult times arise, and anti-Semitism increases—will these non-Jewish people, in these different sectors, truly stand with the Jewish people and with Messianic Jewish Believers? Or, similar to how Peter denied the Lord three times, will these non-Jewish people be seen to deny their involvement with anything "Messianic"?

The Messianic world of today is both wild and wonderful. Our faith community possesses a great deal of potential to make a difference, provided we do not forget its Romans 11:26 trajectory. Are there things involved in the Messianic experience that go beyond Jewish outreach and evangelism? Yes. But things involving non-Jewish Believers entering into the mix, are not solely so such people can be spiritually enriched, and then later leave, do their own thing, and become opportunists. All of us, in spite of some of the confusion that is out there, need to be committed to a future where we remain true to the original mission of the Messianic movement, while still being flexible enough to address the issues of the day.

STUDY QUESTIONS FOR UNIT FOUR

1. How have you been involved in declaring the good news to your friends and neighbors? Why do you think that Jewish evangelism might be somewhat different than reaching other people groups?

2. Why are some of the standard religious terms, used by contemporary Christianity, rather offensive to Jewish people? Have you ever consciously considered how other people might be turned off to the good news, by a word or term that you have used?

3. What are some of the significant ways that you can reach out to your Jewish friends and neighbors with the good news of Messiah? How much do you understand the Jewish struggle in history? How much do you need to improve your understanding of the Jewish experience?

4. In your own words, summarize the importance of Jewish outreach and evangelism. How important is this to your local assembly? How important is it to you, personally?

5. Are you aware of the various non-Jewish movements, associated with the term "Messianic" in some way? Have you ever encountered them? If so, describe your experience.

6. What do you think might be the major problem involved with the various non-Jewish movements associating as "Messianic" or "Hebrew Roots"? Do you think they are facilitating the legitimate purposes of the Messianic mission? Why or why not?

JEWISH OUTREACH AND EVANGELISM
FOR FURTHER READING AND EXPLORATION

Brown, Michael L. *Answering Jewish Objections to Jesus: General and Historical Objections* (Grand Rapids: Baker Books, 2000).

_____. *Answering Jewish Objections to Jesus, Volume 2: Theological Objections* (Grand Rapids: Baker Books, 2000).

_____. *Answering Jewish Objections to Jesus, Volume 3: Messianic Prophecy Objections* (Grand Rapids: Baker Books, 2003).

_____. *Answering Jewish Objections to Jesus, Volume 4: New Testament Objections* (Grand Rapids: Baker Books, 2007).

_____. *Answering Jewish Objections to Jesus, Volume 5: Traditional Jewish Objections* (San Francisco, CA: Purple Pomegranate Productions, 2009).

Glaser, Mitch. *Isaiah 53 Explained* (New York: Chosen People Productions, 2010).

Kaiser, Walter C. *The Messiah in the Old Testament* (Grand Rapids: Zondervan, 1995).

Neusner, Jacob. *The Way of Torah: An Introduction to Judaism* (Belmont, CA: Wadsworth Publishing Company, 1997).

McKee, J.K. *Confronting Yeshua's Divinity and Messiahship* (Richardson, TX: Messianic Apologetics, 2012).

_____. *Israel in Future Prophecy: Is There a Larger Restoration of the Kingdom to Israel?* (Richardson, TX: Messianic Apologetics, 2013).

_____. *Approaching One Law Controversies: Sorting Through the Legalism* (Richardson, TX: Messianic Apologetics, 2016).

_____. *Salvation on the Line, Volume III: The Messiahship of Yeshua* (Messianic Apologetics, forthcoming).

Rydelnik, Michael. *The Messianic Hope: Is the Hebrew Bible Messianic?* (Nashville: B&H Publishing Group, 2010).

OUR PLACE IN THE CONGREGATION

UNIT FIVE

What Does It Mean to Participate in a Messianic Congregation?

Many of us have been told, in our spiritual experiences, and rightfully so, that "There are no Lone Ranger Believers!" Each one of us needs to be in regular fellowship and accountability with fellow brothers and sisters in the Lord, to whom we are not familialy related. By being in weekly fellowship with other Believers, be it during a congregational *Shabbat* service, and/or some other weekly gathering for prayer or Bible study, we can more consciously appreciate the thrust of Proverbs 27:17: "Iron sharpens iron, and one person sharpens the wits of another" (NRSV). It was actually reported of the first Messianic Believers in the Book of Acts, that "all who believed were together, having everything in common" (Acts 2:44, TLV). The first Messianic Believers, in the emergent Body of Messiah, were a very tight knit group of people—so much so that others generously provided for the needs of those who were lacking. Due to the relatively small size of today's Messianic movement, Believers functioning in closer quarters, being aware of the life activities and pursuits of others *for certain*—and able to be there as spiritual support mechanisms during times of difficulty—are dynamics that we frequently encounter.

Each one of us, who find ourselves attending a Messianic congregation or assembly, brings our own series of expectations, needs, and wants. Jewish Believers in Israel's Messiah have certain needs—and indeed requirements—as they involve the local Messianic congregation not only being a "safe space" for

The Messianic Walk

them to maintain their Jewish heritage and traditions, not assimilating into a non-Jewish Christianity, **but most especially as a place where they can bring their non-believing family and friends to be presented with the good news of Yeshua.** Non-Jewish Believers called into today's Messianic movement, from evangelical Protestant backgrounds, bring a selection of needs as they become involved in Messianic congregations. Some of these concern a genuine, supernatural compulsion to reconnect with their spiritual heritage in Israel's Scriptures, participate in Jewish outreach and evangelism, and to some degree reproduce the First Century experience of Jewish and non-Jewish Believers fellowshipping in one accord in mixed assemblies. Other non-Jewish Believers entering into the Messianic movement, do so only for a season, usually being attracted to Messianic congregations because of the music, Davidic dance, intriguing teaching, or the food—but then later move on to something else.

Toward the Restoration of Israel

Today's Messianic congregations actively pray for, and participate in, the restoration of Israel. A self-obvious component of this is how a Messianic congregation is uniquely suited to serve the interests of Jewish evangelism, particularly where Jewish people, who do not recognize Yeshua as Israel's Messiah, can hear the good news presented in a Jewish sensitive manner. Messianic congregations also contribute to Jewish outreach by participating in the affairs of the local Jewish community, and likely also by supporting different endeavors in modern Israel. Messianic congregations certainly make it a regular practice to publicly pray for the salvation of the Jewish people, anticipating what is prophesied in Zechariah 12:10: "Then I will pour out on the house of David and the inhabitants of Jerusalem a spirit of grace and supplication, when they will look toward Me whom they pierced. They will mourn for him as one mourns for an only son and grieve bitterly for him, as one grieves for a firstborn" (TLV; cf. John 19:37; Revelation 1:7).

What is also important to remember, when Messianic congregations serve as outposts for the restoration of Israel, is that we are—to some degree—participating in future prophesied realities, to be consummated at the return of the Messiah. The Disciples' question to Yeshua, as He was preparing to ascend into Heaven, was, "Lord, are you at this time going to restore self-rule to Isra'el?" (Acts 1:6, CJB/CJSB). The Disciples were anticipating Yeshua to restore the Twelve Tribes of Israel, end the Jewish Diaspora, defeat the Roman occupiers of Judea, and establish a permanent Messianic Davidic Kingdom. Yeshua the Messiah hardly dismissed the idea that He would one day restore Israel in all of its intended, Davidic fullness—but the Apostles' assignment was to serve as His witnesses in the whole Earth (Acts 1:8). The salvation of Israel proper *and* the nations were both to be important parts of the anticipated restoration of Israel's Kingdom, as

What Does It Mean to Participate in a Messianic Congregation?

the salvation of the nations was predicated on the raising up of David's Tabernacle, as attested by James the Just at the Jerusalem Council (Acts 15:15-18; Amos 9:11-12). **So, it can be legitimately concluded that we all have a stake in seeing Israel restored!**

Being participants, in some way or another, in the restoration of Israel's Kingdom, the return of Israel's Messiah, and His reign over Planet Earth *is a huge responsibility.* It is probably not emphasized enough in today's Messianic congregations and assemblies, what it actually means to be involved in Israel's restoration! It absolutely involves being representatives of Israel's God and Israel's Messiah in the world: "we are ambassadors of the Messiah; in effect, God is making his appeal through us. What we do is appeal on behalf of the Messiah, 'Be reconciled to God!'" (2 Corinthians 5:20, CJB/CJSB). It also involves is joining into a narrative of salvation history, where each of us is informed—in some way or another—of Ancient Israel in the wilderness, the Kingdom of Israel at the time of David, the split of Israel, the exile of the Northern and Southern Kingdoms, the return of the Jews from Babylon, and the Jewish Diaspora in the Mediterranean. The Messiah was to certainly come to solve the issues and problems that had been caused by the exile, and bring salvation not only to just the Jewish people, but to the entire world. Messianic congregations reconnect with the Torah and Tanach *for far more reasons* than just being educated in Biblical history; Messianic congregations reconnect with the Torah and Tanach because "these things happened to them as a warning, but they were written down for our instruction, upon whom the end of the ages has come" (1 Corinthians 10:11, RSV). **The Scriptures of Israel record many things that the people of God today should not be repeating.**

When you commit yourself to being part of a Messianic congregation, you will naturally bring various expectations for your individual self and your family. *But you are part of something much bigger than your individual self and your family!* When you are a part of a Messianic congregation, you are part of an assembly of men and women who are contributing to the salvation of the Jewish people, and with it the inevitable return of the Messiah. A Messianic congregation is not supposed to be "Saturday Church," where the only thing we do is corporately worship God on Saturday. On the contrary, a Messianic congregation is to be a place where we perform actions reflective of the future world to come, where the King of Israel will reign supreme.

The Place of Messianic Jewish Congregations

When identifying as a Believer in Israel's Messiah to evangelical Christians, Messianic Jews are frequently asked that uncomfortable question: "Where do you go to church?" In the history of the Hebrew Christian movement, which preceded it in the late Nineteenth and early Twentieth Centuries, Jewish Believers or Hebrew Christians, as they were known, almost always were integrated into a mainline

The Messianic Walk

Protestant denominational church. Various Torah prescriptions and Jewish lifecycle events were almost always followed at home, or at various extraneous gatherings of Hebrew Christians. Fidelity to God's Torah was mainly looked at as cultural, and not necessarily as a part of fidelity to a Jewish Believers' Biblical heritage and responsibilities. The Hebrew Christian movement, while an important stage of development, lamentably encouraged a wide degree of assimilation on the part of Jewish Believers into Protestantism. The great-grandchildren of many of the Hebrew Christians of the last century, having been integrated into contemporary evangelicalism *and* being the product of intermarriage, can often have little or no idea—much less appreciation—of their Jewish heritage.

The previous, modern experience, of many Jewish people coming to faith in Yeshua of Nazareth, meant assimilation and intermarriage into Protestantism. It meant looking at God's Torah as being an important part of Jewish culture only, but not as a part of the Jewish people's covenantal relationship with God. After the rebirth of the State of Israel in 1948, and more specifically the recapturing of the Old City of Jerusalem in 1967, things demonstrably shifted with the emergence of the Messianic Jewish movement. Messianic Jewish congregations and synagogues would meet on *Shabbat*, they would have Hebrew liturgy similar to the Jewish Synagogue, the appointed times or *moedim* would be remembered, Jewish national holidays would be observed, a kosher diet would be encouraged, and sons would be circumcised. **Most importantly, Jewish people coming to Messiah faith would not mean assimilation into non-Jewish Christianity,** where one's grandchildren and great-grandchildren would forget their Jewish heritage. Instead, with Jewish Believers maintaining fidelity to their Biblical heritage and ancestral customs, a Messianic Jewish congregation would be an ideal venue for presenting Jewish people with the good news of Israel's Messiah. A Messianic Jewish congregation would be the place to see new Jewish Believers discipled and trained up in the ways of the Lord—*an assembly different than a Sunday evangelical church.*

Messianic Jewish congregations and synagogues were planted throughout North America, in the 1970s and into the 1990s, in places where there are large Jewish populations. The mid-to-late 1990s saw a wide influx of non-Jewish Believers into the Messianic movement, many of whom wanted to substantially connect with their faith heritage in Israel's Scriptures, support Jewish outreach and evangelism, and be in an assembly similar to what would have been seen in the First Century Diaspora. The place of non-Jewish Believers in today's Messianic Jewish congregations varies from assembly to assembly. Many Messianic Jewish Believers, including congregational leaders, have non-Jewish spouses—and so the Messianic community is considered to be ideal for intermarried families, who do not wish to see half-Jewish children assimilate into Protestantism, or worse yet, leave the faith entirely. In more Messianic Jewish congregations than not, non-

What Does It Mean to Participate in a Messianic Congregation?

Jewish Believers are welcomed as fellow brothers and sisters, and co-participants, in the restoration of Israel. Many Messianic Jewish congregations strongly adhere to a philosophy that without Jewish and non-Jewish Believers fellowshipping together in one accord, that some rift in what is intended by the Ephesians 2:15 "one new man" or "one new humanity" can be unnecessarily created. Many Messianic Jewish congregations encourage non-Jewish Believers to embrace their Jewish Roots, provided they guard against legalism, and not pretend that they are somehow ethnically or culturally Jewish.

Congregational Life in a Messianic Jewish Assembly

No two Messianic congregations or assemblies are going to be alike—a partial testimony to the diversity of the worldwide Jewish community. But while there are going to be differences determined by geography and demographics, there are still going to be various constants when you participate in congregational life. **Most Messianic congregations require those who are regularly attending to become formal members.** Much of this involves not only making sure that people are fully committed to the local assembly, but it helps to see that different people—with their gifts and talents and resources—can be best employed to edify the local assembly.

Your Messianic congregation or synagogue may have different expectations for congregational life, than a congregation or synagogue in another city or town. While we are all agreed that the Messiah "loved His community and gave Himself up for her" (Ephesians 5:25, TLV), there are some more specific reasons to be considered by those who are members, or are contemplating membership, in a Messianic congregation. The authors of *Messianic Judaism Class* offer five specific reasons in support of formal membership in a Messianic Jewish congregation:

1. **Biblical reason** (Ephesians 5:25): "The Messiah is committed to the congregation."
2. **Cultural reason**: "It is an antidote to our society...We live in an age where very few want to be committed to anything...a job...a marriage...our country. This attitude has even produced a generation of 'congregation shoppers and hoppers.' Membership swims against the current of America's 'consumer religion.' It is an unselfish decision. Commitment always builds character."
3. **Practical reason**: "It defines who can be counted on...Every team must have a roster. Every school must have an enrollment. Every business has a payroll. Every army has an enlistment. Even our country takes a census and requires voter registration. Membership identifies our family."
4. **Personal reason**: "It produces spiritual growth...The Scriptures place a major emphasis on the need for Believers to be accountable to each

other for spiritual growth. You cannot be accountable when you're not committed to any specific congregation family."
5. **Legal reason**: "It enables formal discipline...We can be sued if we discipline a person who is not a member."[1]

These are all important reasons to reflect upon, if you are presently a member of a Messianic Jewish congregation, who has gone through formal membership procedures—and especially if you are considering becoming a formal member of a Messianic Jewish congregation. **Congregational membership is not a light commitment, but is something to be taken very seriously.**

One of the major differences between today's Messianic congregations, and a wide number of evangelical Protestant churches, is that Messianic congregations tend to be much smaller, and as such they do have some sense of "family" or *mishpachah* to them. But does one's participation in a Messianic congregation as "family," mean that an individual or family of persons, have little or no privacy? Or, does it mean that the congregation serving as a wider "family" of sorts, is there to help and support members of the local faith community, being with them through thick and thin? For certain, most of today's Messianic congregations and fellowships are communities where more people than not, know one another personally, they are involved in the life activities of others, they socialize together, and they are indeed aware of others' life challenges and problems. What this can and does mean, is that various people in the congregation *implicitly trust* others in the congregation, and vice versa. Trust and reliance upon people is not a high commodity in today's religious world; in fact, trust and respect of others is on the considerable decline. *Loyalty to one's own is a virtue that you almost hear nothing about.* While everyone in a Messianic congregation or assembly should be encouraged to participate and socialize with one another—do be aware of the tensions that can be caused by the Messianic movement being relatively small as well, and in some cases demographically imbalanced.

Congregational Purpose in a Messianic Jewish Assembly

When many of us consider what the purpose of a local congregation or assembly may be, we are likely to think that (1) it is to serve as a local support mechanism for brothers' and sisters' spiritual growth and maturation, and (2) to serve as a beacon of God's love and light to a hurting world. Messianic Jewish congregations and synagogues have a certain mandate to be local support mechanisms for the unique needs of Jewish Believers, and non-Jewish Believers specifically called by God into the Messianic movement at this time. Messianic Jewish congregations and synagogues also have a definite mandate to reach out

---

[1] *Messianic Judaism Class*, Teacher Book, 101.

What Does It Mean to Participate in a Messianic Congregation?

with God's love and goodness to members of the local Jewish community, to support Israel, and to stand against anti-Semitism in the world.

Different Messianic congregations will understandably have different mission statements, or varied credos, as they concern the assembly's internal ministries and external outreaches. The authors of the workbook *Messianic Judaism Class*, at one time having been leaders of Congregation Shema Yisrael in Rochester, New York, offer the purpose statement:

> "To proclaim Messiah Yeshua (Jesus) to Jewish and non-Jewish people, connect them personally with the God of Israel through prayer and worship, draw them into fellowship, lead them to spiritual maturity, equip them to serve, and inspire believers everywhere to reconnect with their Jewish roots."[2]

My local congregation, Eitz Chaim of Richardson, Texas, includes the following purpose statement in its weekly bulletin:

> "Eitz-Chaim is called to be a Messiah centered, Spirit-empowered, disciple-making community that reveals the truth of Yeshua (the Jewish Jesus) to both Israel and the nations. We are committed to making Yeshua the L-rd of our life, faith and ministry. Our community seeks to be like the first Jerusalem congregation where both Jew and non-Jew function as one new man, equal before G-d (Acts 2)."

The authors of *Messianic Judaism Class* will then go on to list a number of critical areas where its congregational mission sees some practical, on the ground, activity:

- evangelism
- fellowship
- worship
- prayer and spiritual warfare
- discipleship
- service
- restoring the Body of Messiah to its Jewish Roots[3]

It is possible that your own local Messianic congregation, or fellowship, has these exact same ministry activities, or some variation of them. Each Messianic congregation, while tending to reach out and assist with the purposes of Jewish outreach and evangelism, and seeing non-Jewish Believers properly exposed to their faith heritage in Israel's Scriptures and Judaism, can accomplish these tasks any number of useful ways. Much of what takes place in the spiritual development of Messianic people, understandably occurs in association with the weekly *Shabbat*

---

[2] Ibid., 103.
[3] Ibid., 104.

service, and activities which are scheduled either sometime before or after. Likewise, depending on the demographic makeup of your congregation, there might be some sort of mid-week activity, like a prayer group and/or Bible study, that meets, or there might be various home groups or cell groups that meet outside of your congregation's facility. The available programs and activities accessible via your Messianic assembly—and their related demographics—is almost entirely determinant on the direction of your congregational leadership, in association with the needs of congregational members.

Leadership Structures in a Messianic Assembly

While there are an array of Messianic denominational organizations which exist, such as the International Alliance of Messianic Congregations and Synagogues (IAMCS) and the Union of Messianic Jewish Congregations (UMJC), among others—which do ordain and license Messianic rabbis, pastors, and teachers—the specific leadership structure of one's own local congregation or assembly, is widely going to be determined by the leadership and membership of the local faith community.

The First Century *ekklēsia* inherited a congregational leadership structure, largely from the Second Temple Jewish Synagogue. The requirements issued for elders and deacons by the Apostle Paul, to Timothy in Ephesus (1 Timothy 3), and for elders to Titus on Crete (Titus 1:5-9), are widely adaptations of what would have been likely seen for those in the contemporary Synagogue. Yet as the original Messianic Believers passed away, but most especially as the good news spread throughout the Mediterranean, the need to organize the assemblies in large geographic areas, became apparent. The emergent Christian Church of the Second Century, while inheriting a Jewish leadership model, had to adopt new leadership structures as it would not be as closed and isolated as the Synagogue. As Eastern Orthodoxy and Roman Catholicism would become formal institutions in later centuries, leadership structures involving bishops and archbishops over geographic areas would be established for Church governance and administration. Many of these leadership structures, given many of the complexities of the Middle Ages to be sure, were fused with political governments and European monarchies. Corruption and bribery, among other things, were rampant—and were among the significant causes leading to the Protestant Reformation.

Today's American Protestantism—which whether one wants to consciously recognize it or not, has at least partially affected the Messianic movement—has itself been broadly affected by how the Protestant Reformation took hold in both England and Scotland. When King Henry VIII of England broke with the papacy, because he would not be granted a divorce, he set himself up as the leader of the Church of England. While there were various institutional and theological reforms made to the Church of England, it also maintained much of the semblance of

What Does It Mean to Participate in a Messianic Congregation?

Catholicism, particularly in terms of its leadership structure of archbishops and bishops. The episcopal model of leadership, derived from the Greek *episkopē*, "bishop" or "overseer," has been employed in or adapted for various Protestant denominations, which have their roots in Anglicanism (i.e., the Methodist movement). The Church of Scotland, however, employed a presbyterian model of leadership, taken from the Greek *presbuteros* or "elder," where ordained elders lead the local congregation, and regularly assemble for general sessions to discuss church affairs, with a moderator appointed. Various Protestant denominations today have adopted the presbyterian model of leadership, as it is far less organized.

Today's Messianic congregations will frequently employ Hebrew terminology for their leaders, *zaqein* meaning "elder," and *shammash* being the equivalent of "deacon." While individual assemblies may vary in terms of whom they consider to be qualified as such designated leaders, it is more frequent than not for it to be concluded that the requirements of 1 Timothy 3:1-3 and Titus 1:5-9 are universal prescriptions, rather than situational for Timothy in Ephesus and Titus on Crete. While a strongly discussed and debated issue in contemporary Jewish and Protestant theology, to be certain, on the whole the present Messianic movement tends to take a negative view to females being appointed to formal positions of leadership within the assembly, although the wives of male rabbis and congregational leaders may be incorporated into some congregations' decision making process. (The 2001 compilation book *Voices of Messianic Judaism* did, however, include essays in favor of women serving in leadership,[4] and those favoring male exclusive leadership in the assembly.[5]) Ultimately, the leadership structure of today's Messianic Jewish congregations does come down to an assembly-by-assembly basis. It can, however, be generally observed that there will be three main tiers of leadership: **(1)** elders, **(2)** deacons, and **(3)** ministry/program leaders.

What do you want to get out of participating in a Messianic congregation?

Participation, in the life body of a Messianic congregation, is going to be different than one being a part of a contemporary Jewish synagogue or Protestant church. When one lives in an urban environment, if he or she is dissatisfied with something relatively small or minor in a synagogue or church, he or she can likely consider various alternatives. *Established Messianic congregations and*

---

[4] Ruth Fleischer, "Women Can Be in Leadership," in Dan Cohn-Sherbok, ed., *Voices of Messianic Judaism* (Baltimore: Lederer Books, 2001), pp 151-157.

[5] Sam Nadler, "Male Leadership and the Role of Women," in Ibid., pp 159-168.

Nadler is also the author of *Developing Healthy Messianic Congregations* (Charlotte: Word of Messiah Ministries, 2016).

The Messianic Walk

synagogues are not that frequently accessible to people. When you become a part of a Messianic congregation, there will likely be no other Messianic assembly or group available to you, in your city or town. What this means, more than anything else, is that you cannot bring the same expectations into a Messianic congregation, as you would to a Jewish synagogue or Protestant church. *You will not only have to often think differently in terms of your participation, but you may even have to be innovative.* But also be aware that you are part of a spiritual movement which is going to culminate in the return of Israel's Messiah!

What do you want to get out of participating in a Messianic congregation? Consider this question very seriously as you proceed on the Messianic walk. There are going to be things that you see in today's Messianic congregations and assemblies that you really like, and which genuinely minister to the spiritual needs of yourself and/or your family. There will also be things that you will see in today's Messianic congregations, which you may not like, that may indeed upset and offend you, and can even be insulting at times. If not all of the congregational teaching is to your liking—or more frequently does not address various issues or subjects which matter to you—there are legitimate and approved Messianic teaching ministries that are equipped to address the topics which your local assembly's leaders are not necessarily able to.

Navigating Through a Very Small Messianic Movement

Many of us, at some significant point or another, have been greatly touched by the sentiments of Ephesians 3:17-19: "that Messiah may dwell in your hearts through faith; *and* that you, being rooted and grounded in love, may have strength to comprehend with all the holy ones what is the breadth and length and height and depth, and to know the love of Messiah which surpasses knowledge, that you may be filled to all the fullness of God" (author's rendering).[1] What Paul communicates here is that the love of Messiah is something which is broad and deep, and is undoubtedly something which will take a great deal of effort for Messiah followers to fully comprehend. A parallel passage to this would be Job 11:7-9:

"Can you discover the mysteries of God? Can you find the limits of Shaddai? They are higher than the heavens—what can you do? They are deeper than Sheol—what can you know? Its measure is longer than the earth and wider than the sea" (TLV).

Our God is big, in comparison to us small mortals. Given the greatness and majesty of God and His love for us—and our finality—we should each, as maturing Believers in Israel's Messiah, be able to give others some space and maneuverability as they advance in their understanding of Him and His ways. Throughout a great deal of religious history, both Jewish and Protestant, people have been able to give others—particularly with those whom they might disagree on secondary and tertiary issues—the room that they need to accomplish the particular work or vocation they believe that they have been given by God. This is especially true of the different denominations and theological sectors of Protestantism, which is large

---

[1] This article originally appeared in the November 2018 issue of Outreach Israel News.

The Messianic Walk

enough to permit for there to be differences of opinion on various issues *and* for people to be spread out or part sufficiently so there are not unnecessary clashes or incidents.

A Very Small Messianic Movement

Throughout much of this year (2018), my youngest sister Maggie has been on deployment in the North Sea and Arctic Circle aboard the U.S.S. Farragut. We have been blessed to be able to communicate with her via social media. As we have talked with her about her Navy service, one thing that she told us about her cruise really impacted me: "Human beings were not intended to live in such close quarters for so long!" Keep in mind that the Farragut is a modern destroyer with a crew of around 300; it is not a wooden ship of past centuries where a similarly sized vessel might have a crew of over 1,500. Still, the point was made: **when kept too close together for too long a time, tensions do erupt between people, and the likelihood of there being disagreements and incidents increases.**

Today's Messianic movement is not like evangelical Protestantism, where you have a sufficiently large enough group of people, as well as a wide enough variety of denominations and local assemblies—where if an individual or family does not quite receive what they need in one place, they can go to another. **Today's Messianic movement is small,** and there are not that many options available to people. Today's Messianic movement is much more like the Jewish Synagogue, in that you have a very tight knit group of people—and as the old adage reminds us, "Two Jews, three opinions." Unlike the Protestant world, where if you disagree with the theology of a particular group, you can try another group—in the Jewish world you learn how to maneuver through a plurality of views and positions on a variety of non-essential issues. The Messianic movement is quite similar: on non-essential issues, people have to learn how to be flexible, respectfully disagree, and at least encourage reasonable dialogue on issues so as to decrease unnecessary tensions.

Over the past several years, when people have asked me if there is one thing that I would like to see greatly altered in today's Messianic movement, I have responded with something that has puzzled, if not bewildered many: **We need to fix our demographic imbalance.** When you look out at evangelical Protestantism, you will generally find assemblies where there is a fair balance across age groups, ethnic groups, economic income, and those of different social classes. In today's Messianic movement, a late-thirties single male such as myself, is a niche demographic. There are very few people in today's Messianic movement with whom I can immediately relate, and so I have to make the effort to befriend people who are sometimes still in high school, or who are approaching retirement age, among the various brackets. While I certainly have good and close friends in today's Messianic movement, not all of them are local, as I instead may only see them once or twice a year at a national conference. As it is with all friendships, some people I get along with extremely well, and some people I can only get close with when certain issues or topics are addressed.

Some might say that sometime in the near future, as we get closer and closer to the return of Yeshua—that things will all even out in today's Messianic movement, and we will become more demographically balanced among the Jewish and non-Jewish Believers who compose our ranks. Yet, as what has often been billed as "the end-time move of God," somehow making up "the remnant of her seed" (Revelation 12:17, KJV), I am less optimistic about the numbers of the Messianic movement increasing in the future, than some others might be.

Today's Messianic movement is small, and within such smallness is a wide diversity of opinions and approaches to non-essential theological and spiritual issues. There is more variety on a whole host of topics that face the Bible reader, than tends to be publicly acknowledged. Other than general appeals made like "Behold, how good and how pleasant it is for brothers to dwell together in unity!" (Psalm 133:1, TLV), it is fair to say that we collectively try to avoid or dismiss the psychology of what it means to be a small, and internally diverse, group of human beings. While it is surely important for us to retain unity among brothers and sisters, as we anticipate more challenges as the Messiah's return draws near, how will we be able to successfully navigate through a very small Messianic movement?

Issues Worth Being Divided Over

In my multiple years of being associated with the Messianic movement, I have seen congregations and fellowships where people will divide with others, over the proverbial drop of a hat. They will divide over issues of minutiae, which have no direct bearing on one's salvation, and importance will be given to forms of *halachah* and faith practice, for which there can be a legitimate array of diverse opinions. More frequently than not, one will be prone to find an assembly which is factional, where various cliques in the group place a higher emphasis on non-essentials than is useful.

One of the reasons why we turn to the Apostolic epistles for guidance, is so we can avoid some of the mistakes and limitations of those in the First Century C.E. The Corinthians were one assembly particularly rife with factionalism, yet the Apostle Paul's imperative to them was, "For I determined to know nothing among you except Yeshua the Messiah, and Him executed on a wooden scaffold" (1 Corinthians 2:2, author's rendering). The identity of Yeshua, His sacrifice on the tree, and the salvation He provides to those who trust in Him **constitutes those things which are to separate us from others.**

While in evangelical Protestantism, people are more likely to find another place to worship when discovering what certain people believe about controversies over eternal security, the spiritual gifts, the rapture, or women in ministry—because of

The Messianic Walk

our small size, people in today's Messianic movement do not often have the luxury of leaving one Messianic congregation to find another, on those sorts of issues. *If you are going to divide with other people who bear the label "Messianic" in some way, then it better be over a **major** issue!* In my ongoing studies and research over the past three to four years, the issues which are pressing upon today's Messianic movement—in which we definitely need more refinement and understanding—concern the Divinity and Messiahship of Yeshua. While most people in today's Messianic movement are to be commended for correctly believing that Yeshua is God, and certainly is the anticipated Messiah of Israel—many people in today's Messianic movement are also one conversation away from having their belief in Yeshua at least startled, if not shaken up. *Correct belief has not been followed up with correct doctrine*, and many have a blind faith in Yeshua of Nazareth because some subjective supernatural experience, and not because of their study of Holy Scripture.

Many in positions of congregational leadership and teaching are sufficiently equipped to address the major reasons often lodged by others, against why Yeshua is not God, or even the Messiah. But today's congregational teachers are often constrained to exposit on the weekly Torah portion, or some other ethical or moral issue facing the assembly. While surely important, when these important subjects are not expounded upon regularly in *Shabbat* teaching, one's congregational constituents will often look elsewhere for answers to the questions they pose. Usually accessing social media, individual Messianic people will be presented with scores of free teachings as to why Yeshua cannot be God, or why He cannot be the Messiah. In the past, Messianic congregations would have to guard themselves against a visit from a person passing out unauthorized literature, or a Jewish anti-missionary. While still a looming threat, the electronic tools at one's disposal make the probably of false teaching on the nature of the Messiah, entering into one's congregation, immeasurably high.

I have never hidden the fact that within my teachings, I consider the Divinity and Messiahship of Yeshua to be salvation issues. If I were in a Messianic congregation, where the leadership was questioning whether or not Yeshua was God, I would leave. *To me, the issue is that important.* More probably what we will each be confronted with, are individuals and families within Messianic congregations, who do not believe that Yeshua is God, and congregational leadership which does believe that Yeshua is God. What do you do, when it becomes public knowledge that there are people in your congregation who believe that Yeshua is Messiah, but a created being? It might be one thing if these people stay to themselves, visit on occasion, and say nothing. It might be something else if these have been congregational members for quite some time, have changed their minds, are active in various congregational programs, and have been spreading their ideas to others. The leadership of the assembly will ultimately have to decide how to confront such people, perhaps indeed issuing some disciplinary action, or asking them to leave.

Issues Not Worth Being Divided Over

While many of us can understand how individuals in a Messianic congregation, fellowship, or even ministry, may need to be asked to leave because they have denied Yeshua as God, and may not even be too sure about Yeshua as Messiah—most of the issues that we tend to divide over, and are the result of tensions within our rather small faith community, **do not bear a salvation level significance.** The basic common denominator for believing in the good news or gospel, is, "if you confess with your mouth that Yeshua is Lord, and believe in your heart that God raised Him from the dead, you will be saved" (Romans 10:9, TLV). In view of Romans 10:13 following, quoting from Joel 2:32, one can insist that some recognition of Yeshua's Divinity as the LORD is required for salvation; unfortunately, all of us are at some point guilty of conflating *another issue* with the salvation of someone else.

The world of theology and Biblical Studies is evidence enough how there are many topics and subjects worthy of detailed discussion, analysis, and indeed debate. We are invited as followers of the Messiah to investigate God's Word, to probe the mind of God, and to consider our relationship to both His Creation and wider society. There are issues worthy of our attention, but they are hardly issues which will directly affect whether we spend eternity with the Lord, or separated from Him. For some people, particularly in larger faith communities such as evangelical Protestantism—how you approach certain secondary or tertiary issues of theology, means that if you disagree on an issue, you can find not only another church to attend, but another denomination to be a member of. In today's relatively small Messianic movement, how you approach certain secondary or tertiary issues of theology, means that you may have to proceed very cautiously regarding what you say—or do not say—around certain people. As James 1:19-20 advises, "Know this, my dear brothers and sisters: let every person be quick to listen, slow to speak, and slow to anger—for human anger doesn't produce the righteousness of God" (TLV).

In a small faith community such as the Messianic movement, it would be naïve of us to think that every single person has the same orientation toward a number of secondary and tertiary, non-salvation issues. In fact, I am frequently asked about what I think about various subjects—which some think are entirely "off limits" for being discussed in their local Messianic congregations or fellowships. Yet, some of these subjects are, for certain, entirely legitimate and are indeed discussed in both Jewish and Protestant venues. That there might indeed be more variety in today's broad Messianic community, *beneath the surface*, than a number of leaders and teachers are willing to admit to at present.

The Messianic Walk

Bible Difficulties

The basic rule of good Bible interpretation, is to interpret a text for what it meant to its original audience first, and then to deduce principles for modern times. That is easier said than done! Many people incorrectly read the Bible as though it were written to them *personally and directly*, in the Twenty-First Century. More so than this, we often apply our Twenty-First Century standards of exactness to Holy Scripture. We have each expected certain things of the Bible, which the Bible does not expect of itself.

Too many people in today's Messianic movement, particularly of the older generation, are witnessed to have not engaged that much with how the Scriptures came to be, how texts have been transmitted, much less with the degree of historical accuracy that certain texts have. For a movement which places a high degree of emphasis on the importance of the Tanach (OT), we are largely unconscious of how the further back one goes in history, the less and less evidence one will have for the events recorded.

I certainly hold to a high level of historicity and reliability for the Bible, but more and more younger people—who are receiving a theological education, and are going to be future Messianic leaders—are going to hold to a more diverse array of opinions on an entire array of Bible difficulties. More often than not, opinions which have been kept private, are going to be voiced. How is our small Messianic movement going to handle a diversity of views over the numbers of the Exodus, the extent of Noah's Flood, or over the Genesis chs. 1-2 materials and age of the universe? For better or for worse, there is a greater selection of opinions and positions on these sorts of issues, which we are not willing to publicly recognize at times.

Spiritual Gifts

On the whole, it is fair to say that today's Messianic movement would describe itself as "Spirit filled," meaning that it would generally be positive about the operation of the Spiritual gifts. Today's Messianic movement is broadly not cessationist, the idea that the Spiritual gifts ended with the death of the Apostles, and perhaps their immediate successors. This does not mean, though, that there are not some leaders and teachers who are cessationists—but more often than not today's Messianic leaders, teachers, and people would be continuists. Today's Messianic people generally believe that rather than ceasing with the Apostles, that the Spiritual gifts have continued to the present time.

Yet, among those who believe in the continuation of the Spiritual gifts, are certainly divisions. I am a continuist, but I also believe in the high priority of the fruit of the Spirit (Galatians 5:22-23) and love (1 Corinthians 13:1). While in principle I believe in the operation of the Spiritual gifts, I am also on record as being quite skeptical, and even critical, to the excesses of the charismatic movement—which

Navigating Through a Very Small Messianic Movement

at the very least, I do not believe often exhibits a great deal of discernment of mind. Many people who label themselves as "charismatic," do not tend to be very distinguishing between genuine actions of the Holy Spirit, actions of human flesh, and then actions of nefarious origin. Many of today's charismatics want a subjective spiritual experience, rather than be committed to external acts of grace and holiness.

How do we reach a point of maturity, involving the Spiritual gifts, where God's Holy Spirit is able to transform our hearts and minds—not only to empower us to do good deeds (Ephesians 2:10)—but to get us to think and process increasingly more complicated ideas and concepts? Much of the influence that a charismatic reasoning process has had, on various Messianic people, has hardly been positive. While we genuinely should want God's Spirit to move, we have also been warned, "Many false prophets will arise and lead many astray" (Matthew 24:11, TLV).

The End-Times

All of us who have been involved with the Messianic movement, for any elongated period of time, are aware of our collective interest in the anticipated end-times. Because of our focus on Israel and the Jewish people, it is hardly a surprise that we pay attention to the Middle East and to *when* we are in human history. There are certainly debates—although much friendlier today in 2018 than they were twenty years ago—on whether Yeshua returns to gather the holy ones before or after the Tribulation period. There are different orientations witnessed among those who are convinced we are living in the end-times—with some of the conviction that the return of the Messiah is much closer than others, and should what they do or not do with their lives, be reflective of this. Certainly, if the Messianic movement is to be a significant venue of future Jewish salvation, and in seeing many non-Jewish Believers tangibly connect to their faith heritage in Israel's Scriptures—then some evaluation of what we can legitimately do for the future, would be in order. We might be able to take some solace from Daniel 12:3, "Those who are wise will shine like the brightness of the heavenly expanse. And those who turn many to righteousness will be like the stars forever and ever" (TLV).

The Torah

Today's Messianic movement, although with some exceptions, believes that per Yeshua's word of the Torah or Law not passing away (Matthew 5:17-19), that Moses' Teaching has not been abolished for the post-resurrection era. This does involve a more positive orientation for the role of the seventh-day Sabbath/*Shabbat*, the appointed times or Biblical festivals of Leviticus 23, and the kosher dietary laws—than is seen in today's Christianity. There are debates, however, over the applicability of these instructions to Jewish and non-Jewish

The Messianic Walk

Believers. There are debates over the applicability of many Torah commandments for the Twenty-First Century. Far too frequently, voices trying to divide a rather small Messianic movement, or trying to establish extreme, inflexible positions—drown out those who want to encourage obedience to God's Instruction as a genuine outworking of the good works that born again Believers are to have.

Today's Body of Messiah needs a foundation in Moses' Teaching. Much of the proliferation of sin and ungodliness, lamentably witnessed in contemporary evangelicalism, is a direct result of dismissing the relevance of the Tanach (OT) Scriptures for people of faith. While in the past, much of historical Protestantism artificially divided the Torah's commandments into the so-called moral, civil, and ceremonial law—the Torah's commandments which regulate ethics and morality are being eschewed by too many claiming faith in Israel's Messiah. How today's small Messianic movement can best tackle the extremes of legalism and lawlessness, and truly embody the Torah's principles in its missiology, may be a challenge—but not hopelessly impossible.

Men and Women

One of the biggest theological controversies today, certainly in Protestantism, and to a lesser extent Judaism, regards the role of men and women in spiritual leadership. Customarily from its beginning, the Messianic movement has broadly adhered to a theological position known as complementarianism, which while affirming the ontological equality of males and females (cf. Genesis 1:27-28; Galatians 3:28), also believes that various principal leadership roles, in both the family and Body of Messiah, are only reserved for males. Over the past half-century, for certain, in various branches of both Judaism and evangelicalism, females have been increasingly occupying more and more positions of congregational leadership, with the principle of "mutual submission" (cf. Ephesians 5:20; Philippians 2:4) being highly emphasized, and with females in leadership positions in the Bible a definite feature of study and discussion.

It would be a mistake, as a matter of information at least, to think that one-hundred percent of today's Messianic movement is complementarian, and that there is not a growing sector of egalitarians—who stress the equality of males and females—in our midst. Why have some people been open to egalitarian views on men and women serving as co-leaders of the home and of the assembly? The reasons are likely varied. None of these people, though, have done so for liberal intensions, with the result eventually allowing for homosexual marriage—but instead have considered egalitarian perspectives because complementarian perspectives did not answer certain questions that they raised. In our small Messianic movement, how are we going to handle the knowledge of there being people who hold to either complementarian or egalitarian theologies in our congregations? Are we going to be able to hear one another out, and not immediately dismiss them?

How will you navigate through our small Messianic movement?

Believers in Israel's Messiah are directly admonished, "Pursue peace with everyone, and the holiness without which no one will see the Lord" (Hebrews 12:14, NRSV). A number of the issues which I have noted, have served as dividing lines among different denominations and sects—even though none of them directly affect one's salvation. Of course, each one of these issues does involve how we read and interpret Scripture—and religious history is evidence enough of how not everyone reads and interprets Scripture in exactly the same way.

Today's Messianic movement is small, and that means that there is going to be a diverse array of opinions, on non-salvation, non-essential issues, likely enclosed in tight congregations and fellowships. If there is any issue over which we should divide, it is over the Divinity and Messiahship of Yeshua of Nazareth. While some of us might be seen to have a diversity of opinions and positions on the spiritual gifts, the end-times, or men and women in leadership roles—none of those issues have a direct bearing on whether or not we are forgiven of our sins. These are issues which require us to be diligent students of God's Word, and fair-minded, mature people, who can learn to be a little flexible amongst diversity.

As we approach the return of the Messiah, the need for the Messianic movement to recognize how the Jewish community has stayed coherent for centuries—despite its internal religious and philosophical diversity—will become apparent. The Messianic movement may never be as large, or as demographically balanced, or even as ideal, as some may want it to be. However, we should definitely be seeking the Lord and His ways more and more, and as we do this, ask Him to give us the ability to accomplish His tasks on Earth!

The Messianic Walk

The Calling of Ruth and Non-Jewish Believers in Today's Messianic Movement

The place of non-Jewish Believers, in today's Messianic Jewish movement, has tended to invoke any number of responses or reactions, some of them being positive, and others of them being negative. With only a handful of exceptions, non-Jewish Believers have never been summarily dismissed from attending Messianic Jewish congregations. Most Messianic Jewish congregations would affirm, that in some way, non-Jewish Believers are grafted-in to the olive tree (Romans 11:16-17), and are co-members of the Commonwealth of Israel (Ephesians 2:11-13) along with Jewish Believers. What that means, to be sure, is not entirely agreed. Some think that it means that non-Jewish Believers are "fellow citizens with the saints" (Ephesians 2:19, NASU) in an enlarged Kingdom realm of Israel, per the Tabernacle of David having a rule that extends beyond Israel proper (Amos 9:11-12; Acts 15:15-18). Others think that it means that non-Jewish Believers are part of the Christian Church, which along with the Messianic Jewish community, constitutes one of the two sub-peoples of God. Discussions and debates over ecclesiology, the study of God's elect, will internally continue among Messianic people until Yeshua the Messiah returns.

One common thread that is easily detectable in today's Messianic Jewish movement, regarding the place of non-Jewish Believers, is the wide affirmation **that non-Jewish Believers need to be genuinely called by God into the Messianic movement.** The original vision and purpose of the Messianic Jewish

The Messianic Walk

movement is to serve as a venue for Jewish outreach and evangelism. So, it is not inappropriate, that if non-Jewish Believers are coming into Messianic congregations—even if initially that their reasons for doing so involve their connecting to their faith heritage in Israel's Scriptures—to make sure that such people really are there, because God wants them there. Messianic Jewish leaders, whose main focus rests in focusing congregational activities toward presenting local Jews with the good news that Yeshua is Israel's Messiah, do not want to be overwhelmed with non-Jewish issues so that the main reason for the congregation existing in the first place gets totally forgotten. Even though non-Jewish Believers, who are genuinely supposed to be a part of Messianic congregations, will go through a season of acclimation—**they need to be quite conscious of how they are going to contribute to the mission of reaching out with the good news to their Jewish neighbors.**

The Calling of Ruth

While today's Messianic Jewish movement has been established to be a venue for Jewish outreach and evangelism, throughout its history, the Messianic Jewish movement has always recognized that non-Jewish Believers are going to be attracted to its synagogues and congregations. While the place of non-Jewish Believers, and their participation in the assembly, vary across the spectrum—from full membership to associate membership to welcome visitors—it is widely acknowledged in many Messianic sectors that non-Jewish Believers ,in today's Messianic movement, probably bear some kind of Ruth calling on them. Let us remember that a significant majority of non-Jewish people who come through the door of today's Messianic congregations, are not there to become members, as most are only there to investigate. *They have tried so many denominations and churches, that the Messianic movement is just another place where they can kick tires.* Experientially speaking, many non-Jews who come into a Messianic congregation, leave within three years. But for those who stay, and are fully committed to the Messianic walk and mission, they are often viewed as the figure of Ruth.

What does it mean for non-Jewish Believers in today's Messianic movement to have a Ruth calling upon their lives?

The Book of Ruth is a very important text for understanding the workings of God upon those in desperate situations. The family of Naomi moved to pagan Moab, because of a famine in Israel (Ruth 1:1-2). Elimelech, Naomi's husband, died in Moab, with her two sons having taken Moabite wives (Ruth 1:3), one of them being Ruth (Ruth 1:4). Her two sons die, leaving their two Moabite widows (Ruth 1:5), and so Naomi naturally decides to return to her homeland as the famine had abated (Ruth 1:6). Naomi bids her two daughters-in-law farewell (Ruth 1:7-9), and they actually insist that they return with her to Israel: "'No!' they said to her, 'we will return with you to your people" (Ruth 1:10, TLV). Naomi insists that they should stay in Moab, as she has no future husbands to bear them, and that the future she has in returning home is going to be more difficult than they realize:

"Now Naomi said, 'Go back, my daughters! Why should you go with me? Do I have more sons in my womb who could become your husbands? Go home, my daughters! I am too old to have a husband. Even if I were to say that there was hope for me and I could get married tonight, and then bore sons, would you wait for them to grow up? Would you therefore hold off getting married? No, my daughters, it is more bitter for me than for you—for the hand of ADONAI has gone out against me!'" (TLV).

One of Naomi's daughters-in-law, Orpah, decides to stay behind in Moab (Ruth 1:14), with Naomi informing Ruth, "Look, your sister-in-law is going back to her people and her gods. Return, along with your sister-in-law!" (Ruth 1:15, TLV). Naomi implies that it will be easier for Ruth to return to her people, their gods, and their way of life, than joining her and the people of Israel. The famed response that has received a great deal of attention throughout history, especially when people come together in common cause or solidarity, is Ruth's exclamation, "Do not plead with me to abandon you, to turn back from following you. For where you go, I will go, and where you stay, I will stay. Your people will be my people, and your God my God" (Ruth 1:16, TLV). Ruth insists to Naomi, *ameikha ami, v'Elohayikh Elohai*, "your people are my people, and your God is my God" (ATS). While Bible readers tend to be impressed at Ruth's declaration of being a member of the people of Ancient Israel, just as Naomi, and of monotheism, Ruth's statements do not end there. Ruth made a commitment of being a part of Israel, and of only serving Israel's One God, until her death:

"Where you die, I will die, and there I will be buried. May ADONAI deal with me, and worse, if anything but death comes between me and you!" (Ruth 1:17, TLV).

Ruth is not witnessed just making a claim based on the good feelings and positive sentiments she had in being once married to Naomi's son, and in desiring continued association with Naomi. Ruth is witnessed to make **an all out claim of total loyalty and devotion** to the people of Naomi and to their One God. Naomi cannot dissuade Ruth from staying in Moab, as it is recorded, "When she saw that Ruth was determined to go with her, she no longer spoke to Ruth about it" (Ruth 1:18, TLV). Ruth was "stedfastly minded" (KJV) about her decision.

The story of Ruth continues with Boaz arriving on the scene as the kinsman-redeemer, marrying Ruth, and Ruth actually being an ancestor of King David. That God used a non-Israelite such as Ruth, in an important way, is clear enough. **But Ruth had to be completely committed to Israel, and to Israel's God.** Ruth was not just committed in the sense that she would worship Israel's God, and do her best to stay away from previous religious activities from Moab, but in the event that the Moabites ever attacked Israel, still end up siding with her own people. Ruth

The Messianic Walk

made a commitment to the people of Israel and the One God of Israel which was to last until death, and God was to condemn her if she ever deviated from this.

When non-Jewish Believers, who are genuinely called by God to be a part of today's Messianic movement, are told that they have a Ruth calling upon their lives, what does Ruth 1:16-18 actually translate into?

1. **It means a complete commitment to the Messianic movement, the Messianic mission, and the Messianic walk.** Non-Jewish Believers with a Ruth calling upon their lives should not be members of both an evangelical church and members of a Messianic congregation, as there will be divided loyalties and attentions.
2. **It means that being associated with the Messianic Jewish and the Jewish community requires a non-Jewish Believer's total loyalty, even if it involves death.** Non-Jewish Believers with a Ruth calling upon their lives need to recognize that it may involve dying right alongside of their fellow Messianic Jewish brothers and sisters, especially in these end-times.

Being a part of the Messianic community, is not like being a part of a denomination of Protestantism that happens to be ethnically Jewish, and is only concerned with declaring the good news to the Jewish people in a Jewish way and in a setting more like a synagogue. Being a part of the Messianic community decisively places one's attention on the Romans chs. 9, 10, and 11 trajectory of salvation history: "and in this way all Israel will be saved" (Romans 11:26). This is something which is to culminate in the Second Coming of Israel's Messiah. Non-Jewish Believers have a definite role to play in the anticipated salvation of the Jewish people (Romans 11:11, 31). But should all non-Jewish Believers find themselves one day attending a Messianic congregation? While ultimately a question to be left to God, it is entirely appropriate for today's Messianic Jewish leaders to recognize non-Jewish Believers who have a Ruth calling upon their lives, and those who do not.

If you are a non-Jewish Believer who decisively has a Ruth calling upon your life, then you will demonstrate a complete commitment to the Messianic movement and its mission. While you might still appreciate your evangelical background and upbringing, your church experience is now going to be a part of your past, and not your future. Your future is the Messianic movement, and in contributing something substantial to the Messianic mission of Jewish outreach and evangelism. While your interest in the Messianic movement may have legitimately begun, because of wanting to reconnect to your faith heritage in the Scriptures of Israel, and to be a part of a congregation that was more like the First Century assemblies of Jewish, Greek, and Roman Believers—as you connect to such a dynamic, so should you also be steadfastly compelled by a word such as Romans 11:12: "Now if their transgression is riches for the world, and their failure is riches for the nations, how much more will their fullness be!" (author's rendering). *How do you see a great fullness of Jewish people come forth via their salvation?*

Ruth exclaimed her total loyalty to the people of Naomi and their God, but this went far beyond religious or spiritual loyalty. Ruth exclaimed her total loyalty to the people of Naomi and their God, until death: "Wherever you die, I will die—and there I will be buried. May the LORD punish me severely if I do not keep my promise! Only death will be able to separate me from you!" (Ruth 1:17, NET). Today's Messianic Jewish movement does not often discuss this part of non-Jewish Believers needing to have a Ruth calling, but the ramifications of Ruth's statement are quite severe. Ruth invokes God's condemnation upon her, if Ruth demonstrates herself unwilling to be loyal to Naomi's people and God until death. *Only death was to separate Ruth's integration into the community of Israel.* The significance of this, when considering the persecution and discrimination of the Jewish people throughout history—often at the hands of Christian authorities—are indeed striking. While various political and religious powers have often made promises and commitments to the Jewish community, to be more fair or tolerant, their track record can frequently be one of betrayal. It is hardly a surprise why many Jews throughout history have been very distrusting and suspicious of non-Jewish people! And today's Messianic Jewish community has every right and reason to suspect that not every non-Jewish person in its midst, is going to be loyal to the end.

If you are a non-Jewish person involved in today's Messianic community, have you made a commitment to not only stand by your Messianic Jewish brothers and sisters—but Jewish non-Believers in the wider Jewish community—even if it costs you your life? There are certainly many stories from the Second World War of faithful Christian people, upon witnessing the injustices of Nazi Germany, who hid Jews in their homes, and even took a public stand against Nazism's atrocities. There were those who stood against Nazi Germany's persecution of the Jews, and who went to the concentration camps with their Jewish friends and neighbors, dying right alongside them. **A non-Jewish Believer in today's Messianic movement, having a Ruth calling upon their lives, may require the very same thing sometime in the future.** So, how committed are you to truly being a part of the Messianic movement? Is this something that you will remain a part of, until the end? Or, perhaps just like Peter insisted that he would not deny the Lord (Mark 14:30; Matthew 26:34), and yet did so, might you answer the question "Are you part of the Messianic Jewish movement?" in the negative? Peter said he would die with the Lord, if he had to (Mark 14:31; Matthew 26:35).

Provoking the Jewish People to Jealousy

Provoking Jewish non-Believers to jealousy, that they might come to faith in Yeshua the Messiah, is one of the major, central features of the Messianic

The Messianic Walk

experience. Paul himself expressed the intent in Romans 11:14, "if somehow I might provoke to jealousy my own flesh and blood and save some of them" (TLV). Paul was absolutely distraught over the widespread Jewish dismissal of Yeshua that he witnessed in the First Century, that he said that he would give up his own individual salvation, to see his fellow Jews come to faith (Romans 9:3).

What does it mean to provoke Jewish non-Believers to jealousy? When non-Believers witness born again people experiencing a life of peace and blessing, a life of tranquility, and a life where a person has been reconciled with his or her Creator—non-Believers should be so jealous and envious of it, that they want it too! Paul was the example of someone who recognized that what Yeshua the Messiah had accomplished, was far superior to his own human achievements (Philippians 3:8)—and as one who was a *completed Jew* who knew his Messiah, was to be an example to his fellow Jews who should want to know the Messiah as well.

While Paul in his person demonstrated that Messianic Jewish Believers are to provoke Jewish non-Believers to jealousy for faith in Israel's Messiah—he also stated how non-Jewish Believers have to especially be doing this as well. Communicating to First Century Greeks and Romans, likely having to process why they had received Israel's Messiah into their lives—a Messiah not directly, at least, promised to them—and wanting them to be deflected from harboring any thoughts of superiority to a Jewish community widely dismissive of Him, he directed, "by their transgression salvation *has come* to the nations, to make them jealous" (Romans 11:11, author's rendering). Far from harboring any ungodly prejudices or anti-Semitic venom toward a Jewish community that had broadly rejected Yeshua as Messiah, non-Jewish people to whom He was not directly promised, were to be experiencing lives of great spiritual fullness, peace, love, and mercy—and provoke Jewish people to want a quality of life that was indeed directly promised to them in the Messiah! Non-Jewish Believers in Israel's Messiah have a distinct vocation, because of the mercy shown to them, to demonstrate mercy toward Jewish people who have not yet recognized Him:

"For just as you once were disobedient to God but now have been shown mercy because of their disobedience, in like manner these also have now been disobedient with the result that, because of the mercy shown to you, they also may receive mercy" (Romans 11:30-31, TLV).

The great tragedy, throughout history, is that most (claiming) followers of Israel's Messiah, have not provoked the Jewish people to jealousy *for faith in their own Messiah* by being great beacons of love and grace toward them. As much of the history of historical Christianity has demonstrated, replacement theology or supersessionism has prevailed, where non-Jewish Believers are thought to have totally displaced the Jewish people in God's eternal plans. Misunderstanding and prejudice, discrimination and persecution, have marred institutional Christianity's relationship with the Jewish Synagogue.

The Calling of Ruth and Non-Jewish Believers in Today's Messianic Movement

In today's Messianic community, there is a widespread conviction that Jewish and non-Jewish Believers can fellowship as one in Messiah, with the latter making the significant effort to correct many of the Christian errors of past history. While it is true that many of today's evangelical Protestants, who have been called by God into the Messianic movement, are not directly responsible for mistakes made centuries ago by people long since dead—it is also true that social prejudices and misunderstandings of the Jewish people and Judaism, have still persisted. Many of us have heard it said that non-Jewish Believers in Israel's Messiah, who are a part of today's Messianic community, actually wield more spiritual power than Jewish Believers in Israel's Messiah. Why might this be thought? Because non-Jewish Believers in Israel's Messiah, who are a part of today's Messianic community, have to make sure that they have received correction for any misunderstandings they have had about the Jewish people and Judaism, they must demonstrate great love and mercy for their Jewish neighbors, *and* they must express solidarity with the Jewish community when anti-Semitic acts take place.

From a perspective of individual salvation, non-Jewish Believers hardly have to be a part of Messianic congregations to be saved. There are millions of Christian people in today's world who have never heard, or will ever hear, of the Messianic movement, and they will be in the Kingdom of God. Non-Jewish Believers who come into the Messianic movement, and who indeed stay, are going to raise questions when they come into contact with Jewish non-Believers. These non-Believers might be the extended family of their Messianic Jewish friends, or they might be those they encounter in the marketplace. While these Jewish non-Believers might understand why Jewish Believers in Yeshua would want to express their faith in Yeshua in a Messianic context, these Jewish non-Believers might not fully understand why non-Jewish Believers in Yeshua would want to express their faith in Yeshua in a Messianic context. For those raised in a North American Protestant context, a person gives up a great deal in leaving an established evangelical denominational church, to be part of a very young and still-developing Messianic movement. There are new dynamics present in a Messianic congregation, that are not present in an evangelical church. And, Jewish non-Believers will ask a non-Jewish Believer in the Messianic movement, something to the effect, "Don't you know how difficult it is to be a Jew?", reflecting on historical anti-Semitism.

A big part of non-Jewish Believers provoking Jewish people to jealousy, for faith in Israel's Messiah, is fully grasping the ramifications of the Ruth calling. Technically, you do not have to be a part of a Messianic congregation to be saved. And, if you are a non-Jewish Believer in today's Messianic movement, you will be leaving an established evangelicalism for a young faith community. Are you willing to persevere and see it through? Certainly as one recognizes that the restoration of Israel (Acts 1:6) is the centerpiece of the end-times, then being a part of the Messianic movement will enable someone to be where the center of the action is!

The Messianic Walk

Is the Messianic movement for everyone?

It is very natural for non-Jewish Believers in today's Messianic movement, who tangibly reconnect to their faith heritage in Israel's Scriptures and do things that the First Century Believers surely did—to want this to be something that *everybody needs to do.* In the naiveté of many, it is thought that the Messianic movement is something that should be a universal movement. Perhaps some form of this might indeed be universal, subsequent to the Messiah's return. However, the great influx of non-Jewish Believers into the Messianic movement over the past two to three decades (1990s-2010s), has unfortunately demonstrated that a great majority of these people were not called in to help accomplish the Romans 11:26 trajectory of salvation history, and that many of these people would, sadly, balk at having a Ruth calling upon their lives.

It is indeed to be anticipated from the Tanach Scriptures, that the nations of Planet Earth will stream to Zion to be taught God's Torah (Isaiah 2:2-4; Micah 4:1-3). But what good does it do for non-Jewish Believers to be educated in the truths of Moses' Teaching, if implementing such instruction is not understood within the context of Romans 9-11, and in helping provoke Jewish non-Believers to faith in Israel's Messiah? Today's non-Jewish Torah movements are largely not interested in the salvation of the Jewish people, as you seldom if ever see them talk about Jewish outreach or evangelism, and they tend to make every effort that they can to distance themselves from the mission of the Messianic Jewish movement. Too many of today's non-Jewish Believers, who have reconnected with a Torah foundation of some sort, do not expel the effort to understand mainline Jewish traditions and customs, but instead eschew them. They do not care about studying and understanding the Jewish experience in history. They have not totally Heeded Paul's warning: "do not boast against the branches. But if you do boast, it is not you who support the root but the root supports you" (Romans 11:18, TLV).

Is the Messianic movement for everyone? It is safe to say that many of us have evangelical people we know, who we believe should not only be exposed to the Messianic movement, but should be considering some level of participation in it. But for many of us, this is also wishful thinking. Many evangelical Believers do not have a Ruth calling upon their lives. While they may be considered born again people, they are not able to spiritually and theologically process all of the different dynamics of what it means to know the Jewish Messiah. Forcing people into the Messianic movement, who are not called into it, and are not mature enough to be a part of it, will do more to deter its mission of Jewish outreach, evangelism, and Israel solidarity than accelerate it. And, too many non-Jewish Believers who enter into a Messianic congregation, are only there to experiment because they have been a part of so many other assemblies and groups...

The Calling of Ruth and Non-Jewish Believers in Today's Messianic Movement

Are you a non-Jewish Believer who has a Ruth calling upon your life? This is a very serious question as we consider when we are in human history. It is insufficient for a non-Jewish Believer in today's Messianic movement to simply say that he or she believes in the God of Abraham, Isaac, and Jacob and considers the Jewish people to be kindred in some way (Ruth 1:16). Because of the rising tides of anti-Semitism, even in North America, it will not be convenient for non-Jews to have labels like "Israel" or "Jewish" (or ironically enough, even "Hebrew Roots") associated with them. If you indeed are thrust into a situation where you have to stand in solidarity with a Messianic Jewish Believer, or even a Jewish non-Believer—**and die alongside of them**—will you be able to do it (Ruth 1:17)? How loyal will you truly be to the people of the Messiah of Israel?

The Messianic Walk

STUDY QUESTIONS FOR UNIT FIVE

1. What do you, and/or your family, expect to get out of being a part of a Messianic congregation? Have you fully considered all, or at least most, of the dynamics of what it means to be involved in the restoration of Israel?

2. What might be some of the similarities, but also differences, between a Messianic Jewish congregation, and (a) a Jewish synagogue, (b) an evangelical Protestant church? Speculate if necessary.

3. Are you concerned at the presence of false teachings within the Messianic movement? How might this affect your involvement in a Messianic assembly? (If necessary, describe your experience.)

4. Do you have the perseverance and fortitude to truly see your involvement with the Messianic movement through, to whatever God has intended for it?

5. In your estimation, how important is it for the Body of Messiah to experience unity? Why do you think people have a tendency to divide over what are ultimately minor issues?

6. While Jewish and non-Jewish Believers do have their differences—do you think it is useful for Messianic congregations to focus on differences first, or common faith first? Which approach do you think will encourage unity, mutual honor and respect, and a pooling of gifts and talents?

OUR PLACE IN THE CONGREGATION
FOR FURTHER READING AND EXPLORATION

Beck, James R., ed. *Two Views on Women in Ministry* (Grand Rapids: Zondervan, 2005).

Cowan, Steven B., ed. *Who Runs the Church? 4 Views on Church Government* (Grand Rapids: Zondervan, 2004).

McKee, J.K. *Men and Women in the Body of Messiah: Answering Crucial Questions* (Richardson, TX: Messianic Apologetics, 2018).

Nadler, Sam. *Developing Healthy Messianic Congregations* (Charlotte: Word of Messiah Ministries, 2016).

A SURVEY OF MESSIANIC THEOLOGY

UNIT SIX

A Survey of Messianic Theology

Every one of us, as a mature Believer in Yeshua the Messiah, should recognize the importance of regular, Bible study and reflection. "For the word of God is living and active and sharper than any two-edged sword—piercing right through to a separation of soul and spirit, joints and marrow, and able to judge the thoughts and intentions of the heart" (Hebrews 4:12, TLV). While people in today's Messianic community tend to be committed to a regular study of the weekly Torah portion or other parts of Scripture, **what do we do about theology?** Theology is the technical "study of God," or of matters relating to Biblical doctrine. While theology can, at times, be a term reserved for more academic or scholastic settings, people in today's Messianic community tend to have a genuine interest in more specialized and detailed studies, not only of the Holy Scriptures, but of issues that pertain to their understanding of God, His Word, who we are as His people, and what we are to actually believe.

Today's Messianic movement, as a still-developing and emerging move of God, has many areas of its theology which are sufficiently developed, and others which are presently in various stages of maturation. Over the course of the past two decades, general resources such as *Voices of Messianic Judaism* (Baltimore: Lederer Books, 2001; ed. Dan Cohn-Sherbok) and *Introduction to Messianic Judaism: Its Ecclesial Context and Biblical Foundations* (Grand Rapids: Zondervan, 2013; David Rudolph and Joel Willitts, eds.) have, in broad terms, laid out a number of critical topics, and presented a selection of diverse perspectives. The authors of the workbook *Messianic Judaism Class*, following their local congregation's statement of faith, summarize a number of issues including, but not limited to: the nature of God, the Divinity of Yeshua, the power of grace in salvation, the future resurrection, Jewish and non-Jewish Believers in the Body of Messiah, and even

The Messianic Walk

marriage and homosexuality.[1] This section of our workbook will mention these, and some other issues, presently being discussed in Messianic theology *or* soon to be on our horizon.

When people enter into the Messianic community, whether that be from a background in the Jewish Synagogue or evangelical Protestantism—it would be an understatement to say that there can be some tension, and even fights, over major matters of theology. One's local congregation, or assembly, is likely to be a microcosm, of the diversity of opinion and perspectives witnessed in the wider Messianic world. (This has especially become even more complicated in our information age, and with the wide array of online venues spouting off theological opinions and perspectives.) What are some things that you certainly need to be aware of, as you continue in your Messianic walk?

The Holy Scriptures

To its great credit, the Messianic community tends to have a very high view of Holy Scripture, believing that the Bible is inspired of God, and that the Tanach and Apostolic Writings (also frequently referred to as the B'rit Chadashah by Messianics) are authoritative and reliable for instructing the people of God today (cf. 2 Timothy 3:15-17; Romans 15:4). While Messianic people may tacitly employ terms such as Old Testament or New Testament, at times, for the familiarity of Christians—Messianics today hardly believe that the Holy Scriptures are to be starkly divided in two. Messianic people stress continuity throughout the Word of God, Genesis to Revelation, as God has steadily revealed more and more of His plan for salvation history (cf. Hebrews 1:1-2). While it may seem that Messianics focus heavily on the Torah and Tanach in teaching and preaching, be aware that many of today's Believers do not have any kind of theological foundation in the Tanach. The Bible of Yeshua and His first disciples was the Tanach. Messianic people rightly look for a unifying theme in Scripture, such as the fulfillment of God's promise to send a Deliverer, and the future arrival of the Messianic Age on Planet Earth.

While the authority of the Scriptures tends to be rightly upheld by today's Messianic people, our faith community does not tend to have as well rounded an understanding of *how the books of the Holy Scriptures were composed.* The books of the Bible, while the inspired Word of our Creator, hardly just "popped out" of the sky. Human beings had to actually collect data, transcribe information, catalogue commandments, record history, and copy manuscripts over many centuries to see that they were preserved. Conservative Biblical scholars recognize that the period of the composition of the books of the Bible stretches from the time of the Israelite Exodus from Egypt, the Fifteenth or Thirteenth Century B.C.E., to the close of the First Century C.E. Texts regarded as the Word of God were

---

[1] *Messianic Judaism Class*, Teacher Book, pp 126-160.

A Survey of Messianic Theology

composed in the languages of Hebrew, Aramaic, and Greek. And, while the major players include Ancient Israel prior to the exile, and later the Second Temple Jewish community after the exile—there are other major civilizations which directly intersect with the Biblical story (Sumer, Egypt, Assyria, Babylon, Persia, Greece, Rome).

Today's Messianic movement is in need of significant improvement of its understanding of the composition of the Tanach. A great deal of contemporary Jewish Tanach scholarship is liberal (as would be especially seen in a resource like *The Jewish Study Bible*), and will posit that the Torah or Pentateuch is a compilation of multiple sources from the Sixth Century B.C.E., after the Jewish return from Babylon (the JEDP documentary hypothesis). (Liberal Christian scholars will also be seen to espouse this position.) Being familiar with critical theories of Biblical composition, as a matter of navigating different study Bibles, theological dictionaries, and commentaries, is an area where today's Messianic people need to significantly improve. The past several decades, of critical scholarship, have seen the introduction of liberal proposals which regard most of the Tanach as little more than ahistorical fiction. Our Messianic Torah studies tend to completely ignore the presence of a great deal of such information, and tend to more widely rely upon Orthodox Jewish perspectives, not too interested in areas of Biblical historicity or reliability. Yet, when stressing a Tanach foundation, you inevitably have to deal with issues of when and how many of its events took place, whether there is available archaeological evidence confirming them, and how things might not be as simplistic as an English Bible translation may lead you to believe on first glance.

Today's Messianic movement also needs some greater improvement in its approach to the composition of the Apostolic Writings. No Messianic congregation is immune to somebody brazenly declaring that the New Testament was originally written in Hebrew, even though no original Hebrew New Testament exists from antiquity. All Messianic people agree that there is a genuine Hebraic and Jewish background to the Apostolic Writings, not only including quotations from the Tanach and concepts from Second Temple Judaism, but also various Hebrew idioms such as "whatever you bind on earth shall have been bound in heaven, and whatever you loose on earth shall have been loosed in heaven" (Matthew 16:19, NASU). It is one thing though, to propose an ancient Hebraic and Jewish background to the Apostolic Writings; it is another thing to declare that the Greek Apostolic Writings are to be treated as untrustworthy and uninspired. It is sad to say this, but not enough of today's Messianic congregational leaders possess significant Greek language skills. Being able to better engage with the Greek Apostolic Writings, and hence also with a wide degree of contemporary Protestant scholarship and commentary, is an area where progress must be made in the coming years!

The Messianic Walk

The Nature of God and Divinity of Yeshua

Because of the intersection witnessed in the Messianic movement between Judaism, Christianity, how both religions have approached the Supreme Being—*and* a diversity of people in today's Messianic congregations with their own opinions about the Supreme Being—the nature of God and Divinity of Yeshua is a big issue that can divide people. While the religious traditions of both Judaism and Christianity affirm monotheism, Judaism has widely approached God's oneness as being monolithic, whereas Christianity has approached God's oneness as permitting an internal plurality (most frequently witnessed via the traditional doctrine of the Trinity). Today's Messianic movement certainly does affirm monotheism, but would be seen to employ alternative terms to "Trinity," such as either "tri-unity" or simply "plurality," to describe an internal plurality of *Elohim* or God.

Today's Messianic movement affirms a belief in one Almighty God, Creator of the Universe, and that He has primarily revealed Himself to humanity in three separate, but unified co-existent manifestations: Father, Son, and Holy Spirit (Deuteronomy 6:4; 1 Corinthians 8:6; Matthew 28:19; 2 Corinthians 13:14), although many would leave room for more to be revealed about God in the future eschaton. Recognizing our limitations in evaluating the nature of the Supreme Being, many of today's Messianic people would be keen to emphasize that as mortals we cannot fully comprehend the Godhead and how He chooses to manifest Himself to us, although it is evident from the Scriptures that God is a plurality. This is clear as the main Hebrew word for "God," *Elohim*, is plural; and that He is one or *echad*, denoting a composite, **not** absolute unity. This can create some challenges in not only Jewish outreach and evangelism, but even with the increasingly large number of Unitarians in fringe sectors of the Messianic community. These are people who would widely affirm that Yeshua the Messiah is supernatural, but that ultimately that Yeshua is a created being or entity.

Whether or not Yeshua the Messiah is God, is a major debate among many individual people and families within today's broad Messianic movement. On the whole, today's major Messianic Jewish denominations and ministries affirm that Yeshua is God, but this does not always mean that individual people attending Messianic congregations would follow suit. Certainly while each of us, in our spiritual quest and study of Scripture, have had questions about the nature of Yeshua, which have needed to be answered, it is very disconcerting for many to know that there are probably people sitting near them in their congregational *Shabbat* service, who do not necessarily believe that Yeshua the Messiah is God.

We fully affirm the complete Divinity of Yeshua the Messiah, that Yeshua pre-existed the universe and created the universe (John 1:1-3; Philippians 2:5-7; Colossians 1:15-17; Hebrews 1:2-3), that Yeshua is to be worshipped (Mark 5:6-7; Matthew 2:2, 8, 11; Matthew 14:32-33; 28:9, 17; Luke 24:52; John 9:38; Hebrews 1:6), and even though in Yeshua's human Incarnation the Father is greater than the

Son (John 14:28), that the Son is genuinely God (John 20:28; Romans 9:5; Titus 2:13; 2 Peter 1:1). We believe that acknowledging Yeshua as Lord, meaning YHWH/YHVH, is mandatory for salvation (Romans 10:9; Philippians 2:10-11). We believe that He was conceived of the Holy Spirit, born of the virgin Mary (Isaiah 7:14; Matthew 1:18, 20, 23, 25; Luke 1:26-33), and that He is the prophesied Messiah of Israel (John 1:45). However, as students of the Holy Scriptures, we should not simply accept these tenets on the basis of blind dogma, and must conduct more thorough investigations of the Divinity of Yeshua, and how Yeshua the Son is integrated into the Divine Identity. Fortunately, there are leaders and teachers in today's Messianic movement, who have taken an active interest in seeing our understanding of the nature of Yeshua improve—not only as we spread the good news to Jewish people, but also encounter an increasingly complicated number of false teachings from the independent Hebrew/Hebraic Roots movement, many of whose supporters do not believe that Yeshua is God.

Salvation and the Work of the Holy Spirit

Today's Messianic movement, with a theological tradition inherited from both Judaism and Protestantism, stands at a clear intersection when it comes to evaluating the major issues of salvation. Evangelical Protestantism tends to almost exclusively focus on the salvation of the individual person, and the subsequent work of the Holy Spirit. Judaism has historically focused on the corporate salvation of Israel, something which is to involve the arrival of the Messiah, the restoration of the Davidic monarchy, and the defeat of Israel's enemies. Both of these vantage points of salvation are critical to understand in your Messianic experience. Without the redemption of individuals, there can be no corporate redemption.

Today's Messianic community, in concert with evangelicalism, would affirm that salvation is a free gift of God available through acknowledging Yeshua the Messiah as Lord (Romans 10:9) by repentance and confession of sin (Luke 5:32; Acts 5:31; Romans 2:4; 10:10; 2 Corinthians 7:9-10; 2 Timothy 2:25; 2 Peter 3:9), which results in a person being born again (John 3:3, 7; 1 Peter 1:3, 23) or regenerated by an indwelling of the Holy Spirit. Given our widescale conviction that God's Torah does remain relevant instruction for God's people today, does today's Messianic community at all promote any kind of "salvation by works" doctrine? **Salvation does not come via human action or obeying commandments** (Matthew 5:20; John 1:17; Romans 2:12-13, 25; 3:20, 27; 4:14; 8:3; 10:5; Galatians 2:16, 21; 3:2, 11, 21; 5:4; 6:13; Ephesians 2:8-9; Philippians 3:9), but if one is of the faith, then he or she will have "works" (James 2:14-16) resultant of one's spiritual transformation. The commandments of Scripture define sin (Romans 3:31; 5:13; 6:15; 7:7-9, 12; 8:2; 10:4; Galatians 3:24; Hebrews 7:19; 10:28; James 2:9) and therefore define every person's guilt. God's commandments also provide the basis for the good works that His people are to be actively accomplishing (Ephesians 2:10).

A longstanding debate in Protestantism, since the Reformation, involves whether or not God has predestined some to salvation, and others to damnation, and also whether those who have made a profession of faith in Yeshua can at a later point lose their salvation. All Believers are required to "work out" their salvation (Philippians 2:12), meaning not taking it for granted, and we should all be actively maturing in our walk of faith. However, there is no consensus on the longstanding debate between Calvinists and Arminians in today's Messianic movement, the former advocating a doctrine of eternal security, and the later advocating that, however unlikely, a person can in principle renounce his or her salvation and lose it. Many of today's Messianic congregations and fellowships have individual people reared in both theological traditions. It often follows that congregational leaders and teachers who received theological training at either Calvinist or Arminian institutions, will follow suit.

Another longstanding debate, in evangelicalism today, concerns the continuation of the spiritual gifts from the First Century C.E. (John 14:16l 16:13-14; Acts 1:8). Today's Messianic community has both leaders and people who are cessationists, believing the gifts of the Spirit to have terminated after the death of the Apostles; continuists who believe that the gifts of the Spirit continue in vitality to the present; and today's Messianic community has those who would identify as charismatic, often meaning that the dramatic gifts of the Spirit should manifest themselves at every gathering of Messiah followers. The spiritual gifts are for the corporate edification of all of God's people (1 Corinthians 12:7; Ephesians 5:18-20), most especially involving the virtues commonly called the fruit of the Spirit (Galatians 5:22-23).

Ecclesiology

Ecclesiology is the formal study of the *ekklēsia* or the people of God. In evangelical Protestant settings, ecclesiology often involves the life body of the local faith community. In today's Messianic movement, however, discussions and debates over ecclesiology often involve the place of Jewish and non-Jewish Believers together, in the Body of Messiah. While no one doubts how Jewish Believers in Israel's Messiah remain Jewish, and they clearly are a part of the community of Israel—what is the relationship of non-Jewish Believers to the community of Israel? Much of this involves what it specifically means for non-Jewish Believers in Israel's Messiah to be reckoned as members of the Commonwealth of Israel (Ephesians 2:11-13) or grafted-in to the olive tree (Romans 11:16-18).

Throughout a great deal of academic Messianic Jewish writing, one will commonly see the concept of a **bilateral ecclesiology** promoted. A bilateral

A Survey of Messianic Theology

ecclesiology would affirm that Jewish and non-Jewish Believers are together a part of the Commonwealth of Israel, but that such a Commonwealth of Israel is to be composed of two distinct segments: the Messianic Jewish community, and the Christian Church. The term "commonwealth" is approached from the position of it being like the British Commonwealth of Nations, rather than *politeia* in its classical context of it being, "**the right to be a member of a sociopolitical entity, citizenship**" (*BDAG*).[2] Those who adhere to a bilateral ecclesiology model are not always welcoming of non-Jewish Believers in today's Messianic movement. While Jewish and non-Jewish Believers are not exactly the same, and do have their natural distinctions—those who promote a bilateral ecclesiology can be seen to rigidly emphasize distinctions among God's people, at the expense of the common faith that we are to have in Yeshua.

A competing model that is seen at many Messianic congregations—particularly those which would emphasize that Jewish and non-Jewish Believers are to function as "one new man" or "one new humanity" (Ephesians 2:15)—is probably best labeled as the **enlarged Kingdom realm of Israel** model. In Acts 15:15-18, James the Just placed the salvation of the nations squarely as a component of the restoration of the Tabernacle of David, referencing Amos 9:11-12: "The words of the Prophets agree, as it is written: 'After this I will return and rebuild the fallen tabernacle of David. I will rebuild its ruins and I will restore it, so that the rest of humanity may seek the Lord—namely all the Gentiles who are called by My name—says Adonai, who makes these things known from of old'" (TLV). During the reign of King David, Israel was not only to be regarded at its ideal peak as a state, but as indicated in the Hebrew of Amos 9:12, "That they may possess the remnant of Edom" (NASU), noting how the borders of Israel's jurisdiction reached beyond the Twelve Tribes. An enlarged Kingdom realm of Israel model would regard all of God's people as members of the Commonwealth of Israel, with a restored Twelve Tribes at the center, and enlarged borders to welcome in the righteous from the nations.

For the authors of the workbook *Messianic Judaism Class*, "We believe that the Jews according to the flesh (descendants of Abraham through Isaac; whether through the blood line of the mother or the father) who place their faith in Israel's Messiah Yeshua have not disowned or separated themselves from their race and Judaic heritage, but remain sons and daughters of Israel. Gentiles who place their faith in Israel's Messiah Yeshua are also, spiritually sons and daughters of Israel."[3] For the latter, even though reckoned as "fellow citizens with God's people and members of God's household" (Ephesians 2:19, TLV), they are also strongly warned

---

[2] Frederick William Danker, ed., et. al., *A Greek-English Lexicon of the New Testament and Other Early Christian Literature*, third edition (Chicago: University of Chicago Press, 2000), 845.

[3] Ibid., 148.

The Messianic Walk

against being arrogant to the Jewish people who have yet to receive the Messiah (Romans 11:19-20). **Non-Jewish Believers should not just call themselves "Israel,"** as that can be frequently construed as arrogant, insensitive to the Jewish struggle throughout history, and even supportive of replacement theology. Non-Jewish Believers should qualify their participation within Israel's Commonwealth, as being grafted-in, fellow citizens with Jewish Believers, and most especially co-laborers in the restoration of Israel's Kingdom with Jewish Believers.

Being Patient in Your Theological Studies

Each one of us, as a man or woman of faith, is probably aware of the fact of how our maturation in the Lord is contingent on us being diligent and consistent in terms of praying each day, being in fellowship with brothers and sisters, and regularly studying the Bible. While Qohelet issues the fair warning, "There is no end to the making of many books, and excessive study wearies the flesh" (Ecclesiastes 12:12, TLV), there are necessary books to be read and studies to be conducted, as a part of one's spiritual growth and transformation. Some of these might indeed involve having to wade through some academic and scholarly perspectives, evaluate various Hebrew and Greek language issues, weigh statements made in ancient literature and philosophy, and engage with technical commentaries. Some of the studies conducted in various Messianic congregations and venues today, are not as fruitful or beneficial to one's understanding of God and of His Word, than some others are. But some of the studies conducted in various Messianic congregations and venues today, are indeed required if we are to be a stable and effective Messianic movement, as we approach the final stretch of salvation history.

Many of you, because of your participation—no matter how long or short—in a Messianic congregation and in things Messianic, are aware of the importance of the subjects just summarized. We need to improve our understanding of how we got the Bible. Each one of us unfortunately, is likely to have witnessed or heard about someone, at some time in our Messianic assembly, who denied or at least severely questioned the Divinity of Yeshua. Today's Messianic people need a better approach to their salvation, because even if we are genuinely saved from our sins and proceeding in sanctification—how many of us think of salvation in entirely individualistic terms, and do not really concern ourselves with what is intended for the corporate Kingdom of God? And, when a word like "ecclesiology" appears on our scopes, we tend to have no idea how fraught it can be with controversy among today's Messianics, and the implications it has for Jewish and non-Jewish Believers getting along and respecting one another.

As exciting as it is for many of us to be involved in the Messianic movement—and the great potential is has—none of us has the time or the energy to absorb information and teaching on all the great issues of theology all at once. Each of us, has to deliberately pace ourselves, as we move forward in our individual walks of faith, and as we see the Messianic movement steadily emerge into what the Lord intends for it to become. The issues noted in this chapter are some of those which many of us already know about, or have at least indirectly encountered, in our Messianic experiences. These subjects can be addressed on their own, or can be addressed in segments as people read and study Holy Scripture. *The key is whether you will now consciously remember that these are some of the* known *issues present in Messianic theology.* How will you, as you proceed in your Messianic walk, know that you might need to dig a little deeper with how a particular Biblical book was composed, or that you might need to be on guard with certainly controversial issues? Qohelet advises, "Better the end of a matter than its beginning. Better a patient spirit than a proud one" (Ecclesiastes 7:8, TLV). Where you should ultimately end up as a mature Messianic person, requires you to be patient today, as we steadily and consistently study God's Word, and the theological issues of substance.

The Messianic Walk

How Do You Study the Bible?

Each one of us as a man or woman of faith, continually treading on a spiritual journey, has a certain series of expectations when we read the Holy Scriptures. All of us affirm the great power of the Word of God to change lives, the need for each of us to be diligent students of the Word, and the requirement for us to be informed from the Word as it involves the interactions with God and humanity—and especially what the Bible teaches us about God's character. We can identify with how Paul directed Timothy "Until I come, devote yourself to the public reading of Scripture, to encouragement, and to teaching" (1 Timothy 4:13, TLV). But aside from spiritual people all agreeing that the Holy Scriptures are to be the place where we turn for some decisive answers to life's questions—how do we study the Bible? As we are considering some of the issues present in Messianic theology, it needs to be fairly noted that some of the controversies that we are facing today, come as a result of inadequate, and perhaps even inappropriate, ways of reading and interpreting Scripture.

Many people in today's Messianic movement have been taught, either externally or internally, that the Bible is God's "love letter" to them personally. None of us want to be caught dismissing how the Bible indeed conveys God's good character and good intentions for humanity. Psalm 19:8(7) properly emphasizes, "The teaching of the LORD is perfect, renewing life; the decrees of the LORD are enduring, making the simple wise" (NJPS). There are many passages of Holy Scripture which the Lord has doubtlessly used to help you through a difficult time. Many of you can likely identify with how, when experiencing some crisis, you were guided to a passage like Jeremiah 29:11, "'For I know the plans that I have in mind for you,' declares *ADONAI*, 'plans for *shalom* and not calamity—to give you a future and a hope'" (TLV). However, while it is important that God's love has been conveyed to you via His written Word; those who study Scripture seriously, and especially those who are engaged in technical Biblical Studies, tend to *absolutely*

The Messianic Walk

cringe when someone says that the Bible is God's "love letter" to humanity. The reason, that such persons do not like to hear others saying these sorts of things, is because the Bible was not written directly to Twenty-First Century, modern individuals, who can then interject their subjective feelings into various cherry-picked verses or statements. **The books of the Holy Scriptures were composed for ancient audiences beginning with the Israelites who left Egypt—to the Jewish, Greek, and Roman Believers who made up the First Century *ekklēsia*.**

It is to be commended that a significant majority of the people, in today's Messianic movement, genuinely want to study the Bible at a deeper level. But, in order to study the Bible at a deeper level, a variety of guidelines do have to be followed. Simply picking up an English Bible version, and having a Strong's Concordance by one's side, is entirely insufficient in order for today's Messianic people to study the Bible at the level that they want to study it. Indeed, one needs to be able to read multiple English versions of the Bible and catalogue astute observations, have access to up-to-date Hebrew and Greek lexicons, if necessary be able to access Hebrew and Greek language tools, and also be able to access a selection of up-to-date Bible dictionaries and commentaries. The simple, yet complicated rule, of Biblical interpretation, involves (1) reading and interpreting the text for what it meant to its original audience, and (2) applying it in a responsible manner for modern people. Many of us will find, that when making the significant effort and attempt to read the Bible for what it meant to its original audience(s) first, that Scripture will actually be *more* relevant and critical for us living today, and not less.

Reading the Bible in an Observant Manner

For too many people who want to honestly and sincerely read and appreciate the Holy Scriptures, they tend to be handed a Bible, they are told to be sure to pray before reading the Bible, they are told that the Bible is the inspired Word of God—and that perhaps by reading the Bible, God will communicate something profound to them. Many contemporary Believers start reading the Bible, as though they have just been thrown into the deep end of a pool, without ever having had any swimming lessons. We should hardly be surprised, why not enough of today's Bible Believers do not have as comprehensive or as deep an understanding of Scripture as they ought to have. Because of not having enough guidelines to follow in reading Scripture, people tend to gravitate only toward a selection of Biblical books. For many in evangelical Protestantism, their understanding of God's Word tends to be limited not just to the Apostolic Writings or New Testament, but only a selection of texts in the Apostolic Writings or New Testament. Many Messianic people, in rightly wanting to (re)claim a foundation in the Tanach or Old Testament, can have a reverse problem of only focusing on the Torah or Pentateuch as relevant Scripture. And, many unnecessary and complicated issues have doubtlessly arisen,

How Do You Study the Bible?

because not enough people know how to methodically approach books of the Bible or various (controversial) passages of Scripture.

How should you read the Bible in an observant manner? How can you get a great deal out of the text, as God's Holy Spirit focuses your mind and intellect on what a particular passage communicated to its ancient recipients, and how it applies to you living in the Twenty-First Century? There are some very important guidelines which you need to be aware of, as you read and plumb the depths of Holy Scripture.

1. Read the Biblical text as a whole: While many people have read the whole Bible through via various annual programs, very few, when approaching a known controversial passage, have first started their investigation by sitting down, and reading an entire book, preferably in a single sitting. While it might take a few hours for some books of the Bible, when you are able to sit down and remind yourself that in ancient times, many would first learn the Scriptures by reading them in such a manner, a great deal of information and context will be acquired. If you can believe it, many of the problems that we have with interpreting specific verses, can take place because we fail to read those verses in the context of what is stated before or after such verses. Likewise, as you read an entire Biblical text, it is useful to have a journal handy, where you note various observations on the characters, setting, events, as well as specific questions that the text raises. Do not be fearful if you do not have all of the answers, even when committing a few hours of your life to read through an entire book of the Bible. In order to probe a book of the Bible at a deeper level, reading through an entire book of the Bible is the first necessary step.

2. Compare and contrast various English Bible versions: It is a sad fact, but there are people seen in the religious world today, who will take a single English Bible version, read a passage of Scripture, and stridently insist on various conclusions from it. While English Bible versions have their place, when it is known that there are different theological conclusions drawn from a passage or a verse, such conclusions may originate from how a passage or a verse is translated. When a Bible reader uses a selection of several English Bible versions, in initially approaching a particular passage or verse, it can be easier to detect that there is a variance of opinion with how such a passage or verse should be approached. While many of the differences witnessed among English Bible versions are stylistic, careful Bible readers should be able to detect how various differences witnessed can indeed be theological. Seeing such differences in passages of known controversy is important, before investigating any original language issues. (While there are various parallel Bibles available, where one can have a printed copy of different English versions to compare and contrast, Bible software will often give you the clear advantage of being able to customize which English Bible versions [and others] you can examine at the same time.)

(The recommended English versions that the publishers suggest you use, include, but are not limited to, the 1995 New American Standard Update or NASU, the Revised Standard Version/New Revised Standard Version/English Standard Version family, the New International Version; and for Messianic reading the Complete Jewish Bible and Tree of Life Version. All of these versions have been quoted or referenced in some way, throughout this workbook.)

3. Accessing original languages: Frequently, some of the differences which arise in interpreting Holy Scripture, originate from how Bible translators have chosen to render specific words or terms into English. *There is no "neutral" English Bible translation, as each translator or team of translators brings some presupposition to the text to be communicated from the source language into English.* Jewish translations of the Tanach, in English, will not be reflective of Yeshua of Nazareth being the anticipated Messiah, and as such various Messianic prophecies may be reflective of this. Christian translations of the New Testament, in English, are not too likely to be reflective of the position that the Torah or Law of Moses continues to remain relevant instruction for the people of God in the post-resurrection era. The Messianic Bible reader, in accessing any Jewish or Christian version, needs to keep these factors in mind. It does need to be recognized, that a number of English versions will indicate, in footnotes, where there are differences of opinion among a selection of translations.

There are a number of examples where employing both multiple English versions, as well as accessing the original languages which sit behind English translations, needs to be considered. The Sixth Commandment, as it appears in the venerable King James Version, reads as, "Thou shalt not kill" (Exodus 20:13), but in newer versions such as the New Jewish Press Society Tanakh or New American Standard, Exodus 20:13 reads with, "You shall not murder." An English Bible reader should immediately be able to detect that there is some perspective difference present. Going a little further, it is witnessed that the Hebrew verb translated as either "kill" or "murder" is *ratzach*, noted immediately by the venerable *Brown-Driver-Briggs* lexicon to mean "murder, slay."[1]

A well known difference of translation is witnessed in Romans 10:4, which in a version like the New American Standard reads as, "For Christ is the end of the law for righteousness to everyone who believes," with a footnote also indicating, "Or *goal*." The 2005 Today's New International Version has the slightly different, "Christ is the culmination of the law so that there may be righteousness for everyone who believes," and the 2011 Common English Bible reads, "Christ is the goal of the Law, which leads to righteousness for all who have faith in God." Just among these English versions, it is detectable that some theologians apparently believe that the Torah or Law of Moses is terminated by the Messiah, or that the Messiah is the aim or purpose of the Torah, in that its instructions inevitably point to Him and to His salvation. Not surprisingly, a definition for the Greek *telos*, as provided by *Thayer's Greek Lexicon*, is indeed, "*the end to which all things relate, the aim, purpose.*"[2]

A lesser known part of accessing Hebrew, Aramaic, and Greek resources for Bible study—but an absolutely imperative one—concerns encountering quotations of the Tanach in the Apostolic Writings. Many people, when reading a passage from an English version of the Tanach or Old Testament, and then perhaps encountering a quotation from it later in the Apostolic Writings or New Testament, may not see it quoted word-for-word. Of course, it should be immediately remembered how some quotations of the Tanach in the Messianic Scriptures are only partial quotes, they may be slightly adapted by an author, or they may be amalgamated with other Tanach passages. Romans 11:27, "THIS IS MY COVENANT WITH THEM, WHEN I TAKE AWAY THEIR SINS" (NASU), is a likely amalgamation of Isaiah 59:20-21; Isaiah 27:9; and Jeremiah 31:33-34, with deliberate connections likely to be made to other Tanach passages and expectations as well.

While one can witness partial or amalgamated quotes from the Tanach in the Apostolic Writings, many of the apparent differences that one can encounter, when the Tanach is quoted in the Messianic Scriptures, occur because it is not the Hebrew Masoretic Text being quoted, but instead the Greek Septuagint. What is commonly called the Septuagint (LXX), is an ancient Greek translation of the Hebrew Scriptures, produced approximately two centuries before the arrival of Yeshua the Messiah. The Septuagint was used within the Mediterranean Jewish Diaspora, and

---

[1] *BDB*, 953.
[2] *Thayer*, 620.

so it should hardly be a surprise why the Septuagint is quoted throughout the Greek Apostolic Scriptures. The single longest Tanach quotation, in the New Testament, is how Jeremiah 31:31-34 is quoted in Hebrews 8:8-12. Apparent differences between these two passages in one's English Bible version can be easily explained when it is recognized how Jeremiah 31:31-34 is quoted from the Septuagint. There are printed English translations of the Septuagint available, which you can use as a "crutch" if necessary.

4. Accessing Bible dictionaries and commentaries: While there are many issues regarding a controversial Bible passage or verse which can be resolved by considering translation from the source language into English, many issues cannot, in fact, be resolved by translation. Many of today's biggest theological controversies do not, in fact, concern translation—but they instead involve an evaluation of the location and setting of a text's audience, and potential background witnessed in ancient bodies of extra-Biblical literature, history, or philosophy. Various passages are interpreted differently, simply because different schools of thought have different perspectives in approaching the text. The answer you need for interpreting or applying a passage of Scripture, might actually be found in accessing a Bible dictionary, encyclopedia, or even a technical commentary. These resources should never be accessed *first*, without you having done some homework of reading and wrestling through a Biblical text yourself. Obviously, if the answer you are seeking is found in a quotation from ancient history, or even some archaeological find from Biblical lands, accessing a Bible dictionary or commentary will be necessary.

Tools for Studying the Bible

Each one of us, in our personal quests to study the Bible, does know that we need to have some key tools available at our disposal, for investigating things in more detail, and also for weighing whether or not some of the theological conclusions we might be coming to are at all accurate or appropriate. We are each called to be adequate students of God's Word, and as good students we need to have the right resources to interpret the Bible, understand its background, and be respected in the wider world of ideas. Whether you are someone who will be involved in facilitating various teachings in your local Messianic congregation, helping in a Bible study, or you simply want to be a person who can add useful and constructive thoughts to discussions on Holy Scripture—not enough of today's Messianic people are equipped with a selection of useful tools, to study the Bible, and enter into some conversation of Biblical Studies. While you may not need to

How Do You Study the Bible?

have as an extensive library as I have in my office, there are a few resources which you need to consider adding to your personal library.

Study Bibles

Hebrew-Greek Key Study Bible (ed. Spiros Zodhiates; Chattanooga: AMG Publishers, 1993)

The *Hebrew-Greek Key Study Bible*, available in KJV, NASB, and NIV, has important words underlined and keyed to *Strong's Concordance*. It includes an abbreviated Hebrew and Greek dictionary, and is a good tool to use for Bible studies with those who are completely unfamiliar with the original languages. Each book includes a brief introductory section. Note that it leans toward dispensational theology. The NASB edition due to its literalness in modern English is the preferred edition. *This happens to be the main, personal reading Bible that I use and carry.*

ESV Study Bible (ed. Grudem, Wayne, ed.; Wheaton, IL: Crossway, 2008)

The *ESV Study Bible*, employing the English Standard Version (2001), has become a significant, widely available, evangelical and conservative study Bible. The ESV Study Bible includes extensive introductions, annotations, and essays from many of the well known and appreciated evangelical scholars of the late Twentieth and early Twenty-First Centuries. The *ESV Study Bible* includes a wide selection of perspectives as they involve Biblical historicity, as well as theology. The *ESV Study Bible* does notably lean toward a Reformed or Calvinist perspective in many places, and there are things that today's Messianic people would disagree with. Still, the *ESV Study Bible*, on the whole, is a useful tool for us to engage with a great deal of contemporary evangelical theology.

New Interpreter's Study Bible, NRSV (ed. Harrelson, Walter J.; Nashville: Abingdon, 2003)

The *New Interpreter's Study Bible* should be considered as a token, liberal study Bible. (This resource is actually not as liberal as various volumes in the *Oxford Annotated Bible* series are.) Today's Messianic people do not tend to be well informed that much in critical theories surrounding the composition of the Tanach (OT), nor do they know how to approach various Left of Center schools of thought regarding interpretation of the Apostolic Writings (NT), either. The *New Interpreter's Study Bible*, while not too likely to be used as your primary study Bible, is nonetheless something that you will need, in order to be informed as to what many standard, liberal theological opinions have been, certainly going back to the mid-Twentieth Century. This publication also notably includes the books of the Apocrypha, along with introductions and annotations.

The Complete Jewish Study Bible (Rubin, Barry, gen. ed.; Peabody, MA: Hendrickson, 2016)

The Complete Jewish Study Bible includes an updated edition of David H. Stern's *Complete Jewish Bible*. Most importantly, *The Complete Jewish Study Bible* is a compiled work of both Messianic Jewish and Christian scholars, including introductions, annotations, and select articles. For a number of these Messianic Jewish scholars and pioneers, this will be one of their last major theological contributions to the Messianic movement. There is a diversity of approach to a number of the issues addressed in this resource, and some of you may be surprised what Bible passages include annotations, and which do not. Still, no Messianic library should be without a copy of *The Complete Jewish Study Bible*.

Jewish Study Bible (eds. Adele Berlin and Marc Zvi Brettler; New York: Oxford University Press, 2004

The *Jewish Study Bible* is an ecumenical Jewish resource including perspectives from Reform, Conservative, and Orthodox Judaism based on the NJPS translation. It does represent some liberal theology in various places, but overall is a good, easy-to-access reference source to have for Jewish perspectives on Scripture. Each book includes an introduction, most texts include commentary, essays on various Jewish theological issues are included, and there is a thorough glossary of theological terms unique to Judaism.

Hebrew and Greek Language Tools

Complete Word Study Dictionary: Old Testament (eds. Warren Baker and Eugene Carpenter; Chattanooga: AMG Publishers, 2003)

Easy-to-use volume for referencing Hebrew words for those who are unfamiliar with the Hebrew language. Words are keyed to *Strong's Concordance* numbers and include a brief theological explanation.

Complete Word Study Dictionary: New Testament (ed. Spiros Zodhiates; Chattanooga: AMG Publishers, 1993)

Excellent lay resource to have for referencing Greek words, by a native Greek speaker. Words are keyed to *Strong's Concordance* numbers and include a detailed theological explanation. This dictionary is slightly influenced by dispensational theology.

Bible Dictionaries and Encyclopedias

International Standard Bible Encyclopedia, 4 vols (ed. Geoffrey W. Bromiley; Grand Rapids: Eerdmans, 1988)

ISBE is a good, well respected encyclopedia in both conservative and liberal circles. A revision of the original 1915 edition, the present version reflects new scholarship and many more theological points of view. *ISBE* is generally more conservative than the newer *ABD*, but does not include as many Jewish references.

Anchor Bible Dictionary, 6 vols (ed. David Noel Freedman; New York: Doubleday, 1992)

ABD has become a standard, relatively up-to date Bible dictionary, in many conservative or liberal theological circles. Theologically it is liberal in many places, but is quite factual in terms of archaeology, manuscript information, and history. What is unique about *ABD* is that it is a major work produced with Jewish-Christian dialogue in mind, and Rabbinical opinions and extra-Biblical Jewish sources are referenced every bit as much as Christian opinions and outside sources are referenced.

Dictionary of Judaism in the Biblical Period (eds. Jacob Neusner and William Scott Green; Peabody, MA: Hendrickson, 2002)

Dictionary of Judaism in the Biblical Period is an excellent, one-volume reference work listing critical topics unique to First Century Judaism, their relation to Rabbinical Judaism and the development of early Christianity, and background historical information of the time.

Dictionary of Early Christian Beliefs (ed. David W. Bercot; Peabody, MA: Hendrickson, 1998)

Dictionary of Early Christian Beliefs is a valuable tool to have if you are unfamiliar with the writings of the Church Fathers from Second-Fourth Century Christianity. The Church Fathers' theological positions on a diverse range of subjects are listed by heading with elongated quotations.

Interpreting the Bible as a Messianic Believer

Today's Messianic movement is to be highly commended as having a very high view for the role of Holy Scripture in theology and lifestyle practice. However, as

The Messianic Walk

each of us is probably well aware, there are scores of interpretations and viewpoints present—regarding many issues in the Scriptures—which do not tend to be witnessed in other religious venues. Furthermore, as an emerging faith community—in contrast to much of Judaism and Protestantism—there are an entire array of theological and spiritual issues which today's Messianic movement is internally discussing, (strongly) debating, and even (outright) avoiding. While it is very good that your Messianic congregation or assembly likely has Torah studies, Bible studies, and small groups which encourage open discussion—**learn to be targeted with your remarks.** While there are going to be people who want to add to discussions on important issues and subjects, many of their comments are not going to be as well founded as they ought. When it comes time for you to interject something, make sure that it is based in Holy Scripture, with a number of the guidelines we have just summarized being followed.

The Messianic movement is a very unique move of God, in that we do frequently find ourselves sitting between the great theological traditions of the Jewish Synagogue and evangelical Protestantism. While we should each be willing to always question and reevaluate our beliefs, it is not as though every single tenant of religious faith that is Jewish or Protestant is somehow "wrong." Both the Synagogue and evangelical Church, as human institutions, have their share of mistakes—but they have also contributed, in their own significant ways, to civilization. It is our responsibility, as Messianic Believers interpreting the Word of God, to not haphazardly dismiss the positive virtues of our Judeo-Protestant heritage. If we decide to truly disregard something that has been handed down by Jewish or Protestant interpreters, we need to be able to have a reasoned explanation for doing so. If we are to develop our own, unique, Messianic interpretation of a Biblical book or passage—it needs to be firmly rooted within the text of Scripture, with us able to adequately explain ourselves. For many of you who have studied God's Word for many years, this will not be a problem. For some of you, you do need some help to better focus your attention, as you contribute to our collective Messianic vitality.

Moving Forward in Your Messianic Experience

Today's Messianic movement, because of what it stands for and what it has been doing since the late 1960s, has a great deal of potential to make a difference in the lives of today's Jewish and non-Jewish Believers. The modern Messianic movement's origins are as a missionary movement, focused on reaching out with the good news or gospel, to the Jewish community. Many non-Jewish Believers have been specially called by the Lord into the Messianic movement, not only to join into the purposes of assisting in the restoration of Israel with their talents and resources—but also so that they might tangibly connect with their spiritual heritage in the Scriptures of Israel, and the original faith practices of the Messiah. Attempts have been made since the turn of the Millennium, to correctly evaluate what the next big phase of Messianic development is going to be. What would it mean, specifically, for the Messianic movement to emerge into a post-missionary movement? Various answers have been proposed, some good, some not so good, and almost all of them controversial.

One of the major reasons why the Jews in the synagogue at Berea, tend to be admired by Bible students, is because they demonstrated a genuine open-mindedness at the declaration of the good news, and they weighed the evidence: "they received the message with goodwill, searching the Scriptures each day to see whether these things were true" (Acts 17:11, TLV). While the message of Yeshua of Nazareth had stirred things previously in Thessalonica (Acts 17:1-9), the Bereans, at least for a moment, did not react in an overly-emotional manner to the proposal that a man named Yeshua, had come in fulfillment of Tanach prophecy. *The Bereans demonstrated a fairness, which few in religious history tend to demonstrate.* Far too many of us, in our spiritual experiences, when hearing about

The Messianic Walk

various topics or issues of importance, overreact with our base emotions, and fail to pause and at least hear something or someone out sufficiently.

As we all move forward in the Messianic walk together—while we should continue to be a missionary movement focused on Jewish outreach and evangelism—there are going to be new areas of our mission, and especially our theology, presenting themselves as we move steadily toward the Messiah's return. Many of the issues, on our immediate horizon, have actually been addressed in many Jewish and Protestant venues for the past several decades. For whatever reason or series of reasons, the Messianic movement has a collective tendency to not demonstrate the sensibility of the Bereans in a number of these matters. Furthermore, as we get closer to the return of Yeshua—and with it the anticipated apostasy (2 Thessalonians 2:3)—there will be theological issues pressed upon us by outside forces. It should not matter whether the question or subject was raised by those in the Messianic Jewish movement, the independent Hebrew/Hebraic Roots movement, or some other place. What matters is that as students of God's Word, we demonstrate a willingness to conduct thorough (re)evaluations of our presuppositions and beliefs. We will frequently find that either we have to change certain viewpoints, or indeed that what we have believed was true and has been further confirmed.

Death and the Future Resurrection

A significant majority, of today's independent Hebrew/Hebraic Roots movement, believes that when people die, they enter into a state of complete unconsciousness in the grave, until the resurrection of the dead. Quite contrary to this, and concurrent with a great deal of popular evangelical Protestant thought, today's Messianic Judaism would widely affirm that when Believers in Israel's Messiah die, they go to be with Yeshua in Heaven. How much of this is connected with the anticipation of the future resurrection, though, is hard to say. What is not difficult to deduce, is that in many Messianic congregations and assemblies today, that when the subject of death and resurrection arises—usually because someone has just passed away, or is at least facing the possibility of death—that a number of opinions are likely to surface, that some leaders and teachers have not prepared themselves for. In theological studies, the belief in psychopannychy—more commonly known by the vernacular of "soul sleep"—has never been viewed as theological heresy. In fact, a growing number of evangelical Protestant theologians have expressed a preference for soul sleep, because they believe that it places a proper emphasis back on the future reality of resurrection. But most of the people in the independent Hebrew/Hebraic Roots movement, who are seen to believe in soul sleep, do so because they think that people "going to Heaven" when they die is pagan.

Moving Forward in Your Messianic Experience

No Bible reader can deny the reality that the intended, future condition of those who have died in the faith, is one of resurrection (Daniel 12:2; 1 Corinthians 15:51-53; Philippians 3:20-21; 1 Thessalonians 4:16-18). The intended destiny of Believers is undeniably one of existing in a permanently embodied, immortal state—and the idea that Believers' *permanent* condition is one of being disembodied, floating off to a celestial Heaven, is decisively incorrect. However, is it at all incorrect to conclude that in the intermediate time, between death and resurrection, that Believers will exist in a *temporary* disembodied condition, prior to the resurrection?

Today's Messianic movement widely and correctly affirms that the disembodied consciousnesses of Believers who die in the faith are transported to Heaven to be with the Lord. This is fully consistent with what the Apostles write to us in the Messianic Scriptures and the beliefs of First Century Pharisaical Judaism, which largely advocated an intermediate afterlife prior to the resurrection. As Paul wrote in 2 Corinthians 5:8, "We are confident, I say, and prefer rather to be absent from the body and at home with the Lord" (TLV). The Greek verb that Paul uses for "be at home with," *endēmeō*, actually means "To be at home, to be present in any place or with any person," relating to "one who is at home with. . .or among his own people" (*AMG*).[1] Being separated from one's physical body thus requires a Believer to be present with the Lord.

Paul also writes in Philippians 1:23, "But I am hard-pressed from both *directions*, having the desire to depart and be with Messiah, for *that* is very much better" (NASU), but expressing his need to remain on Earth a little longer to perform the Lord's work. Further on in this same epistle, Paul writes that "our citizenship is in heaven, and from there we eagerly wait for the Savior, the Lord Yeshua the Messiah" (Philippians 3:20, TLV). He wants to die and be in the presence of His Savior, yet clearly recognizes how Yeshua will ultimately come to restore the Earth. The Believer's ultimate place of residence is not a Heaven far off in the sky, but in the restored Kingdom of God on Earth. Heaven is the intermediate place to be with the Lord prior to the resurrection of a Believer's body.

Most leaders and teachers, in today's Messianic Jewish movement, will be seen to widely dismiss any form of "soul sleep" for the righteous, as it is only the Believer's dead body that is "asleep," awaiting for reunification with the consciousness at the resurrection. **Yet we fully affirm the reality of a bodily resurrection!** An intermediate afterlife assures us beyond any doubt that the person, who is resurrected, is the same authentic person who had lived a life on Earth—and not some replica or facsimile of the person.

---

[1] Spiros Zodhiates, ed., *Complete Word Study Dictionary: New Testament* (Chattanooga: AMG Publishers, 1993), 585.

The Messianic Walk

Those in the Messianic community who may believe in "soul sleep" often base it on half-verses such as Ecclesiastes 9:5b, which says "the dead know nothing" (TLV). Yet this is not definitive evidence of no conscious afterlife, as the verse continues describing human life on Earth, and how the dead do not know of any Earth-bound things: "They have no further reward, even the memory of them is forgotten. Their love, their hatred, and their zeal have already perished; never again will they have a share in anything that is done under the sun" (Ecclesiastes 9:5c-6, TLV). Ecclesiastes 9:5-6 does not say anything about the condition of dead persons or where they are, but instead lists specific things that they cannot do because they are dead. These are things that these people had time to participate in on Earth or "under the sun" (Heb. *tachat ha'shamesh*), but cannot participate in beyond the veil of death, hence not "knowing" about them.

It is insufficient for any interpreter, as can be quite commonplace among Messianic advocates of "soul sleep," to only consider references in the Tanach without also weighing them with statements in the Apostolic Scriptures. The Tanach really does not even ask the question about life after death, because it is more widely concerned with the *corporate* nature of God's people and their conduct on Earth, whereas questions of an afterlife are widely *individualistic*. Because the Tanach does not really ask the question, it is not addressed to the same degree as it is in the Apostolic Scriptures. But still, that does not mean that the Tanach is entirely silent about an afterlife. One cannot really "die," and then be "gathered to his people" (Genesis 25:8; 35:29; 49:33; Numbers 20:24, 26; Deuteronomy 32:50), unless one is gathered *somewhere*. It by no means speaks exclusively of internment in a family tomb. When Jacob died, he "was gathered to his people" (Genesis 49:33, NASU), but he was not actually buried for quite some time (Genesis 50:2-14). Moses is said to have been "gathered to your people" (Deuteronomy 32:50, NASU), but he was interred in an unmarked gravesite (Deuteronomy 34:6), certainly not being united with his ancestors' remains in a family tomb.

More controversial, in the discussion over death and the future resurrection, involves what will happen to the unrighteous who reject the salvation of Yeshua. Over the past several decades, a wide number of prominent voices in evangelical Protestantism have embraced a position known as annihilationism, the belief that the condemned will suffer extinction from existence. In theological studies, annihilationism is not viewed as heresy, although various critics of annihilationism, will question the motives and interpretational presuppositions of adherents. It is safe to say that a significant majority of people in the independent Hebrew/Hebraic Roots movement, do believe in annihilationism. And, a number of people in Messianic Judaism have at least been favorable to annihilationism.

In my own personal studies, I have yet to be convinced of the viability of annihilationism—the idea that the unrighteous condemned will suffer non-existence—from the text of Scripture, and in weighing the thoughts of various examiners. Many of today's Messianic people continue to affirm that those who do not repent of their sins and receive Yeshua will spend a conscious eternity in Hell (Deuteronomy 32:22; Job 11:8; 24:19; Psalm 116:3; Isaiah 14:9; Jonah 2:2; Luke 12:5, 16:19-31) and ultimately the Lake of Fire (Revelation 19:20; 20:10; 15). The belief of an annihilation of the condemned is viewed as being widely misguided, allowing the unrighteous to experience no sustainable consequence for their sin. Hell and the Lake of Fire should constitute an ongoing, eternal punishment for the damned (Revelation 20:10), not extinction. However, annihilationists frequently do not recognize that a metaphorical view of eternal punishment has been the majority position in Protestantism, since the Reformation—not the view that the unrighteous condemn have to suffer endlessly in a literal Lake of Fire, with smoke, brimstone, and burning lava. A metaphorical view of eternal punishment more fairly deals with descriptions of both fire *and* outer darkness (cf. Matthew 8:11-12; 13:41-42; 22:13; 24:51; 25:30). This means that eternal punishment may ultimately be considered never-ending banishment, separation, and exile from the presence of the Creator (Revelation 22:15).

The End-Times and Anticipated Tribulation

Because of our focus on Yeshua as the prophesied Messiah, the reconstitution of the State of Israel in 1948, and the present Messianic Jewish revival—there has always been a keen interest in end-time prophecy present, throughout many sectors of the Messianic movement. Some of this interest is rhetorical, and simply emphasizes our faith community as "end-time" and restoring something lost in the First Century C.E. Some of this interest in the end-times is actually quite serious and severe, with people making predictions about the rapture, the rise of the antimessiah and New World Order, and even how to survive the Tribulation period. No Messianic congregation or assembly tends to be immune from people making avid speculations about *when* we are on God's "timeline."

How do today's Messianic people approach the end-times? This, in and of itself, could be its own study. But our purpose here is to only inform you as to what you are likely to encounter in your Messianic congregational experience and participation.

While the end-times can be strongly and vigorously debated among many different positions, on the whole today's Messianic people are mature and fair enough to recognize that eschatology, the study of end things, is not a salvation issue. There is room enough for people to have developed positions and opinions about various aspects of the return of the Lord. At the time time, the considerable majority of today's Messianic movement will be seen to ascribe to some form of pre-millennial eschatology, meaning that it would affirm that Yeshua the Messiah will return to Planet Earth before the thousand-year Millennium. You will not frequently find Messianic people holding to amillennial, post-millennial, or preterist eschatology.

Among pre-millennialists, however, two strong divisions are witnessed between pre-tribulationists and post-tribulationists—although in fairness these are not the only pre-millennial positions. All pre-millennialists in today's Messianic movement will likely affirm that the Messiah will physically return to Earth following the last seven years of Tribulation, more accurately called the Seventieth Week of Israel (Daniel 9:27; Matthew 24:21; Mark 13:19). Messianic pre-millennialists will likely believe that during this final time period that a world leader known as the antimessiah (antichrist) will arise (Daniel 7:15; Revelation 17:11; 17:13), will demand worship (Revelation 13:15), and will require everyone to receive his mark to conduct trade and commerce (Revelation 13:16-17). During this time period, the final judgments of God will be poured out on humanity.

Pre-millennialists in today's Messianic movement will fully affirm a gathering of the holy ones into the clouds to meet the Lord (Matthew 24:29-31; Mark 13:26-27; 1 Corinthians 15:51-52; 1 Thessalonians 4:16-17), and that Believers will be spared from the wrath of God (Romans 1:18; 2:5, 8; Ephesians 5:6; 1 Thessalonians 5:9; Revelation 16:1). Pre-tribulationists will widely conclude that the wrath of God constitutes the whole of the Tribulation period, while post-tribulationists will widely limit it to a series of judgments near the end of the Tribulation period.

Unlike in many evangelical Protestant churches, where the doctrine of an any moment, pre-tribulation rapture, tends to be very popular, and the majority position—the same cannot be said of today's Messianic movement. While there are many Messianic people who believe in a pre-tribulation rapture, there are many other Messianic people who ascribe to some kind of post-tribulational model, where Yeshua the Messiah will return for the Believers in the final days of the Seventieth Week of Israel. It is also to be noted that while in previous decades, pre-tribulationists made up a majority of the Messianic movement, that by the 2020s it can be reasonably deduced that the numbers between pre-tribulationists and those holding to post-tribulational models, are more evenly matched. In fact, those holding to a post-tribulational gathering of Believers may actually be in the majority. **How we encourage constructive and realistic discussions of the end-times**—where we avoid the pitfalls of fear, and in making unwarranted predictions by setting dates—**is something that we all need to carefully navigate.**

The Effect of Post-Modernism

Most of you reading this have never even heard of the term **post-modern**, even though each of us has been affected by it in some (significant) way. The future of the Messianic movement is going to be impacted by post-modernism, whether we like it or not. The 1999 *Pocket Dictionary of Theological Terms* defines post-modernism as, "A term used to designate a variety of intellectual and cultural developments in late-twentieth-century Western society. The postmodern ethos is characterized by a rejection of modernist values and a mistrust of the supposedly universal rational principles developed in the Enlightenment era. Post-moderns generally embrace pluralism and place value in the diversity of worldviews and religions that characterizes contemporary society."[2] As an ideology, post-modernism would hold to the broad position of there being no absolute truth, and that a various religious or philosophical group would hold to its truth, while another would hold to another truth, with neither being better than the other. Post-modernism definitely appeals to liberal Jews and Christians, both of whom may be seen to adhere to an "all paths lead to God" spirituality. A post-modern worldview would stand in stark contrast with Yeshua's explicit claim, "I am the way, and the truth, and the life. No one comes to the Father except through me" (John 14:6, NRSV).

In more practical terms, how might post-modernism affect today's Messianic community? *If post-modernism can be credited with doing anything positive, it is in consciously emphasizing a plurality of views and perspectives that people will encounter in today's world.* The Jewish community throughout history, although small, has tended to be quite pluralistic in terms of the number of views you will encounter on spiritual matters. Protestantism, by virtue of its deeply rooted ideology of how individual people can read and interpret the Bible themselves, does facilitate its own kind of plurality. It is naive and short-sighted of any person today—especially in a still-developing and emerging faith community such as ours—to just *assume things* about other people or about other points of view, without getting to know such people, where they come from, and what their stories are first.

A steadfast rule of Torah jurisprudence is that "a case can be valid only on the testimony of two witnesses or more" (Deuteronomy 19:15, NJPS). From this is derived the necessary principle that a case must be adequately heard before a decision, or at least some preliminary conclusion, can be made. To what degree do we actually follow such a requirement in our personal ethics? How many of us come to quick conclusions about a subject or an issue, which we have scantly examined? How many of us are afraid of publicly saying things like "I don't know" or "I will need to look into that before I come to an opinion"? If you are going to adequately weather the effects of post-modernism, then being "quick to listen, slow to speak, and slow to anger" (James 1:19, TLV), will be imperative. Likewise, learning to place yourself into the position of someone else, will also be required. For whatever reason or series of reasons, Americans tend to have a very difficult time doing this.

---

[2] Stanley J. Grenz, David Guretzki, and Cherith Fee Nordling, *Pocket Dictionary of Theological Terms* (Downers Grove, IL: InterVarsity, 1999), 93.

Future Theological Developments in the Messianic Movement

Today's Messianic movement is still maturing in many areas of its theology and spirituality. Given the fact that people are being called into the Messianic movement from the masses of humanity—and especially given the fact that the Jewish community has a widescale tendency to be liberal and affected by contemporary forces—will require us to address many issues, which at times have been ignored or put aside for "another day." Some of these issues are already acknowledged, at least in part, as needing to be addressed at some time in the future. Every generation of God's people—and especially those who will be present close to the Messiah's return—has frequently had to ask how we got here as human beings, why God created the universe, and especially how God created the universe. Looking toward the future, entirely as a matter of information, it should be anticipated that there will be more known diversity in the Messianic movement regarding Genesis 1-11 issues, than at present wants to be recognized by various leaders and teachers. Likewise, given many discussions and debates present in both Judaism and Protestantism in the past few decades, there will need to be, as a matter of our theology, better and more refined teachings about men and women in the Body of Messiah. This too will be an area, as we move into the future, where there will be an increasing diversity of opinions.

Externally, what will be the biggest challenge facing the Messianic movement in the future? It is, to be certain, difficult to say. For several decades, the Messianic Jewish movement has faced opposition from the Jewish anti-missionary movement, those Jewish organizations which specifically try to convince people that Yeshua is not the anticipated Messiah. Throughout much of its history, the Messianic Jewish movement has received strong support from many in evangelical Protestantism, who not only see Messianic Judaism as an important outreach of the good news to Jewish people, but who especially do not believe that God is finished with Israel, repudiating replacement theology. Evangelical support for Israel, however, has now begun to substantially wane—not only with a new generation of Christian people negatively influenced by liberal trends, post-modernism, LGBTQ, and social justice progressivism—but by the Boycott Divestment and Sanctions or BDS movement. The State of Israel is perceived to be apartheid, and that its actions of self-preservation against Palestinian terrorism are not Messiah like. More and more Christian people, and various established Protestant denominations, have begun to openly oppose the State of Israel, and have at least indirectly been responsible for promoting anti-Semitism. It should go without saying that many of those Christians, who are supportive of the BDS movement, are not too conscious of their faith heritage in Judaism.

Moving Forward in Your Messianic Experience

The future of the Messianic movement is a bright one, because are aiming toward that time in history when "The kingdom of the world has become the Kingdom of our Lord and his Messiah, and he will rule forever and ever!" (Revelation 11:15, CJB/CJSB). At the same time, in order to arrive at that point, there are going to be increasing levels of pressure against the people of God, given the anticipated apostasy and rise of the New World Order and beast system. New waves of anti-Semitism will come, and Jewish Believers will be betrayed by many Christian people who once claimed to be their allies and friends. The loyalty of many non-Jewish people who have entered into the Messianic movement, will be challenged, as we approach the return of Yeshua. Will these people stand in total solidarity with Messianic Jewish Believers, or will they peel away, as it becomes less convenient to be identified or associated with labels such as "Israel" and "Jewish"? These are difficult things to contemplate, but they are nevertheless required things for us to be recognizing today, as we prepare for the final stretch of history, and how the Lord might truly transform the Messianic movement into **a Messianic force** for His righteousness and holiness...

The Messianic Walk

STUDY QUESTIONS FOR UNIT SIX

1. What comes to your mind when you hear the word "theology"? How important is it going to be, in your Messianic experience, to have a more developed approach to various issues and subjects?

2. What specific areas of Messianic theology have you seen discussed or debated in a fellowship setting? Describe your experience. What do you think needs to be investigated or explored further?

3. What guidelines or methods have you followed, for studying the Bible in the past? How have these methods been useful? What are some immediate areas where you know you need to make improvement?

4. How have different Bible studies been conducted at your Messianic congregation or fellowship? Has the teacher been responsible with the text, or is it clear that various corners have been cut? Elaborate.

5. What do you think the next big phase of Messianic theological and spiritual development is likely to involve?

6. How do you think today's Messianic Believers should truly learn to be Bereans, in their approach to studying Scripture or investigating various theological issues?

A SURVEY OF MESSIANIC THEOLOGY
FOR FURTHER READING AND EXPLORATION

Bowman, Jr., Robert M., and J. Ed Komoszewski. *Putting Jesus in His Place: The Case for the Deity of Christ* (Grand Rapids: Kregel, 2007).

Brenton, Sir Lancelot C. L., ed & trans. *The Septuagint With Apocrypha* (Peabody, MA: Hendrickson, 1999).

Bruce, F.F. *The New Testament Documents: Are They Reliable?* (Grand Rapids: Eerdmans, 1981).

Carson, D.A., and Douglas J. Moo. *An Introduction to the New Testament*, second edition (Grand Rapids: Zondervan, 2005).

Cohn-Sherbok, Dan, ed. *Voices of Messianic Judaism* (Baltimore: Lederer Books, 2001).

Dillard, Raymond B., and Tremper Longman III. *An Introduction to the Old Testament* (Grand Rapids: Zondervan, 1994).

Goodrick, Edward W. *Do It Yourself Hebrew and Greek: A Guide to Biblical Language Tools* (Grand Rapids: Zondervan, 1980).

Guthrie, Donald. *New Testament Introduction* (Downers Grove, IL: InterVarsity, 1990).

Harrison, R.K. *Introduction to the Old Testament* (Grand Rapids: Eerdmans, 1969).

Kaiser, Walter C. *The Promise-Plan of God: A Biblical Theology of the Old and New Testaments* (Grand Rapids: Zondervan, 2008).

_____. *Recovering the Unity of the Bible* (Grand Rapids: Zondervan, 2009).

Kitchen, K.A. *On the Reliability of the Old Testament* (Grand Rapids: Eerdmans, 2003).

McKee, J.K. *A Survey of the Apostolic Scriptures for the Practical Messianic* (Messianic Apologetics, 2006/2012).

Unit Six The Messianic Walk

McKee, J.K. *A Survey of the Tanach for the Practical Messianic* (Messianic Apologetics, 2008).

McKee, J.K. *To Be Absent From the Body* (Messianic Apologetics, 2012).

McKee, J.K. *Why Hell Must Be Eternal* (Messianic Apologetics, 2012).

McKee, J.K. *When Will the Messiah Return?* (Messianic Apologetics, 2012).

McKee, J.K. *The Dangers of Pre-Tribulationism* (Messianic Apologetics, 2012).

McKee, J.K. *Are Non-Jewish Believers Really a Part of Israel?* (Messianic Apologetics, 2013).

McKee, J.K. *The Hebrew New Testament Misunderstanding and related issues* (Messianic Apologetics, 2013).

McKee, J.K. *Confronting Critical Issues: An Analysis of Subjects that Affects the Growth and Stability of the Emerging Messianic Movement* (Messianic Apologetics, 2013).

McKee, J.K. *Salvation on the Line, Volume I: The Nature of Yeshua and His Divinity—Gospels and Acts* (Richardson, TX: Messianic Apologetics, 2017).

McKee, J.K. *Salvation on the Line, Volume II: The Nature of Yeshua and His Divinity—The General Epistles, Pauline Epistles, and Later New Testament* (Richardson, TX: Messianic Apologetics, 2018).

Pietersma, Albert, and Benjamin G. Wright, eds. *A New English Translation of the Septuagint* (Oxford and New York: Oxford University Press, 2007).

Provan, Iain, V. Philips Long, and Tremper Longman III. *A Biblical History of Israel* (Louisville, KY: Westminster John Knox, 2003).

Rudolph, David J., and Joel Willitts, eds. *Introduction to Messianic Judaism: Its Ecclesial Context and Biblical Foundations* (Grand Rapids: Zondervan, 2013).

Thompson, David L. *Bible Study That Works* (Napanee, IN: Evangel Publishing House, 1994).

The Messianic Walk

ABOUT THE AUTHOR

John Kimball McKee is an integral part of Outreach Israel Ministries, and serves as the editor of Messianic Apologetics. He is a graduate of the University of Oklahoma (Class of 2003) with a B.A. in political science, and holds an M.A. in Biblical Studies from Asbury Theological Seminary (Class of 2009). He is a 2009 recipient of the Zondervan Biblical Languages Award for Greek. John has held memberships in the Evangelical Theological Society, the Evangelical Philosophical Society, and Christians for Biblical Equality, and is a longtime supporter of the perspectives and views of the Creationist ministry of Reasons to Believe. In 2019, John was licensed as a Messianic Teacher with the International Alliance of Messianic Congregations and Synagogues (IAMCS), and was officially ordained as a Messianic Teacher in 2022.

Since the 1990s, John's ministry has capitalized on the Internet's ability to reach people all over this planet. He has spoken with challenging and probing articles to a wide Messianic audience, and those evangelical Believers who are interested in Messianic things. Given his generational family background in evangelical ministry, as well as in academics and the military, John carries a strong burden to assist in the development and maturation of our emerging Messianic theology and spirituality. John has had the profound opportunity since 1997 to engage many in dialogue, so that they will consider the questions he postulates, as his only agenda is to be as Scripturally sound as possible. John believes in demonstrating a great deal of honor and respect to both his evangelical Protestant, Wesleyan and Reformed family background, as well as to the Jewish Synagogue, and together allowing the strengths and virtues of our Judeo-Protestant heritage to be employed for the Lord's plan for the Messianic movement in the long term future.

John McKee is the son of the late K. Kimball McKee (1951-1992) and Margaret Jeffries McKee Huey (1953-), and stepson of William Mark Huey (1951-), who married his mother in 1994, and who is the executive director of Outreach Israel Ministries. Mark Huey is the Director of Partner Relations for the Joseph Project, a ministry of the Messianic Jewish Alliance of America (MJAA). John is single and has never married. This in no small part due to how the marriage examples modeled to him by his parents, would be very difficult to replicate in our current, and often very small Messianic community.

John has a very strong appreciation for those who have preceded him. His father, Kimball McKee, was a licensed lay minister in the Kentucky Conference of the United Methodist Church, and was a very strong evangelical Believer, most appreciable of the Jewish Roots of the faith. Among his many ministry pursuits, Kim brought the Passover *seder* to Christ United Methodist Church in Florence, KY, was a Sunday school teacher, and was extremely active in the Walk to Emmaus, leading the first men's walk in Madras, India in 1991. John is the grandson of the late Prof. William W. Jeffries (1914-1989; CDR USN WWII), who served as a professor at the United States Naval Academy in Annapolis, MD from 1942-1989, notably as the museum director and founder of what is now the William W. Jeffries Memorial Archives in the Nimitz Library. John is the great-grandson of Bishop Marvin A. Franklin (1894-1972), who served as a minister and bishop of the Methodist Church, throughout his ministry serving churches in Georgia, Florida, Alabama, and Mississippi. Bishop Franklin was President of the Council of Bishops from 1959-1960. John is also the first cousin twice removed of the late Charles L. Allen (1913-2005),

The Messianic Walk

formerly the senior pastor of Grace Methodist Church of Atlanta, GA and First Methodist Church of Houston, TX, and author of numerous books, notably including *God's Psychiatry*. John can also count among his ancestors, Lt. Colonel, By Brevet, Dr. James Cooper McKee (1830-1897), a Union veteran of the U.S. Civil War and significant contributor to the medical science of his generation.

John McKee is a native of the Northern Kentucky/Greater Cincinnati, OH area. He has also lived in Dallas, TX, Norman, OK, Kissimmee-St. Cloud, FL, and Roatán, Honduras, Central America. He presently resides in McKinney, TX, just north of Dallas.

Contributors to this Volume

William Mark Huey became a Believer in the Messiah of Israel in 1978, but it was a Zola Levitt tour to Israel in 1994 with his wife Margaret, which sparked an ardent search for answers about the Hebraic and Jewish Roots of our faith, and the significance of the Torah, Biblical festivals, and the seventh-day Sabbath/*Shabbat*—among other things. By 1995, his family became members of a Messianic Jewish congregation in Dallas, Texas, and their pursuit for truth intensified. Within a year, Mark formed a conference-producing enterprise called "The Remnant Exchange," and began hosting prophecy conferences and seminars with increasing Messianic understanding and emphasis. Mark's business experience, owning a commercial real estate brokerage company, coupled with Margaret's ownership of a cross-stitch design company, led them to form a ministry consulting business which worked with a variety of Messianic ministries from 1997-2002. Mark and Margaret have dedicated their lives to serving the Lord in order to use their God-given gifts, talents, and abilities to advance His Kingdom until the Messiah returns.

By 2002, after years of exposure to tangible evidence that the prophesied "restoration of all things" (Acts 3:21) was becoming a reality, the impetus to focus energy and attention on Israel, the people, the Land, and Torah-centered Messianic teachings merged together. The outcome was the formation of **Outreach Israel Ministries**, of which Mark serves as Director, and Margaret as Business Manager. *From the beginning of Outreach Israel Ministries, the need to educate and to minister to the expanding number of Messianics has always been at the heart of the mission.* The merger with TNN Online in 2003 (now **Messianic Apologetics**) substantially enhanced the capabilities. Today, both Outreach Israel Ministries and Messianic Apologetics have a significant role to play in aiding the people of the broad Messianic movement, in the theological and spiritual issues that they face—as many Jewish people are coming to faith in Israel's Messiah, and many evangelical Christians embrace their faith heritage in Israel's Scriptures in tangibly new ways.

Mark is the author of a number of books which focus on encouraging others to embrace the Hebraic and Jewish roots of our faith. These include the commentaries, *TorahScope, Volumes I, II, & III, TorahScope Haftarah Exhortations, TorahScope Apostolic Scriptures Reflections*, and the devotionals, *Counting the Omer and Sayings of the Fathers: A Messianic Perspective on the Pirkei Avot*.

Mark is a graduate of Vanderbilt University with a B.A. in history, with graduate studies toward a master's degree in aviation management completed at Embry-Riddle Aeronautical University. Mark has served in leadership roles at Messianic congregations and fellowships. Mark serves as the Director of Partner Relations for the Joseph Project, a ministry of the Messianic Jewish Alliance of America (MJAA). Mark and Margaret Huey currently reside in McKinney, TX, just north of Dallas, and have five grown children and three grandchildren.

Contributors to this Volume

Margaret McKee Huey is one of the founders of Outreach Israel Ministries (OIM) and serves on its Board as the Office Manager.

Margaret is a multi-talented woman who exemplifies what a Proverbs 31 woman should be. Besides handling the business responsibilities of OIM and editing assignments with our publications, she operates an internationally known needlework sampler design business that she founded in 1985. Yet, she still finds time to successfully invest in raising her three children.

In addition to her business acumen, Margaret is spiritually gifted as an evangelist. She was actively involved in evangelism through the *Walk to Emmaus, Chrysalis Program* and the *Lay Witness Mission* while in the United Methodist Church. When asked what Biblical character she most identifies with, she demurely responds, "why John the Baptist, of course." The passion of her heart is communicating the "Gospel According to the Torah." In an inspiring and convicting way, she not only helps you understand the sacrifice of Yeshua and your salvation, but also helps you understand the mercy of the Holy One as one follows His Torah.

Margaret comes from a long line of Methodist preachers and teachers. Although raised in a Christian home, she did not come to true saving faith until the age of 30. She was immediately drawn into an appreciation of Israel, the Jewish people, understanding that Yeshua was the Messiah of Israel and even celebrating the Seder Passover with her first husband, Kim McKee, at their Methodist church beginning in 1986.

Lamentably, in 1992 Margaret was widowed at the age of 39 with the responsibility for three young children. This unexpected tragedy did not detour her from her relationship with God, but instead prompted her into even greater dependency upon Him as her provider and comforter. As a result of her life experiences, she is gifted in grief counseling and deliverance issues.

Margaret is the editor for the upcoming Messianic cookbook, *Kosher Your Plate*, as well as editor for the *Messianic Helper Series*. Some of the titles for this series include: *Messianic Winter Holiday Helper, Messianic Spring Holiday Helper, Messianic Fall Holiday Helper,* and the *Messianic Sabbath Helper*.

Margaret is a graduate of Vanderbilt University with a Bachelor of Science degree in Geology. She is the wife of William Mark Huey and the mother of John McKee, Jane McKee, and Maggie Willetts, and now resides in Dallas, Texas.

Margaret can be reached via Outreach Israel Ministries.

The Messianic Walk

Bibliography

Articles
Davies, W.D. "Law in the NT," in *IDB*.

Bible Versions and Study Bibles
Abegg, Jr., Martin, Peter Flint, and Eugene Ulrich, trans. *The Dead Sea Scrolls Bible* (New York: HarperCollins, 1999).
American Standard Version (New York: Thomas Nelson & Sons, 1901).
Barker, Kenneth L., ed., et. al. *NIV Study Bible* (Grand Rapids: Zondervan, 2002).
Berlin, Adele, and Marc Zvi Brettler, eds. *The Jewish Study Bible* (Oxford: Oxford University Press, 2004).
Bratcher, Robert G., ed. *Good News Bible: The Bible in Today's English Version* (New York: American Bible Society, 1976).
Brown II, A. Phillip, and Bryan W. Smith. *A Reader's Hebrew Bible* (Grand Rapids: Zondervan, 2008).
Cabal, Ted, gen. ed. *The Apologetics Study Bible*, HCSB (Nashville: Holman, 2007).
Carson, D.A., gen. ed. *NIV Zondervan Study Bible*, 2011 NIV (Grand Rapids: Zondervan, 2015).
Coogan, Michael D., ed. et. al. *The New Oxford Annotated Bible: Fully Revised Fourth Edition*, NRSV (New York: Oxford University Press, 2010).
Dobson, Kent. *NIV First-Century Study Bible: Explore Scripture in Its Jewish and Early Christian Context*, 2011 NIV (Grand Rapids: Zondervan, 2014).
Ecclesia Bible Society. *The Voice Bible: Step into the Story of Scripture* (Nashville: Thomas Nelson, 2012).
Garrett, Duane A., ed., et. al. *NIV Archaeological Study Bible* (Grand Rapids: Zondervan, 2005).
Goodrich, Richard J., and Albert L. Lukaszewski. *A Reader's Greek New Testament* (Grand Rapids: Zondervan, 2007).
Green, Jay P., trans. *The Interlinear Bible* (Lafayette, IN: Sovereign Grace Publishers, 1986).
Green, Joel B., ed. *The Wesley Study Bible* (Nashville: Abingdon, 2009).
God's Game Plan: The Athlete's Bible 2007, HCSB (Nashville: Serendipity House Publishers, 2007).
Grudem, Wayne, ed. *ESV Study Bible* (Wheaton, IL: Crossway, 2008).
Harrelson, Walter J., ed., et. al. *New Interpreter's Study Bible*, NRSV (Nashville: Abingdon, 2003).
Holman Christian Standard Bible (Nashville: Broadman & Holman, 2004).
Holy Bible, King James Version (edited 1789).
Holy Bible, New International Version (Grand Rapids: Zondervan, 1978, 1984, 2011).
Kohlenberger III, John R., ed. *The NIV Integrated Study Bible* (Grand Rapids: Zondervan, 2013).
LaHaye, Tim, ed. *Tim LaHaye Prophecy Study Bible*, KJV (Chattanooga: AMG Publishers, 2000).
Lattimore, Richmond, trans. *The New Testament* (New York: North Point Press, 1996).
May, Herbert G., and Bruce M. Metzger, eds. *The New Oxford Annotated Bible With the Apocrypha*, RSV (New York: Oxford University Press, 1977).
Meeks, Wayne A., ed., et. al. *The HarperCollins Study Bible*, NRSV (New York: HarperCollins, 1993).
Messianic Jewish Shared Heritage Bible, JPS/TLV (Shippensburg, PA: Destiny Image, 2012).
Messianic Jewish Family Bible—Tree of Life Version (Snellville, GA: Messianic Jewish Family Bible Society, 2014).
Newman, Barclay M., ed. *Holy Bible: Contemporary English Version* (New York: American Bible Society, 1995).
New American Standard Bible (La Habra, CA: Foundation Press Publications, 1971).

The Messianic Walk

New American Standard, Updated Edition (Anaheim, CA: Foundation Publications, 1995).
New English Bible (Oxford and Cambridge: Oxford and Cambridge University Presses, 1970).
New King James Version (Nashville: Thomas Nelson, 1982).
New Revised Standard Version (National Council of Churches of Christ, 1989).
Packer, J.I., ed. *The Holy Bible, English Standard Version* (Wheaton, IL: Crossway Bibles, 2001).
Peterson, Eugene H. *The Message: The Bible in Contemporary Language* (Colorado Springs: NavPress, 2002).
Phillips, J.B., trans. *The New Testament in Modern English* (New York: Touchstone, 1972).
Pietersma, Albert, and Benjamin G. Wright, eds. *A New English Translation of the Septuagint* (Oxford and New York: Oxford University Press, 2007).
Rubin, Barry, gen. ed. *The Complete Jewish Study Bible* (Peabody, MA: Hendrickson, 2016).
Ryrie, Charles C., ed. *The Ryrie Study Bible*, NASB (Chicago: Moody Press, 1978).
Scherman, Nosson, and Meir Zlotowitz, eds. *ArtScroll Tanach* (Brooklyn: Mesorah Publications, 1996).
Siewert, Frances E., ed. *The Amplified Bible* (Grand Rapids: Zondervan, 1965).
Suggs, M. Jack, and Katharine Doob Sakenfeld, and James R. Mueller, et. al. *The Oxford Study Bible*, REB (New York: Oxford University Press, 1992).
Stern, David H., trans. *Jewish New Testament* (Clarksville, MD: Jewish New Testament Publications, 1995).
_____, trans. *Complete Jewish Bible* (Clarksville, MD: Jewish New Testament Publications, 1998).
Tanakh: The Holy Scriptures (Philadelphia: Jewish Publication Society, 1999).
The Holy Bible, Revised Standard Version (Nashville: Cokesbury, 1952).
The Jerusalem Bible (Jerusalem: Koren Publishers, 2000).
The Keter Crown Bible Jerusalem: Chorev, 2006).
The NET Bible, New English Translation (Dallas: Biblical Studies Press, 2005).
The Voice Bible: Step into the Story of Scripture (Nashville: Thomas Nelson, 2012).
Today's New International Version (Grand Rapids: Zondervan, 2005).
Tree of Life Messianic Family Bible—New Covenant (Shippensburg, PA: Destiny Image, 2011).
Walton, John H., and Craig S. Keener, eds. *NIV Cultural Backgrounds Study Bible*, 2011 NIV (Grand Rapids: Zondervan, 2016).
Williams, Charles B., trans. *The New Testament: A Private Translation in the Language of the People* (Chicago: Moody Publishers, 1937).
Wright, N.T. *The Kingdom New Testament: A Contemporary Translation* (New York: HarperCollins, 2011).
Young, Robert, trans. *Young's Literal Translation*.
Zodhiates, Spiros, ed. *Hebrew-Greek Key Study Bible*, NASB (Chattanooga: AMG Publishers, 1994).

Books
Appel, James, Jonathan Bernis, and David Levine. *Messianic Judaism Class* (Copenhagan, NY: Olive Press, 2011).
_____. *Messianic Judaism Class*, Teacher Book (Copenhagan, NY: Olive Press, 2011).
Beck, James R., ed. *Two Views on Women in Ministry* (Grand Rapids: Zondervan, 2005).
Boyd, Gregory A., and Paul R. Eddy. *Across the Spectrum: Understanding Issues in Evangelical Theology* (Grand Rapids: Baker Academic, 2002).
Brown, Michael L. *Our Hands Are Stained With Blood* (Shippensburg, PA: Destiny Image 1992).
_____. *Answering Jewish Objections to Jesus: General and Historical Objections* (Grand Rapids: Baker Books, 2000).
_____. *Answering Jewish Objections to Jesus, Volume 2: Theological Objections* (Grand Rapids: Baker Books, 2000).

Bibliography

————————. *Answering Jewish Objections to Jesus, Volume 3: Messianic Prophecy Objections* (Grand Rapids: Baker Books, 2003).

————————. *Answering Jewish Objections to Jesus, Volume 4: New Testament Objections* (Grand Rapids: Baker Books, 2007).

————————. *Answering Jewish Objections to Jesus, Volume 5: Traditional Jewish Objections* (San Francisco, CA: Purple Pomegranate Productions, 2009).

Bruce, F.F. *New Testament History* (New York: Doubleday, 1969).

————————. *The New Testament Documents: Are They Reliable?* (Grand Rapids: Eerdmans, 1981).

Carson, D.A., and Douglas J. Moo. *An Introduction to the New Testament*, second edition (Grand Rapids: Zondervan, 2005).

Cohn-Sherbok, Dan, ed. *Messianic Judaism* (London and New York: Continuum, 2000).

————————, ed. *Voices of Messianic Judaism* (Baltimore: Lederer Books, 2001).

Chernoff, David. *An Introduction to Messianic Judaism* (Havertown, PA: MMI Publishing, 2012).

Chernoff, Yohanna, with Jimi Miller. *Born a Jew, Die a Jew: The Story of Martin Chernoff A Pioneer in Messianic Judaism* (Hagerstown, MD: EBED Publications, 1996).

Cowan, Steven B., ed. *Who Runs the Church? 4 Views on Church Government* (Grand Rapids: Zondervan, 2004).

Dillard, Raymond B., and Tremper Longman III. *An Introduction to the Old Testament* (Grand Rapids: Zondervan, 1994).

Donato, Christopher John, ed. *Perspectives on the Sabbath: Four Views* (Nashville: B&H Academic, 2011).

Eby, Aaron. *Biblically Kosher: A Messianic Jewish Perspective on Kashrut* (Marshfield, MO: First Fruits of Zion, 2012).

Egan, Hope. *Holy Cow! Does God Care About What We Eat?* (Littleton, CO; First Fruits of Zion, 2005).

Engle, Paul E., ed. *Understanding Four Views on the Lord's Supper* (Grand Rapids: Zondervan, 2007).

Glaser, Mitch. *Isaiah 53 Explained* (New York: Chosen People Productions, 2010).

Goldberg, Louis, ed. *How Jewish is Christianity? 2 Views on the Messianic Movement* (Grand Rapids: Zondervan, 2003).

Goldingay, John. *Old Testament Theology: Israel's Gospel* (Downers Grove, IL: InterVarsity, 2003).

Grudem, Wayne. *Systematic Theology: An Introduction to Biblical Doctrine* (Grand Rapids: Zondervan, 1994).

Gundry, Robert H. *A Survey of the New Testament*, third edition (Grand Rapids: Zondervan, 1994).

Guthrie, D., and J.A. Motyer, eds. *The New Bible Commentary Revised* (Grand Rapids: Eerdmans, 1970).

Guthrie, Donald. *New Testament Introduction* (Downers Grove, IL: InterVarsity, 1990).

Harvey, Richard. *Mapping Messianic Jewish Theology: A Constructive Approach* (Milton Keynes: Paternoster, 2009).

Harrison, R.K. *Introduction to the Old Testament* (Grand Rapids: Eerdmans, 1969).

Hegg, Tim. *The Letter Writer: Paul's Background and Torah Perspective* (Littleton, CO: First Fruits of Zion, 2002).

————————. *Fellow Heirs: Jews & Gentiles Together in the Family of God* (Littleton, CO: First Fruits of Zion, 2003).

Juster, Daniel C. *Growing to Maturity* (Denver: The Union of Messianic Jewish Congregations Press, 1987).

————————. *Jewish Roots: A Foundation of Biblical Theology* (Shippensburg, PA: Destiny Image, 1995).

————————. *Jewish Roots: Understanding Your Jewish Faith*, revised edition (Shippensburg, PA: Destiny Image, 2013).

Kaiser, Walter C. *Toward an Old Testament Theology* (Grand Rapids: Zondervan, 1978).

————————. *Toward Old Testament Ethics* (Grand Rapids: Zondervan, 1983).

The Messianic Walk

_____. *The Messiah in the Old Testament* (Grand Rapids: Zondervan, 1995).

_____. *The Promise-Plan of God: A Biblical Theology of the Old and New Testaments* (Grand Rapids: Zondervan, 2008).

_____. *Recovering the Unity of the Bible: One Continuous Story, Plan, and Purpose* (Grand Rapids: Zondervan, 2009).

_____, Peter H. Davids, F.F. Bruce, and Manfred T. Branch. *Hard Sayings of the Bible* (Downers Grove, IL: InterVarsity, 1996).

Kasdan, Barney. *God's Appointed Times: A Practical Guide for Understanding and Celebrating the Biblical Holidays* (Baltimore: Lederer, 1993).

_____. *God's Appointed Customs: A Messianic Jewish Guide to the Biblical Lifecycle and Lifestyle* (Baltimore: Lederer: 1996).

Kinzer, Mark S. *Post-Missionary Messianic Judaism: Redefining Christian Engagement with the Jewish People* (Grand Rapids: Brazos Press, 2005).

Kitchen, K.A. *Ancient Orient and Old Testament* (Madison, WI: InterVarsity, 1966).

_____. *On the Reliability of the Old Testament* (Grand Rapids: Eerdmans, 2003).

Lancaster, D. Thomas. *The Mystery of the Gospel: Jew and Gentile in the Eternal Purpose of God* (Littleton, CO: First Fruits of Zion, 2003).

_____. *Restoration: Returning the Torah of God to the Disciples of Jesus* (Littleton, CO: First Fruits of Zion, 2005).

_____. *Grafted In: Israel, Gentiles, and the Mystery of the Gospel* (Marshfield, MO: First Fruits of Zion, 2009).

_____. *From Sabbath to Sabbath: Returning the Holy Sabbath to the Disciples of Jesus* (Marshfield, MO: First Fruits of Zion, 2016).

Liberman, Paul. *The Fig Tree Blossoms: The Emerging of Messianic Judaism* (Kudu Publishing, 2012).

Martin, Walter R. *The Kingdom of the Cults* (Minneapolis: Bethany House Publishers, 1985).

McKee, J.K. *Torah In the Balance, Volume I* (Kissimmee, FL: TNN Press, 2003).

_____. *James for the Practical Messianic* (Kissimmee, FL: TNN Press, 2005).

_____. *Hebrews for the Practical Messianic* (Kissimmee, FL: TNN Press, 2006).

_____. *A Survey of the Apostolic Scriptures for the Practical Messianic* (Kissimmee, FL: TNN Press, 2006).

_____. *Philippians for the Practical Messianic* (Kissimmee, FL: TNN Press, 2007).

_____. *Galatians for the Practical Messianic*, second edition (Kissimmee, FL: TNN Press, 2007).

_____. *Ephesians for the Practical Messianic* (Kissimmee, FL: TNN Press, 2008).

_____. *A Survey of the Tanach for the Practical Messianic* (Kissimmee, FL: TNN Press, 2008).

_____. *Colossians and Philemon for the Practical Messianic* (Kissimmee, FL: TNN Press, 2010).

_____. *Acts 15 for the Practical Messianic* (Kissimmee, FL: TNN Press, 2010).

_____. *The Pastoral Epistles for the Practical Messianic* (Kissimmee, FL: TNN Press, 2012).

_____. *1&2 Thessalonians for the Practical Messianic* (Kissimmee, FL: TNN Press, 2012).

_____. *Are Non-Jewish Believers Really a Part of Israel?* (Richardson, TX: TNN Press, 2013).

_____. *James for the Practical Messianic* (Richardson, TX: TNN Press, 2013).

_____. *Romans for the Practical Messianic* (Richardson, TX: TNN Press, 2014).

_____. *Torah In the Balance, Volume II* (Richardson, TX: TNN Press, 2015).

_____. *1 Corinthians for the Practical Messianic* (Richardson, TX: Messianic Apologetics, 2015).

_____. *2 Corinthians for the Practical Messianic* (Richardson, TX: Messianic Apologetics, 2016).

_____. *Salvation on the Line, Volume I: The Nature of Yeshua and His Divinity—Gospels and Acts* (Richardson, TX: Messianic Apologetics, 2017).

_____. *Salvation on the Line, Volume II: The Nature of Yeshua and His Divinity—The General Epistles, Pauline Epistles, and Later New Testament* (Richardson, TX: Messianic Apologetics, 2018).

———. *Men and Women in the Body of Messiah: Answering Crucial Questions* (Richardson, TX: Messianic Apologetics, 2018).

Michael, Boaz, with Jacob Fronczak. *Twelve Gates: Where Do the Nations Enter?* (Marshfield, MO: First Fruits of Zion, 2012).

———. *Tent of David: Healing the Vision of the Messianic Gentile* (Marshfield, MO: First Fruits of Zion, 2013).

Moseley, Ron. *Yeshua: A Guide to the Real Jesus and the Original Church* (Baltimore: Lederer Books, 1996).

Nadler, Sam. *The Feasts of Israel: God's Appointed Times in History & Prophecy* (Charlotte, NC: Word of Messiah Ministries, 2002).

———. *Developing Healthy Messianic Congregations* (Charlotte: Word of Messiah Ministries, 2016).

Neusner, Jacob. *The Way of Torah: An Introduction to Judaism* (Belmont, CA: Wadsworth Publishing Company, 1997).

Payne, Philip B. *Man and Woman, One in Christ: An Exegetical and Theological Study of Paul's Letters* (Grand Rapids: Zondervan, 2009).

Provan, Iain, V. Philips Long, and Tremper Longman III. *A Biblical History of Israel* (Louisville, KY: Westminster John Knox, 2003).

Richardson, Susan E. *Holidays & Holy Days* (Ann Arbor, MI: Servant Publications, 2001).

Rudolph, David J., and Joel Willitts, eds. *Introduction to Messianic Judaism: Its Ecclesial Context and Biblical Foundations* (Grand Rapids: Zondervan, 2013).

Rydelnik, Michael. *The Messianic Hope: Is the Hebrew Bible Messianic?* (Nashville: B&H Publishing Group, 2010).

Shannon, Jill. *A Prophetic Calendar: The Feasts of Israel* (Shippensburg, PA: Destiny Image, 2009).

Stern, David H. *Restoring the Jewishness of the Gospel* (Clarksville, MD: Jewish New Testament Publications, 1990).

———. *Messianic Judaism: A Modern Movement With an Ancient Past* (Clarksville, MD: Messianic Jewish Publishers, 2007).

Strickland, Wayne G., ed. *Five Views on Law and Gospel* (Grand Rapids: Zondervan, 1996).

Tessler, Gordon. *The Genesis Diet* (Raleigh: Be Well Publications, 1996).

Thompson, David L. *Bible Study That Works* (Napanee, IN: Evangel Publishing House, 1994).

Wilson, Marvin R. *Our Father Abraham: Jewish Roots of the Christian Faith* (Grand Rapids: Eerdmans, 1989).

Wolff, Robert F., ed. *Awakening the One New Man* (Shippensburg, PA: Destiny Image, 2011).

Christian Reference Sources

Alexander, T. Desmond, and David W. Baker, eds. *Dictionary of the Old Testament Pentateuch* (Downers Grove, IL: InterVarsity, 2003).

Arnold, Bill T., and H.G.M. Williamson, eds. *Dictionary of the Old Testament Historical Books* (Downers Grove, IL: InterVarsity, 2005).

Bercot, David W., ed. *A Dictionary of Early Christian Beliefs* (Peabody, MA: Hendrickson, 1998).

Boda, Mark J., and J. Gordon McConville, eds. *Dictionary of the Old Testament Prophets* (Downers Grove, IL: InterVarsity, 2012).

Bromiley, Geoffrey, ed. *International Standard Bible Encyclopedia*, 4 vols. (Grand Rapids: Eerdmans, 1988).

Buttrick, George, ed. et. al. *The Interpreter's Dictionary of the Bible*, 4 vols. (Nashville: Abingdon, 1962).

Cairns, Alan. *Dictionary of Theological Terms* (Greenville, SC: Ambassador Emerald International, 2002).

The Messianic Walk

Crim, Keith, ed. *Interpreter's Dictionary of the Bible: Supplementary Volume* (Nashville: Abingdon, 1976).

Elwell, Walter A. *Evangelical Dictionary of Theology* (Grand Rapids: Baker Academic, 2001).

Evans, Craig A., and Stanley E. Porter, eds. *Dictionary of New Testament Background* (Downers Grove, IL: InterVarsity, 2000).

Evans, C. Stephen. *Pocket Dictionary of Apologetics & Philosophy of Religion* (Downers Grove, IL: InterVarsity, 2002).

Feldmeth, Nathan P. *Pocket Dictionary of Church History* (Downers Grove, IL: InterVarsity, 2008).

Freedman, David Noel, ed. *Anchor Bible Dictionary*, 6 vols. (New York: Doubleday, 1992).

_____, ed. *Eerdmans Dictionary of the Bible* (Grand Rapids: Eerdmans, 2000).

Geisler, Norman L., ed. *Baker Encyclopedia of Christian Apologetics* (Grand Rapids: Baker, 1999).

Goodrick, Edward W. *Do It Yourself Hebrew and Greek: A Guide to Biblical Language Tools* (Grand Rapids: Zondervan, 1980).

Green, Joel B., Scot McKnight, and I. Howard Marshall, eds. *Dictionary of Jesus and the Gospels* (Downers Grove, IL: InterVarsity, 1992).

_____, ed. et. al. *Dictionary of Scripture and Ethics* (Grand Rapids: Baker Academic, 2011).

Grenz, Stanley J., David Guretzki, and Cherith Fee Nordling. *Pocket Dictionary of Theological Terms* (Downers Grove, IL: InterVarsity, 1999).

_____, Jay T. Smith. *Pocket Dictionary of Ethics* (Downers Grove, IL: InterVarsity, 2003).

Harrison, Everett F., ed. *Baker's Dictionary of Theology* (Grand Rapids: Baker Book House, 1960).

Hawthorne, Gerald F., Ralph P. Martin, and Daniel G. Reid, eds. *Dictionary of Paul and His Letters* (Downers Grove, IL: InterVarsity, 1993).

Holmes, Michael W., ed. and trans. *The Apostolic Fathers: Greek Texts and English Translations*, third edition (Grand Rapids: Baker Academic, 2007).

Kapic, Kelly M., & Wesley Vander Lugt. *Pocket Dictionary of the Reformed Tradition* (Downers Grove, IL: InterVarsity, 2013).

Keener, Craig S. *The IVP Bible Background Commentary: New Testament* (Downers Grove, IL: InterVarsity, 1993).

Longman III, Tremper, and Peter Enns, eds. *Dictionary of the Old Testament Wisdom, Poetry & Writings* (Downers Grove, IL: InterVarsity, 2008).

Martin, Ralph P., and Peter H. Davids, eds. *Dictionary of the Later New Testament & its Developments* (Downers Grove, IL: InterVarsity, 1997).

McKim, Donald S. *Westminster Dictionary of Theological Terms* (Louisville: Westminster John Knox, 1996).

McLay, R. Timothy. *The Use of the Septuagint in New Testament Research* (Grand Rapids: Eerdmans, 2003).

Patzia, Arthur G., and Anthony J. Petrotta. *Pocket Dictionary of Biblical Studies* (Downers Grove, IL: InterVarsity, 2002).

Provance, Brett Scott. *Pocket Dictionary of Liturgy & Worship* (Downers Grove, IL: InterVarsity, 2009).

Roberts, Alexander, and James Donaldson, eds. *The Apostolic Fathers*, American Edition.

Schaff, Philip. *History of the Christian Church*, 8 vols. (Grand Rapids: Eerdmans, 1995).

Tenney, Merrill C., ed. *The New International Dictionary of the Bible* (Grand Rapids: Zondervan, 1987).

Walton, John H., Victor H. Matthews, and Mark W. Chavalas. *The IVP Bible Background Commentary: Old Testament* (Downers Grove, IL: InterVarsity, 2000).

Greek Language Resources

Aland, Kurt, et. al. *The Greek New Testament, Fourth Revised Edition* (Stuttgart: Deutche Bibelgesellschaft/United Bible Societies, 1998).

Bibliography

Aland, Barbara and Kurt, Johannes Karavidopoulos, Carlo M. Martini, Bruce M. Metzger, eds. *Novum Testamentum Graece, 28th Revised Edition* (Deutsche Bibelgesellschaft: Stutgart, 2012).

Black, David Alan. *Learn to Read New Testament Greek* (Nashville: Broadman and Holman, 1994).

_____. *It's Still Greek to Me* (Grand Rapids: Baker Books, 1998).

Brenton, Sir Lancelot C. L., ed & trans. *The Septuagint With Apocrypha* (Peabody, MA: Hendrickson, 1999).

Bromiley, Geoffrey W., ed. *Theological Dictionary of the New Testament*, abridged (Grand Rapids: Eerdmans, 1985).

Brown, Robert K., and Philip W. Comfort, trans. *The New Greek-English Interlinear New Testament* (Carol Stream, IL: Tyndale House, 1990).

Comfort, Philip W. *New Testament Text and Translation Commentary* (Carol Stream, IL: Tyndale House, 2008).

Danker, Frederick William, ed., et. al. *A Greek-English Lexicon of the New Testament and Other Early Christian Literature*, third edition (Chicago: University of Chicago Press, 2000).

Liddell, H.G., and R. Scott. *An Intermediate Greek-English Lexicon* (Oxford: Clarendon Press, 1994).

Marshall, Alfred. *The Interlinear KJV-NIV Parallel New Testament in Greek and English* (Grand Rapids: Zondervan, 1975).

Metzger, Bruce M. *A Textual Commentary on the Greek New Testament* (London and New York: United Bible Societies, 1975).

Mounce, William D. *Basics of Biblical Greek Grammar* (Grand Rapids: Zondervan, 2009).

Mounce, William D., and Robert H. Mounce, eds. *The Zondervan Greek and English Interlinear New Testament (NASB/NIV)* (Grand Rapids: Zondervan, 2008, 2011).

Nestle, Erwin, and Kurt Aland, eds. *Novum Testamentum Graece, Nestle-Aland 27th Edition* (New York: American Bible Society, 1993).

Nestle-Aland Greek-English New Testament, NE27-RSV (Stuttgart: United Bible Societies/Deutche Bibelgesellschaft, 2001).

Newman, Jr., Barclay M. *A Concise Greek-English Dictionary of the New Testament* (Stuttgart: United Bible Societies/Deutche Bibelgesellschaft, 1971).

Rahlfs, Alfred, ed. *Septuaginta* (Stuttgart: Deutsche Bibelgesellschaft, 1979).

Rogers, Cleon L., Jr., and Cleon L. Rogers III. *The New Linguistic and Exegetical Key to the Greek New Testament* (Grand Rapids: Zondervan, 1998).

Thayer, Joseph H. *Thayer's Greek-English Lexicon of the New Testament* (Peabody, MA: Hendrickson, 2003).

Vine, W.E. *Vine's Expository Dictionary of New Testament Words* (Nashville: Thomas Nelson, 1968).

Wallace, Daniel B. *Greek Grammar Beyond the Basics* (Grand Rapids: Zondervan, 1996).

Zodhiates, Spiros, ed. *Complete Word Study Dictionary: New Testament* (Chattanooga: AMG Publishers, 1993).

Hebrew Language Resources

Arnold, Bill T., and John H. Choi. *A Guide to Biblical Hebrew Syntax* (New York: Cambridge University Press, 2003).

Baker, Warren, and Eugene Carpenter, eds. *Complete Word Study Dictionary: Old Testament* (Chattanooga: AMG Publishers, 2003).

Brown, Francis, S.R. Driver, and Charles A. Briggs. *Hebrew and English Lexicon of the Old Testament* (Oxford: Clarendon Press, 1979).

Davidson, Benjamin. *The Analytical Hebrew and Chaldee Lexicon* (Grand Rapids: Zondervan, 1970).

Dotan, Aron, ed. *Biblia Hebraica Leningradensia* (Peabody, MA: Hendrickson, 2001).

Elliger, Karl, and Wilhelm Rudolph, et. al., eds. *Biblica Hebraica Stuttgartensia* (Stuttgart: Deutche Bibelgesellschaft, 1977).

The Messianic Walk

Gabe, Eric S., ed. *New Testament in Hebrew and English* (Hitchin, UK: Society for Distributing the Hebrew Scriptures, 2000).

Harris, R. Laird, Gleason L. Archer, Jr., and Bruce K. Waltke, eds. *Theological Wordbook of the Old Testament* (Chicago: Moody Press, 1980).

Holladay, William L., ed. *A Concise Hebrew and Aramaic Lexicon of the Old Testament* (Leiden, the Netherlands: E.J. Brill, 1988).

Jastrow, Marcus. *Dictionary of the Targumim, Talmud Bavli, Talmud Yerushalmi, and Midrashic Literature* (New York: Judaica Treasury, 2004).

Kelley, Page H., Daniel S. Mynatt, and Timothy G. Crawford, eds. *The Masorah of Biblia Hebraica Stuttgartensia* (Grand Rapids: Eerdmans, 1998).

Koehler, Ludwig, and Walter Baumgartner, eds. *The Hebrew & Aramaic Lexicon of the Old Testament*, 2 vols. (Leiden, the Netherlands: Brill, 2001).

Kohlenberger III, John R., trans. *The Interlinear NIV Hebrew-English Old Testament* (Grand Rapids: Zondervan, 1987).

Lambdin, Thomas O. *Introduction to Biblical Hebrew* (Upper Saddle River, NJ: Prentice Hall, 1971).

Pratico, Gary D., and Miles V. Van Pelt. *Basics of Biblical Hebrew Grammar* (Grand Rapids: Zondervan, 2007).

Seow, C.L. *A Grammar for Biblical Hebrew*, revised edition (Nashville: Abingdon, 1995).

The New Covenant Aramaic Peshitta Text with Hebrew Translation (Jerusalem: Bible Society in Israel, 1986).

Tov, Emanuel. *Textual Criticism of the Hebrew Bible* (Minneapolis: Fortress Press, 1992).

Torah Nevi'im Ketuvim v'ha'Brit haChadashah (Jerusalem: Bible Society in Israel, 1991).

Unger, Merrill F., and William White. *Nelson's Expository Dictionary of the Old Testament* (Nashville: Thomas Nelson, 1980).

Van Pelt, Miles V. *Basics of Biblical Aramaic* (Grand Rapids: Zondervan, 2011).

Historical Sources and Ancient Literature

Bettenson, Henry, and Chris Maunder, eds. *Documents of the Christian Church* (Oxford: Oxford University Press, 1999).

Eusebius of Caesarea: *Ecclesiastical History*, trans. C.F. Cruse (Peabody, MA: Hendrickson, 1998).

González, Justo L. *The Story of Christianity*, Vol. 1 (San Francisco: Harper Collins, 1984).

_____. *The Story of Christianity*, Vol. 2 (San Francisco: HarperCollins, 1985).

Irvin, Dale T., and Scott W. Sunquist. *History of the World Christian Movement*, Vol. 1 (Maryknoll, NY: Orbis Books, 2001).

Josephus, Flavius: *The Works of Josephus: Complete and Unabridged*, trans. William Whiston (Peabody, MA: Hendrickson, 1987).

Judaeus, Philo: *The Works of Philo: Complete and Unabridged*, trans. C.D. Yonge (Peabody, MA: Hendrickson, 1993).

Shanks, Hershel, ed. *Ancient Israel: From Abraham to the Roman Destruction of the Temple* (Washington, D.C.: Biblical Archaeology Society, 1999).

Jewish Reference Sources

Bridger, David, ed. et. al. *The New Jewish Encyclopedia* (West Orange, NJ: Behrman House, 1976).

Chill, Abraham. *The Mitzvot: The Commandments and Their Rationale* (Jerusalem: Keter Books, 1974).

Cohen, A. ed. *The Soncino Chumash* (Brooklyn: Soncino Press, 1983).

Cohen, Abraham. *Everyman's Talmud: The Major Teachings of the Rabbinic Sages* (New York: Schoken, 1995).

Eisenberg, Ronald L. *The JPS Guide to Jewish Traditions* (Philadelphia: Jewish Publication Society, 2004).

Bibliography

_____. *The 613 Mitzvot: A Contemporary Guide to the Commandments of Judaism* (Rockville, MD: Schreiber Publishing, 2005).

Encyclopaedia Judaica. MS Windows 9x. Brooklyn: Judaica Multimedia (Israel) Ltd, 1997.

Frank, Daniel H., Oliver Leaman, and Charles H. Manekin, eds. *The Jewish Philosophy Reader* (London and New York: Routledge, 2000).

Friedman, Richard Elliot. *Commentary on the Torah* (New York: HarperCollins, 2001).

Harlow, Jules, ed. *Siddur Sim Shalom for Shabbat and Festivals* (New York: Rabbinical Assembly, 2007).

Hertz, J.H. *Sayings of the Fathers* (New York, Behrman House, 1945).

_____, ed. *Pentateuch & Haftorahs* (London: Soncino, 1960).

_____, ed. *The Authorised Daily Prayer Book*, revised (New York: Bloch Publishing Company, 1960).

Isaacs, Ronald H. *Mitzvot: A Sourcebook for the 613 Commandments* (Northvale, NJ: Jason Aronson Inc., 1996).

Kolatch, Alfred J. *The Jewish Book of Why* (Middle Village, NY: Jonathan David Publishers, 1981).

_____. *The Second Jewish Book of Why* (Middle Village, NY: Jonathan David Publishers, 1985).

Kravitz, Leonard, and Kerry M. Olitzky, eds. and trans. *Pirke Avot: A Modern Commentary on Jewish Ethics* (New York: UAHC Press, 1993).

Levine, Amy-Jill, and Marc Zvi Brettler, eds. *The Jewish Annotated New Testament*, NRSV (Oxford: Oxford University Press, 2011).

Lieber, David L. *Etz Hayim: Torah and Commentary* (New York: Rabbinical Assembly, 2001).

Neusner, Jacob, trans. *The Mishnah: A New Translation* (New Haven and London: Yale University Press, 1988).

_____, ed. *The Tosefta: Translated from the Hebrew With a New Introduction*, 2 vols. (Peabody, MA: Hendrickson, 2002).

_____, and William Scott Green, eds. *Dictionary of Judaism in the Biblical Period* (Peabody, MA: Hendrickson, 2002).

Scherman, Nosson, ed., et. al. *The ArtScroll Chumash, Stone Edition*, 5th ed. (Brooklyn: Mesorah Publications, 2000).

Telushkin, Joseph. *Jewish Literacy* (New York: William Morrow and Company, 1991).

Werblowsky, R.J. Zwi, and Geoffrey Widoger, eds. *The Oxford Dictionary of the Jewish Religion* (New York and Oxford: Oxford University Press, 1997).

Wigoder, Geoffrey, ed. et. al. *The New Encyclopedia of Judaism* (Jerusalem: Jerusalem Publishing House, 2002).

Software Programs

BibleWorks 7.0. MS Windows XP. Norfolk: BibleWorks, LLC, 2006. CD-ROM.

BibleWorks 8.0. MS Windows Vista/7 Release. Norfolk: BibleWorks, LLC, 2009-2010. DVD-ROM.

BibleWorks 9.0. MS Windows 7 Release. Norfolk: BibleWorks, LLC, 2011. DVD-ROM.

E-Sword 9.9.1. MS Windows Vista/7. Franklin, TN: Equipping Ministries Foundation, 2011.

The Babylonian Talmud: A Translation and Commentary. MS Windows XP. Peabody, MA: Hendrickson, 2005. CD-ROM.

The Jerusalem Talmud: A Translation and Commentary. PDF-compatible MS Windows and Mac OS. Peabody, MA: Hendrickson, 2009. CD-ROM.

The Messianic Walk

OUTREACH ISRAEL MINISTRIES
MESSIANIC APOLOGETICS

STATEMENT OF FAITH

The goal and purpose of Outreach Israel Ministries and Messianic Apologetics is to gain a fully Biblical and Messiah-like approach toward our faith, life, and position in the world that desperately needs the good news of salvation in Messiah Yeshua.

THE BIBLE

We fully affirm that the Holy Scriptures or Bible (Genesis—Revelation) comprise the inspired, infallible Word of God as revealed in the original Hebrew, Aramaic, *and* Greek texts. We believe that it is the final authority for faith and practice (Deuteronomy 30:14-16; Psalm 103:20; 105:8; 119:11, 28, 38, 105, 133, 160, 172; Proverbs 30:5; Romans 9:28; 2 Corinthians 6:7; Ephesians 6:17; Philippians 2:16; 2 Timothy 3:16; 4:2; Hebrews 4:12; James 1:22-23; 1 Peter 1:25; 1 John 2:5, 14;).

While we certainly employ English Bible translations in our examinations of the Scriptures, these translations are subject to the theological presuppositions of their translators. We believe that a literal, or literal-free translation, is the best method of translation, as opposed to dynamic equivalence which can sometimes skew the text. Ultimately though, final authority rests with the Hebrew and Greek texts. We also affirm the importance and necessity of reading Scripture in its original historical and cultural context.

THE PLURALITY OF GOD

We affirm a belief in one Almighty God, Creator of the Universe, and that He has primarily revealed Himself to humanity in three separate, but unified co-existent manifestations: Father, Son, and Holy Spirit (Deuteronomy 6:4; 1 Corinthians 8:6; Matthew 28:19; 2 Corinthians 13:14). We emphasize that as mortals we cannot fully comprehend the Godhead and how He chooses to manifest Himself to us, although it is evident that God is a plurality. This is clear as the Hebrew word for "God," *Elohim*, is plural; and that He is one or *echad*, denoting a composite, **not** absolute unity.

THE MESSIAH

We fully affirm the complete Divinity of Yeshua the Messiah (Jesus Christ), that Yeshua pre-existed the universe and created the universe (John 1:1-3; Philippians 2:5-7; Colossians 1:15-17; Hebrews 1:2-3), that Yeshua is to be worshipped (Mark 5:6-7; Matthew 2:2, 8, 11;

The Messianic Walk

Matthew 14:32-33; 28:9, 17; Luke 24:52; John 9:38; Hebrews 1:6), and even though in Yeshua's human Incarnation the Father is greater than the Son (John 14:28), that the Son is genuinely God (John 20:28; Romans 9:5; Titus 2:13; 2 Peter 1:1). We believe that acknowledging Yeshua as Lord, meaning YHWH/YHVH, is mandatory for salvation (Romans 10:9; Philippians 2:10-11). We believe that He was conceived of the Holy Spirit, born of the virgin Mary (Isaiah 7:14; Matthew 1:18, 20, 23, 25; Luke 1:26-33), and that He is the prophesied Messiah of Israel (John 1:45).

While on Planet Earth Yeshua observed the Torah or Law of Moses perfectly (Matthew 5:17; 22:36-40) becoming our blameless Passover Lamb (1 Corinthians 5:7). We believe that through His sacrifice He took away the curse of the Law, or eternal damnation, for humanity (Galatians 3:13), thus atoning for all sin. We believe that the Messiah was resurrected on the third day (Matthew 28:6-7; Mark 16:6; Luke 24:34; 2 Timothy 2:8), that He ascended into Heaven (Acts 1:9-11), is presently sitting at the right hand of the Father interceding for us (Psalm 110:1; Mark 16:19; Luke 20:42; 22:69; Acts 2:25, 33-44; 5:31; 7:55-56; Romans 8:34; Colossians 3:1; Hebrews 1:3, 13; 8:1; 10:12; 12:2; 1 Peter 3:22), and is awaiting His return to rule for a thousand years from Jerusalem (Matthew 24:29-31; 26:34; Mark 12:36; 13:24-27; 14:62; Revelation 20:4; 6).

SALVATION

We affirm that salvation is a free gift of God available through acknowledging Yeshua the Messiah as Lord (Romans 10:9) through repentance and confession of sin (Luke 5:32; Acts 5:31; Romans 2:4; 10:10; 2 Corinthians 7:9-10; 2 Timothy 2:25; 2 Peter 3:9), which results in a person being born again (John 3:3, 7; 1 Peter 1:3, 23) or regenerated by an indwelling of the Holy Spirit. Salvation does not come via human action or obeying commandments (Matthew 5:20; John 1:17; Romans 2:12-13, 25; 3:20, 27; 4:14; 8:3; 10:5; Galatians 2:16, 21; 3:2, 11, 21; 5:4; 6:13; Philippians 3:9), but if one is of the faith, then he or she will have "works" (James 2:14-16). The commandments of Scripture define sin (Romans 3:31; 5:13; 6:15; 7:7-9, 12; 8:2; 10:4; Galatians 3:24; Hebrews 7:19; 10:28; James 2:9) and therefore define every person's guilt.

While a forcefully debated theological issue, we believe that God gives each one of us a free will and choice whether to choose or reject His salvation and to serve Him (Joshua 24:15). All Believers are required to "work out" their salvation (Philippians 2:12), meaning not taking it for granted, and we should all be actively maturing in our walk of faith. We do believe that a person can lose his or her salvation (Hebrews 6:4-6; 10:26-27), but that God is the only One who can make the ultimate determination regarding the eternal destiny of anyone.

We believe that those who receive Yeshua as their personal Savior will spend eternity with Him, whether in Heaven, during His Millennial reign on Planet Earth, or in the New Heavens and the New Earth.

RETRIBUTION

We fully affirm that those who do not repent of their sins and receive Yeshua will spend a conscious eternity in Hell (Deuteronomy 32:22; Job 11:8; 24:19; Psalm 116:3; Isaiah 14:9; Jonah 2:2; Luke 12:5, 16:19-31) and ultimately the Lake of Fire (Revelation 19:20; 20:10; 15).

Statement of Faith

We totally disavow the belief of an annihilation of the condemned and believe that such a concept is misguided, allowing the unrighteous to experience no sustainable consequence for their sin. Hell and the Lake of Fire must constitute an ongoing, eternal punishment for the damned (Revelation 20:10), not extinction. It is possible, though, that a metaphorical view of eternal punishment more fairly deals with descriptions of both fire *and* outer darkness (cf. Matthew 8:11-12; 13:41-42; 22:13; 24:51; 25:30). This means that eternal punishment may ultimately be considered never-ending banishment, separation, and exile from the presence of the Creator.

THE TORAH

We fully recognize that Yeshua must have observed the Torah or Law of Moses contained in Genesis—Deuteronomy perfectly to be the prophesied Messiah and be sinless (Matthew 5:17; 22:36-40). We believe that through His sacrifice, the Messiah has filled the Torah with His Spirit (Matthew 5:17-20), not annulled it, and has given it greater understanding.

We do not believe that meticulous observance of the Torah is mandatory for salvation (Matthew 5:20; John 1:17; Romans 2:12-13, 25; 3:20, 27; 4:14; 8:3; 10:5; Galatians 2:21; 3:2, 11, 21; 5:4; 6:13; Philippians 3:9), but rather that it is the Torah which has defined sin for humanity (James 2:9; Romans 3:31; 5:13; 6:15; 7:7-9, 12; 8:2; 10:4; Galatians 3:24; Hebrews 7:19; 10:28). By further studying the Torah we can better understand what the Messiah died for and therefore we can enhance our spiritual walk. After salvation, via the enacting of the New Covenant in our lives, with the Holy Spirit supernaturally writing the commandments onto the heart (Jeremiah 31:31-34; Ezekiel 36:25-27), we should want to not knowingly break God's commandments and we should naturally be led into greater obedience (Psalm 1:2; 40:8; 119:92, 174; Romans 7:12; 8:4; 1 Timothy 1:8). The Torah forms the foundation of the entire Bible, and is necessary to understand for properly understanding and interpreting the Prophets, Writings, and Apostolic Scriptures (New Testament). The Torah helps us to understand God's holiness and character, and thus how we too can be holy (Exodus 19:6; Leviticus 11:44-45; 19:2; 20:26; Deuteronomy 7:6; 14:2; 26:19; Isaiah 8:3; 1 Peter 1:15-16).

We encourage Believers to obey God's Instruction as they are legitimately able, but most especially as they are *genuinely led* by His Spirit. Unfortunately, many of those who make a point to call themselves "Torah observant" are not, in fact, genuinely led by the Holy Spirit, being quite legalistic and inflexible, and are not too tempered by the critical commands of love of God and neighbor (Deuteronomy 6:5; Leviticus 19:18; cf. Matthew 19:19; 22:39; Mark 12:31; Luke 10:27; Romans 13:9; Galatians 5:14; James 2:8).

THE NAME OF GOD

We affirm that the Almighty God of the Universe has a proper name which in Hebrew is YHWH/YHVH (Exodus 3:15; 6:3; 1 Samuel 24:21; 2 Kings 21:4, 7; 2 Chronicles 33:4; Isaiah 42:8; 52:6; Malachi 1:11, 14), commonly rendered in most English Bibles as "the LORD." We believe that its exact pronunciation has been lost to antiquity.

In Second Temple Judaism, the verbalization of the name YHWH was reserved only for the high priest on *Yom Kippur* or the Day of Atonement (m.*Yoma* 6:2), and it was not used as a common name. It became common to refer to YHWH by terms such as the

The Messianic Walk

Almighty, the Power of Heaven, the Temple, the Kingdom, *HaShem* (meaning "the Name"), and the ever-common *Adonai* (Lord) or *Elohim* (God). It was considered blasphemous in Second Temple times to speak the name YHWH, and it was punishable by death (b.*Sanhedrin* 56a). We can find no objective evidence in the Apostolic Scriptures that the Messiah or the Apostles ever used the name YHWH, as these writings use the Greek terms *Kurios* (Lord) and *Theos* (God), which were employed by the Septuagint translators who rendered the Hebrew Bible into Greek approximately three centuries before Yeshua.

The Third Commandment tells us that we are not to bring God's name to nothingness, or use it in a profane way (Exodus 20:7; Deuteronomy 5:11). We recognize that there are many Messianics who are discovering that the God of Creation indeed has a proper name, but do not believe that we should use His name casually in respect for Jewish tradition and the fact that we do not know exactly how to say it. We believe that the name YHWH can be used in a scholastic sense, but should not be spoken aloud frequently. We certainly do not believe that it is necessary that one know the name YHWH to be saved, as the God of the Universe looks at the heart of one who is seeking salvation, not whether or not such a person knows how to pronounce His proper name correctly.

We also recognize that the Messiah was fully Hebrew in a First Century context, and that His original name was *Yeshua* meaning "He saves" or "Savior/Salvation" (Matthew 1:21). The Greek transliteration of *Yeshua* was *Iēsous*, originating with the Septuagint Rabbis, and appears as the title for the Book of Joshua in the LXX. The name *Iēsous* is the name from which the English name Jesus is derived. **We totally reject** the concept that the Messiah's English name "Jesus Christ" is pagan because of its Greek linguistic origins. While we encourage use of the Messiah's original Hebrew name Yeshua, we recognize that many have come to faith through His English name Jesus.

THE PEOPLE OF GOD

We affirm that there exists a universal body of Believers (Romans 12:5; 1 Corinthians 10:17; 12:12-13; Ephesians 4:4). The redeemed in Israel's Messiah compose the Commonwealth of Israel (Ephesians 2:11-12) or Israel of God (Galatians 6:16), which incorporates together the physical descendants of the Biblical Patriarchs Abraham, Isaac, and Jacob/Israel, today's Jewish people, and those from the nations. Those who are not physical descendants of Abraham, can claim his promises through faith in Yeshua (Galatians 3:8-9, 16). We certainly believe that God's promises to Ancient Israel and the contemporary Jewish people are valid and remain in force—including the existence of the State of Israel in fulfillment of Bible prophecy (Isaiah 66:8)—but also that non-Jewish Believers by their faith in the Jewish Messiah are to be regarded as "grafted in" to Israel's olive tree (Romans 11:17-18). Jewish and non-Jewish Believers in Yeshua are to constitute a "one new humanity" (Ephesians 2:15).

While Jewish and non-Jewish Believers do have their distinctions and differences, they also have far more in common than not. Per the prophesied restoration of David's Tabernacle (Amos 9:11-12; Acts 15:15-18), the reconstituted Twelve Tribes of Israel will be at the center of this Commonwealth of Israel, yet with enlarged borders and a farther reaching rule to welcome in the righteous of the nations. Non-Jewish Believers in today's Messianic community, need to be especially called into this unique faith community, in its present phase of development, as they should not only be concerned with being enriched from their faith heritage in Israel's Scriptures, but to be actively participating in Jewish outreach and evangelism (Romans 11:11, 30-31).

THE LAST DAYS

While recognizing that eschatology is not a salvation issue, we hold to eschatological views consistent with historical pre-millennialism, and we do not hold to amillennial, post-millennial, or preterist eschatology.

We believe that the Messiah will physically return to Earth following the last seven years of Tribulation more accurately called the Seventieth Week of Israel (Daniel 9:27; Matthew 24:21; Mark 13:19). We believe that during this final time period that a world leader known as the antichrist/antimessiah will arise (Daniel 7:15; Revelation 17:11; 17:13), will demand worship (Revelation 13:15), and will require everyone to receive his mark to conduct trade and commerce (Revelation 13:16-17). We believe that during this time period, the final judgments of God will be poured out on humanity.

We fully affirm in a gathering of the saints into the clouds to meet the Lord (Matthew 24:29-31; Mark 13:26-27; 1 Corinthians 15:51-52; 1 Thessalonians 4:16-17) and that Believers will be spared from the wrath of God (Romans 1:18; 2:5, 8; Ephesians 5:6; 1 Thessalonians 5:9; Revelation 16:1). However, we believe that the wrath of God is poured out on a literal Day of the Lord, promoting the idea of a pre-wrath/post-tribulational gathering of the elect, and that ultimately the "wrath" of God is eternal condemnation in the Lake of Fire reserved for the condemned.

The Messianic Walk

Made in the USA
Coppell, TX
14 September 2024

37262831R00151